MW01700440

With best wishes

Briefest Encounters

Canterbury Court Library

February 2018.

First published in 2016 By Quadrant Books

Copyright © Pip Burley 2016
Cover © Pip Burley 2016

Design by Spiffing Covers

ISBN: 978-0-946894-08-6

The author asserts his moral right under the Copyright, Designs and Patents Act, 1988, to be identified as the author of this work.

All Rights reserved. No part of this publication may be reproduced, copied, stored in a retrieval system, or transmitted, in any form or by any means, without the prior written consent of the copyright holder, nor be otherwise circulated in any form of binding or cover other than that in which it is published and without a similar condition being imposed on the subsequent purchaser. All brand names and product names used in this book are trademarks, registered trademarks, or trade names of their respective holders.

A CIP catalogue record for this title is available from the British Library.

Printed in the United Kingdom

Briefest Encounters

From chance meetings to working with the stars - a rare insight into the world of music, showbiz and celebrity.

PIP BURLEY

Canterbury Court Library

QUADRANT BOOKS

"There should be a Society for the Prevention of Cruelty to Musical Instruments".

NOEL COWARD, 'BRIEF ENCOUNTERS' 1945

Contents

Saturday 7th September, 1963

ON Saturday 7th September 1963 at 1pm The Beatles began a three-hour recording session at The Playhouse Theatre in London for the fifth birthday edition of 'Saturday Club'. Around 4 o'clock the group drove to Croydon where they were scheduled to appear at the Fairfield Halls. After the show about 500 screaming teenagers mobbed the band as they tried to leave. A policeman said: "I've never seen anything like it. It's a miracle no one was killed".

The 'Croydon Advertiser' later wrote: "They demonstrated why they have shot to the top at such a rapid pace. They were self-assured, smart in appearance and gave the customers what they wanted - although what this precisely *is* poses rather a doubtful question. It has been said somewhere that 'The quality of Mersey is not strained'... It was very severely strained - the Noise Abatement Society would have had a hey-day! Continuous high-pitched screaming throughout the group's entire act from a capacity audience, composed mainly of teenage girls, prevented any attempt at a critical assessment of the Beatles' performance. During their 30-minute appearance on stage, the numbers they played included, *I Believe, Please, Please Me, From Me To You,* a frenetic *Twist And Shout* and their current success *She Loves You*".

You'll note there was absolutely no reference to the 'The Quiet Five', the group I was in at the time - and we were on the same bill!

A bit of background. I had only recently left school at the time. My education had been entirely science based. I had achieved good grades in Physics, Maths and Chemistry at A-Level and already been offered a place at Bristol University to study engineering. This was pre-destined - my father had been an engineer and we had both always assumed that I would follow in his footsteps.

But, just as I was about to go to university, my mother died. It changed everything. I was shocked into asking myself for the first time what I actually wanted to do with my life. I'd played the piano since I was four and a half and, although I was largely self-taught, must have been pretty good. So much so, that by the time I was in my teens I was kept busy playing for school productions - I would be asked to do anything light that needed a piano accompaniment and, because I was 'unknown' to the music department, this caused a bit of a stir! Anyway, whilst I was studying physics, maths and chemistry during the daytime, I was doing all this other stuff after school hours - singing, playing, acting, writing and appearing in reviews. It was all fun and I loved it.

My father was understandably very cut up after my mother's death and, as an only child, I didn't feel comfortable about traipsing off to Bristol and leaving him on his own. So, I went to see the Headmaster to ask if I could stay on for a further year. He agreed. Then I wrote to Bristol to see if they could defer my place for a year, which they kindly agreed to do. As a result I stayed on at school until I was eighteen and, during that year, changed my mind about everything. It became crystal clear that I didn't want to be an engineer, didn't want to do any more science. What I *did* want was to play the piano and somewhere in that strangely nebulous way that youngsters think I saw a career for myself in the media and performing arts. Looking back, though tragic, the death of my

mother changed my life. My charted route had been interrupted, and that's what gave me the opportunity to re-think.

'The Quiet Five' was formed by a school friend, Pat Adamson, in 1962. We started off by playing around the Croydon and South London areas and were popular as a live band, performing mainly cover versions of current hits with a few originals thrown in. When the well-known DJ, Shaw Taylor, took an interest in us we had a couple of attempts at recording and produced some good demos but we never made it as a recording band. Although we had ambition, it was really only our bass player, Richard Barnes, who wanted to make a career in music. The rest of us had found 'respectable' jobs which naturally curtailed our progress musically. And, anyway, I wasn't a great fan of rock n'roll. But, back to the Beatles.

I remember that night half a century ago very clearly. The building itself was fresh, new and exciting at the time, comprising a 1,700 seat concert hall, a theatre and art gallery; in fact, it had only been opened officially the previous November by the Queen Mother. We did most of the first act to a wild, tumultuous reception from the very young, largely female audience who were clearly practicing for what was to come! 'Croydon Advertiser was right, the screaming was so loud we could hardly hear what we were doing. Then, as we made our exit stage right, we passed the Fab Four in the wings waiting to go on. They were small - that's the thing that sticks in my mind. To a man they were at least four inches shorter than us, their southern counterparts (or so we liked to think). We didn't have any other interaction with them - I wish we had - but we'd been allocated our own dressing rooms, we were on at different times and it was, quite literally, passing like strangers in the dark. An encounter can't get much briefer than that, but the effect on me (and, as it transpired, most of the Western world) was massive.

At the time Paul, John, George and Ringo were freshly embarked upon what was to become the biggest roller-coaster since Elvis, complete with sharp suits and muppet haircuts. As we stood in the wings waiting for them to begin, we had no idea what to expect. We'd played a good set and received a huge ovation and I remember wondering what they could do that we couldn't. Well, we didn't have to wait long to find out. Within a few bars there it was - the unmistakable originality, the sound, the wit, the sense of mischief - so different and so much better than us.

Performing with them was a life-changing experience. It brought it home to me that, even though we were still just out of our teens, something had changed, things had moved on and the popular music scene would never be the same again. Just as we had got started, we were being left behind! Of course we weren't the only ones; The Beatles were unique and represented the beginning of an entirely new era that was to last for the next twenty-five years, some would argue much longer. And that new era began for me in 7th of September 1963.

As the world was to discover they were a daunting quartet, particularly McCartney and Lennon, and you just knew that they were intelligent, accomplished, original, creative people and they weren't coming from anywhere except the recesses of their minds and souls. That came across not just in their music but in their interviews and personal appearances - it was all so fresh and new.

In the early sixties we weren't used to youngsters being assertive, yet here they were having views and opinions and wrong-footing people two or three times their age! It all came so naturally and effortlessly and, coupled with their great sense of humour, made it impossible not to like them - which why they got away with it. It was as if they'd been there and done it all before, born with wisdom well beyond their years. This was evident in everything they did and inspired everyone they met. How did Mozart know how to write symphonies by the age of ten? It was the same with The Beatles. True originality is unmistakable and you don't need to be clever to recognize it.

With the benefit of hindsight we now see that The Beatles were part of something much larger; the whole world of music, film, television and art was changing. There was a huge youth-driven revolution going on, particularly in this country, so it was an exciting time to be entering what previously had been considered a hopelessly insecure line of work. Before the sixties, anything 'artistic' was 'flamboyant' and 'exotic' and to be discouraged at all costs.

Happily, it didn't turn out that way for me working as a musician in the 60's, in publishing and advertising in the 70's and 80's and, later, producing television shows in the 90's.

Thirty years later the music I wrote for 'The Darling Buds Of May' won an Ivor Novello Award - just about the only thing I can claim to share with John, Paul, George (oh yes, and Ringo).

Introduction

"Knowledge is knowing that a tomato is a fruit.
Wisdom is not putting it in a fruit salad"

I am sometimes asked if I discovered Catherine Zeta-Jones - which is much less than half the story. If the question was: "were you involved in Ms Z-J landing the role of Mariette in "The Darling Buds of May"? - then the answer would certainly be 'yes'. Nearly everything in the world of entertainment is a team effort and casting a TV series is no exception.

We are all curious about the rich and famous, what they're really like, what makes them tick. Furthermore, we have a compelling desire for them to be like us; absurd, of course, since it is precisely because they are *not* like us that makes them fascinating in the first place. Of course, the confusion is compounded by the media who, whilst generally careful not to break the law, are adept in trading in what might be called 'suspended truth'. So, our appetite remains – what are they *really* like, these famous faces, remorselessly flitting across our screens and front pages? Having spent most of my life around the edges of show business and the media and occasionally in the thick of it, I have gained some insight into these curious creatures and what makes them tick. It is these impressions, right or wrong, which inform the pages of this book.

Let me explain something; I was brought up not to be suspicious of people. As a child my father told me to look for the best in others and so, without thinking, I find myself giving a new acquaintance the benefit of the doubt. Looking back, I can't recall many instances where this has let me down. Also, I have hardly, if ever, disliked someone at first sight, which has made following the old man's advice a lot easier.

When I meet famous people, I start with the assumption that they are indeed special. Why else would they be celebrated, successful and possibly very rich? They must have been good at something in the first place and then worked damned hard at it. And if that sounds naïve, so be it - but my experience has been that a genuinely trusting, positive approach to others is more than likely to elicit a generous reaction .

I've also learned that famous people are as unsure of themselves as the rest of us, often more so. Knowing that all eyes are on you the moment you walk into a room is hardly likely to make you feel relaxed and self-assured! They may be practised at disguising their unease, but that doesn't excuse the rest of us from making the effort to help them feel comfortable - whereas, perversely, we always expect it to work the other way round!

Of course, you can never be sure when you are going to meet a star. Such encounters mainly happen by chance. But occasionally - for example, if you have advance notice of the seating plan for a dinner - it is a good idea to find out something about a celebrated dining companion ahead of time. Nowadays, with everything online, this is easy. There is nothing worse than telling an actor how good he was in a thirty-year-old film; it's tantamount to saying he hasn't done anything of merit since! Far better to mug up on his latest effort - if he's shrewd enough to spot that you've been on the internet, no matter, he'll still be flattered.

Since these people generally have short attention spans, it's unlikely you will grab them with some time-consuming anecdote - even if it is about them. So, the apt one-liner is a great help if you can conjure the right one up at the right time. Not long ago I quite literally bumped into a particularly beautiful actress who I guessed thought she was being cast for her looks rather than her talent (a frequent anxiety amongst leading actors particularly as they get into their mid-thirties). I said: "You don't know me, Ms K*****, but I've always admired your work and considered you to be a most underrated actor." Well, that certainly rang the bell and I spent the remainder of the evening at her table with her equally glamorous friends!

Lest all this suggests that I have gone out of my way to meet and get to know celebrities, I must assure you nothing could be further from the truth. It has happened in the course of the job, whatever it may have been at the time - musician, publisher, advertising executive or TV producer. And maybe that's part of it too, for whilst respecting their skills and status, I have not treated them as demi-gods - truthfully, no-one likes fawns and acolytes. As a certain Colonel Stephen Bauer (US rtd), who served in close proximity to five US presidents, once told me - "These people are just like us. We all put our pants on in the morning and take them off at night. The difference is they have folk to help them".

This book isn't about me - quite simply because hardly anyone beyond my family and friends would be in the least bit interested. Instead I have written about "the team" - the people I have been privileged to encounter, spend time with and exchange ideas, even, in a few cases, been fortunate to get to know. To stitch all this together, however, means that a bit of me might show through.

So, there it is, we all know what celebrities are. Enjoy them, obsess about them if you will - but do keep them away from the fruit salad!

PIP BURLEY, FEBRUARY, 2016

We have to stop meeting like this...

WHEN I was twelve my father took me to the Radio Show (or 'Radio Olympia' to give it it's correct title) which, in 1955, was quite an event. It had been going since 1927 and was still hugely popular. Despite all manner of new radio sets, gramophones, radiograms and other home entertainment devices on display, the real attraction were the daily live BBC broadcasts from Olympia, featuring the radio stars of the day. Many of these artists were normally just voices to the public, so to see them performing in person was particularly exciting. All in all, it was a must for radio enthusiasts, including my father, who used to build radios and amplifiers as a hobby - and me, an avid listener.

We had a number of treats in store for us that day, including a live transmission of the Goon Show and a personal appearance of a young, emerging international singing star called Frankie Vaughan. The Goons were great fun. As a twelve-year-old avid radio listener, to actually watch Peter Sellers, Harry Secombe and Spike Milligan delivering their crazy, funny material in front of a single microphone, discarding the pages of their scripts onto the floor as they went along and generally messing about, was spell-binding. Seeing the sound effects man at the side of the stage with his mysterious array of gadgets and watching Ray Ellington and his band effortlessly interpose the musical segments was nothing less than a revelation.

Then there was Frankie Vaughan making a guest appearance on some Light programme variety show, I can't remember which. Although we had no television at home, I was, of course, familiar

with his appearance through endless publicity pictures in the Radio Times and the tabloids. He would have been in his early thirties at the time and, onstage, immaculately turned out in light grey slacks, blazer and tie, dark-haired and olive skinned, he looked every inch the tall, handsome, rugged star. Relaxed and engaging, with a palpable physical presence, he sang a couple of numbers (including 'Give Me the Moonlight', his big hit at the time) and, quite literally, serenaded the audience. He had us in the palm of his hand.

He was, of course, the closing act, and it was time for an enthusiastic young lad to make a dash for what, in theatrical terms, would be designated as the stage door - except at Olympia there wasn't one, just a set of steps leading up to the temporary stage and a few drapes that afforded the artists scant privacy to make their entrances and exits. Leaving my father behind, I made a beeline for this 'offstage' area in the hope of catching a glimpse of the star. Over the years I have had a few such encounters, simply by being in the right place at the right time and this was one of them - for who should emerge and stand right next to me chatting to a colleague but Mr Vaughan himself. He gave me a huge smile and a nod before concentrating on the conversation in hand. Of course, I was far too star-struck to make any approach and a few seconds later, with another friendly grin he had gone. The only thing that registered was that he was no taller than me, about 5ft 7ins - an early lesson in how show business is an illusion and one which came back haunt to me years later when we were casting 'A Touch of Frost' – no male actors over 5ft 6ins, no females over 5ft 3ins. Otherwise David Jason was looking up all the time! On set it was like filming with the little people but it all looked perfectly normal on the screen.

Forty-four years later, in 1999, Frankie Vaughan died. He was seventy-one. It was during my year as Chief Barker of the Variety Club of which Frank and his wife Stella had been life-long supporters. Although I had only met him a few times over the years, I had followed his career with great interest. Born in Liverpool and a qualified art teacher, he was a greatly talented man and a fine singer - not of Italian extraction as he was often mistakenly thought, but Jewish. As well as a string of hit records, he had been a big act in Las Vegas, moving on to Hollywood where he starred alongside Marilyn Monroe in the film 'Let's Make Love'. After that experience, he returned to the UK, later saying it was a decision he never regretted for a moment. Not long before he died I heard him sing at the Savoy. It was a skilful and moving performance. He was awarded the OBE in the '50's and the CBE twenty years later.

So, when he died and the BBC telephoned me out of the blue for a quote I was well prepared. At the time, I was driving through the East End so had no notes or references. When everyone else would be saying what a great guy Frank was, I wanted to make the point that he was also a great professional and fine musician. That short radio tribute remains on the internet to this day.

* * *

Another enlightening 'backstage' encounter I enjoyed many years later was in the downstairs foyer of the Savoy Hotel. This time it was Eric Sykes, to my mind one of the truly great comic actors and writers of our generation. I had stepped out of the dinner to visit the cloakroom and, returning to the River Room, found myself standing next to Mr Sykes who was waiting to make his entrance.

I knew that he had just finished shooting a series called 'The 19th Hole' for television, the late Johnny Speight's de-bunking take on the elitism of golf and golf clubs. Originally written as a play, with Eric in the lead as the hapless but hilarious club secretary, it had completed a highly successful tour and was quickly snapped up by ITV. Whilst he waited to be announced, I asked him how it was going - would ITV be commissioning a second series? His sight was pretty restricted by then and I am sure he had no idea who he was talking to.

"Not optimistic," he replied, "they don't really understand Johnny's comedy. They should never have dropped 'Til Death Us Do Part'. They thought it was racist. They didn't get the fact that Johnny was doing exactly the opposite – trying to draw attention to the stupidly bigoted views of people like Alf Garnett. It didn't mean he agreed with them! So, we'll probably get the same reaction to a low handicap transgender golfer playing off the ladies' tees. Enjoy the rest of the evening." With which he returned to the top table where he made a brilliantly funny (and clever) appearance.

And he was right about 'The 19th Hole'. It never made a second series.

That's me on the left with the 'Shaw Taylor' glasses

Overture and Beginners

WE had finished our act and left the floor to a pleasing round of applause. It was just before Christmas and the ballroom at the Hilton on Park Lane was packed, with everyone enjoying a jovial night out of dining, cabaret and dancing to the Claude Cavalotti Orchestra. Now it was our turn to race round the service corridor to the back of the room to watch the star turn, the famous Liverpudlian comedian, Ted Ray.

At the time I was leading a group of eight young male singers, all in our early twenties, called 'The Semitones'. Believe me, in 1964 that name sounded a lot better than it does now. We had been going for about six months working around the West End hotels singing foot-tapping arrangements of popular songs in four-part harmony accompanied by two guitars and, when available, the band. Our 'signature tune', which concluded our thirty-minute set, was called *'One Finger Lift Up, Keep Moving'*, a furiously energetic number involving eight chairs and much standing up and sitting down. Whatever had gone before, it invariably brought the house down and this night had proved to be no exception.

Now, standing at the back of the room drinking in the atmosphere, we looked forward to seeing a real professional at work. Ted Ray was a household name having worked his way up the showbiz ladder to his own immensely popular radio series 'Ray's a Laugh', which itself had come out of an earlier wartime series called 'Variety Bandbox' in which Ted Ray had starred. Now, fifteen years or so later, Ted was cashing in on his well-deserved fame and was much in demand for television, film and cabaret.

The Toastmaster approached the microphone and with some ceremony introduced the great man, the band struck up a rousing version of Ted's signature tune and the spotlight swung stage right. And that was it. Of Mr Ray there was no sign. The applause faltered to a halt, the Toastmaster disappeared into the wings and, with great presence of mind, Claude Cavalotti struck up a chorus of *'There Was I Waiting at the Church'*. After a few minutes, the man in the red coat reappeared, repeated the introduction and, lo and behold, smiling broadly in the spotlight, violin at the ready, appeared the man himself.

Needless to say, his act was flawless as he effortlessly interwove anecdotes, jokes and stories with some accomplished violin playing. Three false tabs and forty minutes later, Ted Ray took his last bow and exited back to his dressing room amidst a huge ovation. Bar the dancing, the show was over and we followed him backstage to change and gather up our stuff ready to go home. As we were collecting the band parts together and sorting our white tuxedos into plastic suit hangers, there was a light knock on the door. A few seconds later Mr Ray was in our midst telling us how much he had enjoyed our act.

Thanking him for his kind remarks, I mentioned that we had been completely unaware that he had been watching us as, indeed, we had watched him. He explained that he had come down on the train from Liverpool and had arrived at the Hilton in good time. He was, he added, a stickler for punctuality. He could see immediately from our expressions how ironic his remark must have sounded in the light of his missed entrance. Chuckling, he explained that having watched the first part of our act, he had been having a quick 'pony and trap' before he went on. On the other hand, he added, it would have been courteous if someone had called him before introducing him!

The whole experience was delightful for us beginners and we felt we were being taken into the confidence of this big star. After a few more engaging pleasantries he again wished us well and bid us goodnight.

A week later we each received a handwritten Christmas card. An extraordinary gesture bearing in mind that he would have had to contact our agent for all eight names and addresses.

A few years later when I was running a publishing business, I dropped a line to him asking whether he would allow me to put together a coffee table book based on his colourful life and experiences. A day or so later he telephoned to say that he was very flattered but he didn't think anyone would be interested. I assured him he was wrong but he had made up his mind.

I look back on that as a lucky early encounter with a true celebrity: a successful, talented, modest, professional man who had worked hard to master his craft and given great pleasure to millions throughout a long and distinguished career.

The Bandleaders - The End of an Era

WHILST I ran the musical side of "The Semitones", choosing and arranging the material, rehearsing the group, etc, my old school friend and close neighbour Richard Arscott was our business manager.

It was he who found us an agent and, it transpired, a rather good one. His name was Sydney Lipton.

All eight original members of the group had been at school together where we had sung in a Glee Club. When we left – all at about the same time to embark upon our various careers – it seemed like a good idea to keep the Glee Club going. In those days nearly every home had a piano so we simply met up once a week courtesy of our long-suffering parents to carry on where we'd left off. It was good fun and, equally important, inexpensive since none of us had any money. My first job working in a small publishing office paid £8 a week. The others were similarly placed and it wasn't long before our minds turned to the possibility of earning an extra shilling or two from our musical activities.

I had already been supplementing my meagre income by playing keyboards with "The Quiet Five" so I was already familiar with the idea of 'moonlighting'. It was the sixties and our early rock/pop style was acquiring a bit of a following. Joe Meeke had just produced "Telstar" with "The Tornados", a revolution in popular music was under way, and everyone wanted to be part of it. Girls had got the pill and it was the beginning of women's lib. As the DJ David Hamilton once said to me: "Before rock n'roll we had love songs, afterwards we had sex songs".

With the benefit of hindsight "The Quiet Five" was the future; "The Semitones" definitely not. And for a while, things went well. The quality of our gigs got better, culminating at that concert at the Fairfield Halls in Croydon when we appeared on the same bill as "The Beatles".

I had a bigger problem. I didn't really like rock 'n roll, although I certainly did my stint playing those loud, monotonous three chord songs in sharp keys, stuck behind a keyboard with three guys out front playing guitars, singing and soaking up the adulation of our largely female teenage audience! For me, with my preference for the music of Jerome Kern, George Gershwin and Cole Porter, the cabaret circuit was far more appealing. "The Semitones" were getting busier and so for the time being I waved goodbye to rock n' roll.

Meanwhile, our new agent, Sydney Lipton, was working hard for us - and for him. Syd was an elegant, urbane character, tall, handsome and, at that time, probably in his early sixties. He had built a considerable reputation before and after the war as resident bandleader at the Grosvenor House in Park Lane where his position seemed unassailable. Not only did he provide the band for all the dinner dances and other social events at the Grosvenor House, he also booked the cabarets.

Syd was an interesting man. Born in London in

1904, he had learned to play the violin as a child and by his early teens was playing in pit bands accompanying silent films. His interest in dance band music led him to work in the 20's with Murray Hedges and Billy Cotton, before forming his own band in the early 30's. His first recordings were released in 1932, and from then, until the war, Sydney Lipton and His Orchestra were resident at the Grosvenor House, from where he made regular broadcasts.

After serving in the Royal Artillery and the Royal Signals during the war, Syd returned to the Grosvenor House, and continued to purvey his particular brand of sophisticated dance music until 1967. It was then that he formed his entertainment agency, as well as serving as musical director for various prestige venues and cruise ships. Top musicians who played in his bands over the years included Ted Heath, Bill McGuffie, Freddy Gardner, George Evans, Max Goldberg, Billy Munn and many more, along with vocalists including Anona Wynn, Les Allen and Syd's daughter, Celia Lipton. When he finally retired he went to live with Celia and her family in Florida, where he died in 1995. He was a one-off and I liked him.

The Great Room at the Grosvenor House was by far the largest banqueting facility in London holding nearly two thousand people for a sit down meal at full capacity. When set up for dancing the capacity was much reduced but it was still a cavernous space with the larger part of the audience remote from the stage. Whilst this didn't matter too much for the band, it was a nightmare for cabaret performers, especially solo acts. In fact, it was not uncommon for some very famous entertainers to fall flat in the Great Room. I recall that fine comic Dave Allen coming off almost in tears. He had simply been unable to command the attention of the audience and they had gone on talking through his act. Professional that he was, he battled on and completed his forty minutes, but I doubt he ever returned to the Great Room. And he wasn't the only one.

What was needed were 'big' acts, not just 'big' names, and these were hard to come by. There were some good troupes of dancers around at the time, 'Pan's People', led by the charismatic Flick Colby, who had made their name on 'Top of the Pops', being one of the best - but then the well ran pretty dry. Syd knew this only too well. So, when 'The Semitones' auditioned in front of the great man, he was quick to see the potential. Here were eight well-spoken, smart, good-looking young men with an 'easy-listening' sound and a belter of a closing number. He signed us on the spot taking 10% agent's commission on all our bookings. It didn't take us long to realise that since most of the time he *was* the booker, so the 10% was more of a discount! Still, that didn't matter and within a couple of weeks, we had our first gig in the Great Room.

Syd had taken a chance and been proved right. 'The Semitones' went down a storm and from then on we found ourselves at the Grosvenor House once or twice a week. We were professionals! Well, nearly.

Syd's West End reputation, partly due to his natural poise and presence onstage, had been enhanced by his many broadcasts on radio after the war. This meant that he and the band were in great demand for private events outside London. I got the firm impression that he turned most of these down – firstly because he was so committed in town, but also because it guaranteed that he remained exclusive and his price stayed high. However, from time to time one of these would turn up, usually in Cheshire or Goodwood or some other country seat involving several hours travelling, and, increasingly, we were asked to go too.

This presented us with a problem. As our schedule had got busier, two members of the group had already left (and been replaced) due to the pressure of their day jobs and, since we were all in the same boat, it was one thing working in London in the evenings, quite another meeting up early in the afternoon for a three-hour coach journey to some stately pile in the sticks and getting back at 3.30am. The straw that broke the camel's back was an appearance at the Bath Festival which, although prestigious and gratifying, had meant us all having to take two days off work. It had also led to an appearance on a TV show hosted by Pete Murray, which, again, whilst exciting and great for our West End bookings, meant more time out of the working week.

Now, other members of the group began to have second thoughts as well.

Syd, bless him, understood and tried to accommodate our predicament by finding us more jobs in and around London. He clearly had good working relationships with the other well known bandleaders of the time – Cyril Stapleton, Claude Cavalotti (who was Syd's equivalent at the Hilton), Joe Loss, who was playing everywhere and had a virtual monopoly of the cruise market, and Ken Mackintosh - to name but a few. Many of these acted as agents in their own right and had their own cabaret artists to promote. So we found ourselves appearing at The Savoy, The Dorchester, The Hilton, The Inn on the Park, The Royal Garden, as well as some lesser-named hotels, in front of different audiences and different bands. Little did I realise how useful this would prove to be in the months to come. Without realising it, we had become members of an exclusive little group of performers circuiting the West End. Great fun and a most useful way of supplementing my £8 a week.

Since we were now performing in front of people who had most likely seen us before, Syd was putting pressure on us to come up with new material and, as the group's musical director, it fell to me not only to come up with ideas but to arrange the vocal parts and provide the orchestrations as required.

One of the pieces I chose was that haunting spiritual *"Brown is the Colour of My True Love's Hair"* which I set, unusually for us, to a piano accompaniment. I explained to Syd that we would need a small grand piano situated on the dance floor and that when we came to the new number we would break the line and group around the piano with me playing. Syd looked quizzical and said that he had no idea I was a pianist. I briefly explained my qualifications and the stage was duly set

for our next performance. It went well. We did the new number as our penultimate piece and the audience seemed to appreciate the lull before the storm which, of course, was our usual barnstorming rendition of *"One Finger Lift Up"*. Afterwards, Syd came up to me and (again) said: "I didn't know you played the piano." But this time he was smiling.

Syd was not the only star in the Lipton family. As I mentioned earlier, his daughter, Celia, a ravishing redhead, was for some time the singer in his band and, indeed, made a real impression on the West End stage, becoming known as the UK's Judy Garland. She was also the apple of her father's eye. So, when she married American multi-millionaire Victor Farris and went off to live in the States (where she became a successful actress and celebrated socialite), Syd was not only devastated personally, but had also lost a valuable business asset. Since her departure he had employed a number of female vocalists but failed to settle on any of them.

After I left school I had done quite a bit of amateur dramatics both as a performer and musical director and had been impressed by one of the local company's leading ladies. Her name was Joy Willison, she was in her late twenties had a fine singing voice and looked great. She also had a three-year old daughter, worked for the Midland Bank and was about to get divorced. Desperate to get away from this humdrum existence – but without the first idea how to do it – she asked me for advice. Frankly, I didn't know either, but got as far as suggesting she might go about finding an agent. I helped her produce some leaflets and photos and wrote an accompanying letter.

We then sent this little package out to twenty or thirty agents whose names and addresses I had got from a trade directory. Of course, I had no idea who these people actually were.

I suspect due more to the photographs than the letter, she received a large number of invitations to audition. After the first couple – for reasons she was reluctant to spell out but required little imagination – she refused to do any more. Faced with this predicament for which I felt partially responsible, I did the only other thing I could think of. I introduced her to Syd.

It might be an exaggeration to say that Syd fell in love with Joy, but he was certainly smitten. She may even have reminded him of Celia, his 'lost' daughter. Still, there was clearly something in his make-up that inclined him to encourage new talent and, within a couple of weeks, she had her first gig with the Sydney Lipton band. He had found his singer and, I sometimes wondered, his surrogate daughter, too.

A week or so later, as if to return the favour, Syd asked me if I would like to try playing with the band and did I have an organ? Now, I should explain that at this time the electric keyboard was a new phenomenon and piano players were increasingly expected to play (and provide) an electric organ as a matter of course. These were not the light, portable digital keyboards of today, but heavy, bulky items requiring two or three people to lift and set them up. In fact, one keyboard player I knew used to transport his two-manual Hammond organ on a trailer! So, from being the only one in the band who never had to take an instrument to a job, the pianist became the one with the heaviest, most inconvenient encumbrance of all! The irony of this was not lost on the others - especially the drummers, bass players and guitarists who had been carting their equipment around without any help for years - so assistance was not always forthcoming.

Add to this the difficulty of getting such heavy kit into the building – the older hotels had not been built with this in mind –

and the dawn of the electronic era made life physically strenuous for keyboard players. Just as when the electric bass had replaced the steam bass, making many of the older bass players redundant, so the same thing applied to pianists. As it happened, I had recently traded in an old Hofner President guitar (a classic which today would have been worth a great deal of money) in exchange for a Bird organ, complete with two keyboards and pedals, which I had set up in my bedroom at home and was practising on hard. So, I was able to answer Syd's question with an honest 'yes'. How I would ever get this monstrous piece of kit into the Great Room remained to be seen.

All the bandleaders, Syd included, knew that with the advent of rock music, the end of the big band era was inevitable. However, since that was what he did, he had to somehow keep up with the times for as long as he possibly could. That meant playing the tunes of the day (difficult though it was with a conventional brass and sax line up), incorporating more electric instruments and, most important of all, employing younger musicians to give the band a more youthful and energetic appearance. It was a time of flux.

The average age of the musicians in Syd's band was in the late 50's and, excellent instrumentalists that they were, they were not going to adapt easily to new musical conventions. Conversely, whilst there were plenty of younger players around, they were not necessarily able or wanted to play the conventional big band repertoire. Syd needed younger players who could do both. He had already taken on a young bass guitarist who sang the current hits as well as managing the old dance band pad. There was already a guitarist in the band and he was experimenting with younger guitar players who could stand up and knock out the pop stuff. It seemed that it was time for a change in the keyboard department and I appeared to be firmly in the frame.

Syd's piano player at the time was an elderly, balding, substantially overweight man in his sixties, whose proud boast was that he could play any song in any key. Having watched and listened to him many times, I had always thought that whilst his claim may have been justified, the reason was because he played everything wrong anyway! It may seem surprising but it is comparatively easy for a poor player to "hide" in a big band, especially in the rhythm section.

Before the days of the much more precise, fretted electric bass, a bass player could easily get away with playing a series of fluffed notes so long as they were in time. I remember one bass player who had earned himself a big house in Weybridge and drove to work in a new Jaguar. He was a session player and could only play from music. I never heard him play a right note on electric bass unless he had the dots in front of him. Guitar players, too, could get away with what we called "quacking" – simply making a percussive noise on the beat without actually fingering the right chord. Even piano players got away with murder, the unamplified sound of an acoustic piano often getting lost behind the rest of the band. Of course, none of this worked in the studio which is why most if not all of the bandleaders used different musicians for broadcasts and recordings, much to the chagrin of their regular band members.

However, it worked the other way round, too. Broadcasting and recording (generally called session work) required musicians who could read music accurately and quickly with minimal rehearsal and play very precisely, not necessarily with any great feeling or expression. Live music was quite different. If someone asked the band to play a well-known tune, you were expected to know it – with or without music. Not only that, but in pretty well any key. For example, although most of the ten-piece band repertoire was played from the pad and mainly in a pre-set order, there were also longish 'busked' sequences where we would play a medley of numbers in the same tempo with the singers or one of the front line players taking the solos. For example, we might do three waltzes on the trot with the lead trumpet choosing the first piece, the singer taking the second and maybe the tenor sax winding up with the third.

Every popular tune is published in its own key, the "written" key.

However, this might not suit the range of a vocalist or, for that matter, the trumpet player. So, using a system of coded signals - three fingers down for E flat, two fingers up for D, hand on head for a minor key, etc - the soloist would let the rhythm section know which key he was going into a few seconds before the previous song finished. Usually, it was the keyboard player's job to make the modulation into the new key, often without knowing what song it was going to be.

When I first started playing in the big band, some of the older members used to enjoy trying to catch me out by signalling a key and then going into a tune that had never been played in that key before. Easy for them, they were only playing one note at a time; I was playing six or seven! Left to transpose on the spot, sometimes I didn't make too good a job of it. Still, this was all fair game to the older guys as they put me through a kind of initiation ritual; the audience never seemed to notice. Whenever this happened I would go home that night, sometimes at two or three in the morning, and practise that song in every key imaginable to make sure they wouldn't catch me out again. But they always did.

By now the natural life of "The Semitones" was drawing to a close. We had enjoyed a great couple of years but it was becoming clear that as we edged towards our middle twenties, the demands of our day jobs – not to mention girlfriends and partners - were increasingly in conflict with our musical activities. Inevitably the moment came when we had to tell Syd not to take any more bookings. He was genuinely disappointed but understood that we had reached a crossroads where only a couple of us were prepared to make the commitment to a highly insecure future in the music business and, although Syd was getting us at least a booking a week, this did not represent enough income for us plan our futures around.

As for me, I was enjoying my day job in the little publishing company well enough and regarded myself as a professional musician first and a trainee businessman second. I was certainly earning more from my musical activities than I was from publishing but, there again, not enough to see a real future ahead. Besides, now that I was getting an increasing amount of work from playing the piano (albeit with the inconvenience of carting around my Bird organ), there was no urgency to make a choice.

By now I had come to realise that there was more to Syd's business than I had first thought. Far from the Sydney Lipton Band playing exclusively at the Grosvenor House three or four nights a week, there were Sydney Lipton bands playing all over London – sometimes four of five a night! How did he do this? Well, it answered another question that had been in the back of my mind from the outset, namely, why was it that Syd disappeared halfway through the evening only to re-appear when the job was about to finish? As I subsequently discovered, on a busy night, he would spend half the evening dashing about town from one hotel to another putting in a brief appearance at all the jobs booked under his name.

To make this highly lucrative aspect of his business work, he needed other people around him who could step into his shoes when he wasn't there. In the case of the big band, Syd always made sure that he left an indelible impression on the clientele before he slipped off. He would be there at the start, play a couple of violin pieces himself, smilingly acknowledge the seemingly dozens of faces in the crowd he recognised and then hand over to his right-hand man, Syd Taylor, the lead alto player, to run things while he was away. Syd Taylor was an accomplished bandleader in his own right with a style of introducing numbers and running the band which, when required, was almost indistinguishable from Syd's. As I mentioned, Syd would always be back to wind the evening up.

Syd also needed another group of hand-picked musicians who could lead the other jobs – and this was not so easy. Although billed as "Sydney Lipton" bands, these would usually be smaller groups – four of five piece at most – and, of course, playing to smaller audiences. This was a different type of work requiring a different style, both musically and in terms of presentation.

When I was with "The Quiet Five" I had also worked around the Croydon area for a man called Ken Tapper, a dapper little chap who, whilst holding down a responsible job in the Finance Department of Croydon Council, had built up a profitable sideline supplying bands and cabaret artists to the Fairfield Halls and in the hotels around Croydon; very much a miniature version of what Syd was doing in the West End. As Croydon-based groups, both "The Semitones" and "The Quiet Five" had done a lot of work for him in their early days.

Ken used to send me out with small bands locally knowing that I would organise the musical programme, make the announcements and generally run the evening. Like Syd he would turn up immaculately dressed in black tie at some point in the evening, speak to the management and, if we were lucky, hand us our money in a brown paper envelope. There were normally a couple of pounds extra for me for running the evening. So, when Syd suggested that I might like to take on the job of leading some of his smaller bands I wasn't entirely unprepared.

There were two other people involved in Syd's office, housed rather impressively on the first floor of Steinway Hall, just off Bond Street. One of them, a delightful and devoted grey-haired lady called Betty, was Syd's faithful secretary whom we had known all along. The second was a man called Ronnie Lanchbury, who, until that time, I had only recognised as the drummer in Syd's number one band. In truth he was not a very good drummer and I'd often wondered why Syd had not replaced him in his quest for youth and modernity. Well, I was about to find out.

Ronnie was a tough, wiry little man in his late forties. He was Syd's 'fixer', the man who booked the musicians for all the bands put out through Syd's office. It worked liked this: Betty would tell Ronnie how many bands were required in the weeks or months ahead and Ronnie's job would be to ring around telling the musicians where they had to be, when and at what time. Whether Ronnie ever got paid any extra for providing this service I have no idea, but his main reward was that he could book himself on all the best jobs ahead of all the other drummers.

He also arranged transport (mostly for himself) and many a the time I found myself diverting via Crystal Palace where Ronnie lived on my way up to the West End. Ronnie's drums, plus my electric keyboard and amplifier, added up to quite a carload but at least we had each other to help unload at the other end. I cannot recall him ever contributing to the petrol. In Ronnie's mind, he was giving me all this work so the least I could do was give him a lift!

On a good night when Syd had, say, half a dozen bands out, as well as the big band at the Grosvenor House, Ronnie would be looking for six keyboard players, drummers and bass players, and at least another twelve assorted trumpet and sax players, plus a few guitarists and singers – between thirty and forty musicians in addition to the ten or so at the main West End venue. Plus, at least six of those had to be capable of running the band and acting as MC for the evening. Because Syd's reputation demanded that he employed the best musicians available, and that all the other bandleaders were doing the same thing, Ronnie had quite a job – day in, day out.

The fact that he made it work was due simply to the principal of supply and demand. If he was able to provide more work than anyone else, then he could demand loyalty from the players he wanted. This, in turn, relied on the office producing enough bookings in the first place. I can remember more than once Ronnie wanting me on a certain night when I had already accepted a job from elsewhere. When I told him this, Ronnie's reply was invariably the same: "Put a dep in - try Jim Smith, I know he's free." So, in order to honour my first loyalty to Ronnie, I would be left to explain to, say, Claude Cavalotti that I had arranged for Jim to do his job in my place since I was needed by Mr Lipton. Claude wouldn't be too happy, but since he was almost certainly playing the same game with his regulars, would normally grin and bear it. Like any other

business, if you are any good, you quickly become known and by now I was getting plenty of offers of work from different people. One of them was Joe Loss.

Joe was another of the broadcasting bandleaders who, like Syd, had built up a sizeable business during the years when the big bands reigned supreme. Joe had come up via a different route, playing in dance halls and recording. He was also born in London, the youngest of four children. His parents, Israel and Ada, were Russian Jews and first cousins. His father was a cabinet-maker who had an office furnishing business. Joe was educated at the Jews' Free School, Trinity College of Music and the London College of Music. He started violin lessons at the age of seven and later played violin at the Tower Ballroom, Blackpool and also with Oscar Rabin.

Joe started band-leading in the early 1930's, working at the Astoria Ballroom and soon breaking into variety at the Kit-Cat Club. In 1934 he topped the bill at the Holborn Empire but in the same year moved back to the Astoria Ballroom where he led a twelve-piece band. With broadcasting, recording and annual tours in addition to the resident work the band became highly popular over the next few years. In the 1950's he was resident bandleader at the Hammersmith Palais His adopted signature tune, Glenn Millar's *"In the Mood"*, would often be requested three or more times a night. He died in 1990.

Although he had his residency at the Hammersmith Palais, Joe didn't have a prestigious West End gig like Syd. What he did have was the next best thing – a virtual monopoly with the top cruise lines, Cunard and P&O. At the time Cunard were running scheduled trips across the Atlantic on QE2 and were setting themselves the same onboard standards as the top London hotels. The Joe Loss Band was very much a part of that aspiration.

In both cases, not only did Joe provide the resident dance band, but also at least one guest band and usually a number of solo players, harpists, pianists, classical string quartets as well as cabaret acts. One day I had a 'phone call from a man called Doug Perry, who I knew as a guitarist and bass player, asking if I would be interested in playing with the 'Joe Loss Ambassadors' on board the P&O ship, "Oriana". She was sailing in a couple of months' time from Southampton on a two-week cruise, up through the Norwegian fiords to North Cape, the land of the midnight sun. The pay was reasonable and, with all expenses thrown in, the opportunity irresistible. What's more, I wasn't required to take my wretched electric organ!

I soon discovered that cruising, even as a working musician, is a hugely enjoyable experience. There were even one or two unexpected bonuses. As a guest band we were accorded 'junior officer' status, meaning that we were accommodated 'above deck' with access to the same areas and dining facilities as the passengers. This was a huge plus, assigned only to the guest entertainers onboard - the lecturers, cabaret performers and, in our case, musicians who were, quite literally, 'guesting' for two weeks only. So, while we were swanning around upstairs, the resident musicians who were on board all the time, were treated as crew with their quarters firmly established 'below deck'. Of course, we seldom knew these guys for the obvious reason that they had chosen, in some cases at the outset of their musical careers many years ago, to spend long periods at sea, thereby effectively opting out of a land-based life.

What's more we weren't expected to work very much, maybe only three or four times during a week at sea. The rest of the time was our own. This was designed to make our performances 'special' and it did seem they were eagerly anticipated by the passengers. Whenever and wherever we performed, the room was full to overflowing. Why was this, you might ask? We weren't a rehearsed band – in fact, only two of us had even met before – so, it certainly wasn't because we had a coherent, well thought out routine. Nor did we have the opportunity to rehearse on board. No, it was because we were able to adapt and be flexible to the demands of the audience. We all knew roughly the same repertoire and if an elderly American lady asked us to play a number from her favourite Broadway show, we would manage it. Similarly, should there have been a popular dance craze around at the time, all those nights in the West End would come into their own. We could, in fact, (as Syd Lipton's old pianist used to claim but this time for real) play pretty much any tune in any key.

I tried to work out once how many tunes I was carrying around in my head at the time. It came to several hundred. So keen was I to keep up with new material that I actually had a portable tape recorder wired up to my car radio so that I could catch new releases whilst driving around. Later, at home, I would play them back and jot down the words and the chords. Talk about devotion to duty! But at the time I regarded it as professional and part of the job.

That cruise was the first of several and gave me a taste for seagoing life that I have retained to this day. Except now I pay the cruise line rather than them paying me! Life was good, I was busy. Then something happened which changed everything.

* * *

So far I have said very little about the day job. In a sense, there hasn't been much to tell. I would turn up at the office in Norfolk Street near the Aldwych every day and get on with what I was asked to do. I was learning on the job, it was interesting and enjoyable and pretty much fitted in with my musical activities.

Mostly, I was 'laying out' the pages of the magazines - meaning that I would send the copy off to the typesetter, get the galley proofs back and, literally, paste up the type and photographs into pages. My layouts would then go back to the printer to be made up, proofed, checked again and then, finally, assembled with the advertisements into the magazine ready for press.

Now, if that all sounds very unfamiliar, let me explain that in the 50's and 60's, before litho printing and computers were widely available, print was a very different industry. Those were the days of letterpress printing and 'hot metal' typesetting when type was cast in solid lead and the compositor would use his 'stick' to assemble the type and make it up into pages in metal frames. Photographs and illustrations were made into metal 'blocks' by specialist firms of blockmakers and inserted within the pages alongside the metal type. When all this had been done and passed by the client, the frames, each containing a page, were made up into four or eight page (or even sixteen page) sections ready to print. This whole process, with its pots of molten metal and laborious manual labour was the way it had been done for a century or more and the way I learned the publishing and printing business.

But, changes were afoot. Litho printing, a more sophisticated and much cleaner process, was coming on in leaps and bounds and, despite the protests and dying gasps of the letterpress printers - who were still claiming nonsensically that if you wanted real quality you had to use them - hot metal was fast becoming extinct. Almost overnight a whole industry was dissembling, together with the fortunes of many individuals who saw their (in some cases rather 'plush') lifestyles deserting them. Printers, specialist typesetters - who had been quite happily charging £50 to set a headline in a typeface you particularly wanted - and blockmakers were effectively out-of-work overnight. Instead, there was a rapidly expanding business in litho printing, especially with the introduction of web presses, fast-running rotary machines, not unlike the gravure presses used by newspapers and long run magazines. The lid on the coffin of the old letterpress industry was finally nailed down by the widespread use of the desk-top computer which enabled anyone to produce professional looking typesetting in a wide range of typefaces at virtually no cost at all.

The advertising industry changed, too, as highly skilled visualisers – artists who would render a mock-up of an advertisement or brochure using magic markers, pencils and paint – found themselves made redundant by Apple Macs which could do the same job in a fraction of the time with a more finished (although some would argue less creative) result.

Part of my job was to go round the advertising agencies selling advertising in the magazines. This was great experience, although I'm not sure I thought so at the time! I was not short of confidence, but found selling pretty tough. Especially selling advertising which is as close as you can get to selling thin air! Still, like most things, you learn as you go along and soon I found the knack of giving clients what they wanted - even if I had to find a way of supplying it later!

At this time, the little publishing company embarked upon a new venture. A rather elegant lady called Elisabeth Anderson had somehow got to know the boss, Stephen Pilton, and come up with a new idea for a magazine. She had been a beauty editor on various glossies and believed that there was a need for a trade magazine for department stores and chemists shops to 'educate' sales staff in the retailing of cosmetics, perfumes and beauty products in general. The name she had come up with was "Beauty Counter".

This was to be a monthly publication, with a ten thousand circulation and, frankly, compared to the rather more specialised, low run technical magazines we had been producing, was in a different league. Still, to my surprise, Mr Pilton agreed to take it on.

To cut a long story short, the financing of this venture put the little company and its founder under considerable strain, enough, in fact, to make him ill. At the time Mr Pilton was probably in his middle sixties, although to me he was an old man. He was himself a printer turned publisher and ran his little business as a genial fiefdom. He had an elderly secretary, Miss James, and had taken on a young man called Jimmy Lear, the son of a friend, who he had trained up to be Managing Director. We didn't see Mr Pilton every day, largely due to the fact that his wife was an invalid, severely afflicted by arthritis. In fact, by the time I was on the scene, it was rare for him to come in more than once or twice a week, so it was Jim's job to run the business on a day-to-day basis. Then there were two young girls who acted as general typists and Girl Fridays.

I liked Mr Pilton. He had a pleasant, friendly manner and great charm. He also had a good line in epigrams. "The way to make money out of print," he would say, "is not to do any printing!" - very true as a lot of prosperous advertising agencies, design studios and publishers already knew only too well. "Get it off to the printer!" was another of his war cries, meaning, don't let anything sit on your desk doing nothing, let the printer sort it out. And then, on a more human note: "There are plenty of nice people in the world, Philip, you don't have to do business with the nasty ones." That one stuck with me.

After twelve months or so with 'Beauty Counter' making heavy demands on the firm's fragile cashflow - not to mention Mr Pilton's limited capital resources - the strain got too much for him and he took to his bed. It wasn't that 'Beauty Counter' wasn't doing okay, it was just that the rest of the business was too small to support it. I didn't see him for a while and when I did, it was to visit him in hospital. He was pleased to see me and assured me that he would be back running things very soon, meanwhile he was confident that everything was safely in Jim's capable hands. Of course, whilst all this was of some interest to me, I didn't lose any sleep over it: in my mind I was still a professional musician and an amateur publisher, whatever that meant. Remember, I was turning up at the office most mornings with my evening suit and electric keyboard in the back of the car.

Then a strange thing happened. Jim called me into his office (well, it was Mr Pilton's office actually, which he had commandeered during the old man's absence). He asked me to sit down as he had something important to tell me. The conversation went something like this:

Jim: "Pip, you must realise that things aren't going too well here?"

Me: "Yes, I think I've cottoned on to that, I'm sorry."

Jim: "Well, to be frank, the business can't support both of us."

Me: "I quite understand and I'll miss it..."

Jim: "So, I'm leaving. I've got a wife, a mortgage and a baby. I can't hang around here waiting for this ship to sink."

Me: "I see. When are you going?"

Jim: "End of the week. I've got something else lined up. The old man would like you to go and see him."

And that was that.

My next conversation at the hospital was of a rather different nature. Pilton was clearly shaken. He had received Jim's resignation and asked me very nicely if I could hold the ship for a week or two after which he expected to be back at the office and able to take charge. It was to be a year before I saw him again.

During that time I set about the job of trying to salvage what was left of the business. With no experience of running anything, this was a fast learning curve which I had no idea whether I could ride. Still, I liked the old man and didn't want to see him or the business left high and dry. Saving Jim's salary was a help and, suffice to say we tottered on, on the one hand trying to maximise the revenue by selling as much advertising as I could and, on the other, keeping the costs to an absolute minimum.

Gradually, as much by luck as judgement, things improved and the business was no longer in crisis. It had taken a lot of effort but, as a novice businessman, it gave me a surprising degree of satisfaction - and some pride - to have succeeded in 'rescuing' the little company.

Imagine my surprise then when, suddenly, one morning, completely out of the blue, Mr Pilton turned up! Chipper, full of good cheer and the joys of spring with a newly plucked rose in his button hole.

"Right, young Pip, let's get down to business," he said as though the last twelve months had never happened. I glanced at Miss James who had been hovering nervously by the door.

"Miss James, I wonder if you would kindly leave us for a few minutes?" I said. In hindsight this must have sounded rather pompous but I honestly had no idea how I was supposed to respond - although something told me that whatever happened next was best confined to the two of us.

What followed was a row. I was indignant and hurt that he couldn't even come up with a few words of thanks for my efforts on his behalf. Remember, I was only in my early twenties and still unaware that life was seldom fair. He, I suppose, may have felt some guilt for leaving me stranded for such a long time and was anxious to give the impression of being fully recovered and keen to resume the reins of what – rather academically it seemed to me - he referred to as 'his' business. The difference in our positions (and ages) meant that a resolution was unlikely and, to his credit, he must have seen this.

"Very well," he said after ten minutes or so of angry to-ing and fro-ing, "If you want the business you'd better buy it from me."

I was flabbergasted. Whilst just about getting the drift of his proposal, I had no idea what it might involve.

"How much do you want for it?" I asked trying to muster more confidence than I felt.

"Five thousand pounds," he responded immediately. Rather too immediately, I thought, wondering if he had planned this in advance. Besides which, it was an awful lot of money in 1968.

"How am I supposed to afford that?" I asked.

"You can pay me over a period of time," he responded, "or, if you can manage it all upfront, I'll reduce the figure to £3,000. That's a generous deal, Philip, 'Beauty Counter' alone is worth that."

"But I haven't got £3,000," I replied – honestly enough, I really hadn't. £300 would have been nearer the mark.

"Alright," he said, "You've got six months. Let me know how you get on." And with that, he turned and left.

I thought about little else for the rest of that day and the next. Was this what people described as 'an opportunity' or was it an elderly, experienced man trying to unload a failing business onto a naïve youngster? I've since learnt that ninety per cent of opportunities are like that.

To this day I really don't know what made me go for it but, encouraged by the modest success I had enjoyed over the last year, I did. The first problem was how to get my hands on the enormous sum of £3,000.

First stop was my father, at that time in his late sixties and retired. He had been an engineer all his life and done well working for the same company for more than forty years. I knew well enough that he had been bitterly disappointed when I turned my back on a career in engineering, and here I was asking him to help me buy a little half-cock failing publishing business! But he was hugely supportive, trusting that I knew what I was doing. He said he would give me half of the money but I would have to find the rest. A tall order, but a step forward.

During the next six months I worked like I'd never worked before; during the day selling advertising space in our motley collection of magazines so that I could pay myself a bit more out of the business and, at night, in every dive, club, pub and dancehall in the South-east of England - hen parties, stag do's, accompanying strippers and comics – you name it, I did it. Not particularly enjoyable (in fact playing at hen parties led to some of the scariest experiences of my life!) but, as the end of the six months approached, I had nearly reached my target. I was exhausted, physically and mentally, but the end was in sight. Mr Pilton was as good as his word and instructed a solicitor, B.D.Laddie, who worked in an adjoining office to us in Norfolk Street, to draw up the papers.

To digress slightly, Mr Laddie was a funny man. No more that five feet three, with a shock of wavy, greying hair, he cut a Dickensian figure and his office reflected this. I had never seen a place so stacked with paper and books. Not only were there piles on the floor, but his desk was covered with heaps of files too, so tall that you could hardly see the diminutive Mr Laddie sitting behind them!

Next to his desk, mounted firmly on the wall on metal brackets, was one of those huge rolls of brown wrapping paper that you used to see in department stores. Before starting a meeting, he would tear off a large sheet of paper and lay it on top of whatever was on his desk at the time, thus 'clearing the decks' for his next client. At the end of the meeting he would rise, shake hands, put your file on the floor with all the others and flamboyantly sweep the sheet of brown paper off the desk before noisily crumpling it up and consigning it to WPB. But, he knew his job and within a day or so the papers were ready for signature.

There were a few remaining hassles to resolve but, in essence, the deal was done and I was the owner and sole shareholder of a little magazine publishing company which was to prove the foundation for my subsequent efforts in business, which included setting up a design business and the acquisition of an advertising agency. This was the sixties and the same sense of optimism and excitement that was prevalent in the music business was driving the world of media in general. I had taken on a substantial task but, as it transpired, at a very good time.

But, for the moment I still thought of myself as a professional musician with a day job and so it was to remain for some time.

Barry Humphries

ONE of the fun things about being in advertising is creating the ads. In this respect it is no different to show business.

Whether you are working for maximum visual impact within a confined space as with printed advertisements, finding the fewest words to express an idea in a headline, or creating a miniature drama for a TV or radio commercial, the whole process requires discipline and economy. You also need to quickly grasp the essence of what the client is trying to say and crystallise it down to its most minimal form. Sometimes more easily said than done.

One of my clients was the Financial Times who, as well as publishing the famous newspaper, had a division that, amongst other things, produced the FT Diary, an upmarket item, very much in demand amongst the business community. This commercial arm of the FT group frequently came up with new products and it was our job to advertise and market them. One such product was the FT Shareline. The idea was simple – by subscribing to this service anyone with a portfolio of shares could telephone a number, enter a unique code, and get the current value of their investments or, if they wished, of any individual share they held. Remember, this was before the widespread use of PC's and desktop computers so the idea, made possible by plugging into the FT's existing database, had the potential to be useful to the increasing army of shareholders encouraged to invest in the stock market by Mrs Thatcher.

The target audience was everyone who held a portfolio of shares, many of whom would be readers of the FT anyway. The problem was how to reach the others! As usual the available budget was well short of the money required to run a truly national campaign and so we had little choice but to concentrate our efforts principally on the FT itself and other specialised publications. Nevertheless, we were reluctant to give up on the rest of the market and managed to persuade the client to spend some money on local radio advertising, concentrating in and around London and the south-east.

Needless to say, the product itself, although practical, was 'dry' and unlikely to make our audience sit up and take much notice – unless we could come up with something pretty special. Which I think we did.

Only a few weeks before this my wife, Christine, and I had been to see the brilliant Australian female impersonator Barry Humphries at the Theatre Royal in Brighton where we were living at the time. His show was clever and hugely entertaining as his two principal characters, the famous Dame Edna Everedge and Les Patterson (the Australian Cultural Attache) regaled us with anecdotes, puns and – in Les's case - a good deal of spittle. I know - we were sitting in the second row!

If you have been to one of Barry's shows you'll appreciate that it is hazardous to be a few minutes late – as we were. Christine and I took our seats a minute or two after Dame Edna had finished her introductory remarks and weren't allowed to forget it. Still, gentleman that Dame Edna is – if that's not a contradiction – I took the brunt of his numerous pointed and offensive remarks during the first act and then, as one of the hapless half dozen members of the audience to be dragged up onstage, later in the show.

As the youngest male in the group, Dame Edna set about 'flirting' with me salaciously to the great amusement of the audience who relished my discomfort. It was, as you would expect, an entirely one-sided exchange. In fact, at one point I unwisely attempted to respond to one of his more outrageous innuendos when, to my surprise and with his back to the audience and out of earshot, the great dame quietly snarled 'shut up'. Which I did.

On subsequent reflection I realised he was absolutely right. Mr Humphries was treading a tightrope with his act and, of course, like all great performers, was working to a well-rehearsed and proven routine. To allow an uncharted exchange with a member of the audience could easily detract from the fragile illusion that he had so carefully constructed up to that point. It was not an option. Needless to say, when we were sent back to our seats, he was careful to thank us with great courtesy so that none of us retired hurt or took away a bad impression.

But that night set me thinking. Could Dame Edna be the face of the FT Shareline? It was certainly feasible that she would have some of her great wealth invested in stocks and shares and so I started to think of how such a campaign might come together. The radio ads practically wrote themselves: the press ads were a little tougher.

I decided to feature a photograph of Dame Edna's bedside table where, amongst the detritus of her life – hair rollers, spectacles, diary, sleeping tablets, Prozac and the obligatory tub of Vaseline – resided her pink FT Shareline card. Next to the picture would be the benefits of subscribing to the service in Dame Edna's own words. The headline would read something like:

"Really, Possums, I wouldn't sleep soundly
at night without my FT Shareline..."

I wrote a series of four press ads in which she made mention of her sidekick, the long-suffering Madge, not to forget her late husband, the much lamented Norman. There were also eight 30-second radio commercials. This all took some time and I had no idea whether Mr Humphries would agree to do it. When I thought I had it about right, I sent the whole lot off to his agent and awaited a reply. It was not long coming. Mr Humphries would be happy to oblige - and for what I thought was a reasonable and affordable fee. Having secured our star, I put the whole proposition to the FT. Since Barry was enjoying a lot of TV exposure at the time, they thought it was a great coup and gave me the go-ahead.

When I went back to the agent, I made the point that if his client wished to make any changes to the scripts or the copy, then, of course, he was welcome to do so. Everything was in character so I naturally assumed that he would want to re-write my material to suit himself. I was surprised when the response came back: not only had he enjoyed reading it, he would like to pass on his congratulations to the copywriter for so accurately getting inside Dame Edna's head. There was no need to change a word. I took that as a great compliment.

The day came to make the radio commercials at a studio in Soho. Mr Humphries turned up dead on time. It was the first time I had met him as himself and, as with all drag artists, my first impression was that he was smaller than I recalled.

The next weird thing was to see him through the control room window as himself with Dame Edna's voice coming out of the speakers. I'd half expected him to turn up in costume! Needless to say he did a wonderful job bringing the scripts to life. As we shook hands I refrained from mentioning our previous meeting in Brighton.

The campaign was a great success and the FT was inundated with subscribers. Within two years it had been overtaken by the burgeoning use of computers, those odd looking miniature televisions with curved screens and pointed backs produced mostly by the young Alan Sugar in collusion with the BBC, a bit like "The Apprentice". But look at him now.

As for Barry Humphries, he sustained a long, stellar career, not only as a light entertainer but as a serious actor; a rare achievement for any artist. He will go down as one of the great, if not greatest, female impersonators of all time and certainly the most original. And as history has shown time and time again, it's originality that counts.

A Day at the Beeb

WHEN I was in my last year at school after my mother had died, I knew exactly what I wanted to do. Whether I would be able to do it was another matter entirely.

My father had only got round to buying a television set when I was in my early teens. We were great listeners to the radio and, like many in those days, he thought the new-fangled invention was intrusive and self-indulgent. In fact, the first occasion I can recall watching television was when my aunt persuaded him to let us watch the coronation at her house up the road. By the time he finally resigned himself to the inevitable and purchased a set, British television was well into its stride and I was hooked. I loved the whole idea of making and transmitting programmes into people's homes, especially light entertainment and drama.

In those early days, before the advent of commercial broadcasting, television *was* the BBC, still heavily influenced by the vision of its founder, Lord Reith, namely to educate through entertaining. A far cry, I am sorry to say, from the BBC of today.

I wanted desperately to work in this new world of words and pictures, behind the camera, thinking up and making programmes, working with writers and stars. Creating. There were two problems. Firstly, I wasn't alone, there were thousands like me, all fascinated by the new medium and wanting jobs at the newly built Television Centre at Shepherds Bush. Secondly, I had totally the wrong qualifications. I was heading for three A-levels in science, maths and chemistry which meant the only way I could get into the Corporation was as an engineer, and that held no interest for me whatsoever.

I wrote two letters, one to the engineering department and one to the head of light entertainment. Both elicited quick responses. Engineering sent me a job application pack through the post, the other telephoned me to ask if I would like to visit TV Centre to meet a producer who would be pleased to show me around. Quelle difference.

I cannot remember being so excited and full of anticipation as when I arrived for my tour of the studios. I was treated with warmth and courtesy and led around those unfamiliar circular corridors by a pretty young woman who smiled a lot. As we passed door after door, most of them left open, I could hear the sounds of creativity, including much laughter. Every office had the names of its occupants on the door – we passed the office of comedy writers Frank Muir and Denis Norden, Marty Feldman and Barry Cryer before stopping at one labelled 'Johnny Stewart, Producer, Top of the Pops'.

Puzzled, I enquired of the pretty assistant what that meant. As a keen follower of popular music I had never heard of such a programme. She told me that Johnny would explain and ushered me in.

He was a lean, wiry man, I guessed in his early forties, with blond hair, dressed in a T-shirt and jeans. He greeted me with a huge smile and I felt instantly at home. He immediately launched into the details of his current project, code named 'Top of the Pops', a new idea to capture the interest of the youth market by putting together a chart of the most favourite hits in order of popularity based on record shop sales. "Come and see the studio," he said with enthusiasm.

That was the start of a magical day for a schoolboy. Not only did

I see the 'Top of the Pops' studio, all set up, ready to film a pilot later in the day, but he also took me to a smaller studio where Benny Hill was rehearsing his show. It was set up with a number of small sets and, of course, the banks of seating where the audience would sit for the recording later that day. Only Benny, his small cast of supporting players, the floor assistant and two or three cameramen were visible from the gallery where Johnny had taken me.

The eerie thing was there was no laughter. This was a master craftsman perfecting his performance which involved running lines and scenes several times, not only for the benefit of the performers, but so that the director could set up his shots. It made me realise what a deadly serious business comedy is.

The real treat was yet to come. At the time the BBC owned the Shepherd's Bush Theatre just down the road from the Television Centre, which was used regularly for big light entertainment productions. On that particular day they were rehearsing the Andy Stewart Show, a classic LE format where the star would host the show, perform himself and introduce a number of guests. Andy was a Scottish singer who was enjoying a spell of popularity and had been given his own TV series.

Entering the theatre I was struck by how much of what would have been the stage area and stalls had been taken over by crew, cameras and musicians. In fact, the whole thing looked far more like one of the TV studios I had already visited that the theatre it once was.

Everything was going on at the same time. The musical director, the portly Eric Robinson, was rehearsing the orchestra, stage-hands were arranging props and scenery, Andy, in full tartan regalia, was having his make-up refreshed, and the cameras were jostling into position for the next sequence of the show. I found the whole thing very exciting.

Andy was ready to rehearse a novelty song which, if I recall correctly, began 'We've All Come Back from the Isle of Skye' with each verse ending: "Donald Where's Yer Troosers?"- not entirely to my taste but performed with great gusto and energy. He was hardly into the first verse when Eric Robinson stopped the number with a curt "That's fine, save your voice". Immediately, the stage crew were onstage setting up for the next act, which required them to trundle on three grand pianos. As a budding pianist I was intrigued and asked Johnny what was going on. He told me that three well-known players of the day were performing a trio on three pianos, something that had not been done on television before.

The artists turned out to be Denis Wilson, Bill McGuffie and Steve Race (left), all of whom I had heard of, watched and admired.

The piece they'd chosen was a well-known standard which, firstly, they played together then followed by each of them taking a chorus in their own inimitable style - Bill McGuffie jazzing it up, Denis introducing his trademark altered harmonies and Steve adding his unmistakable latin beat. To me it was wondrous and when they had finished, I made a beeline for Mr Race who had taken a seat in what was left of the stalls.

How youthful and naïve I must have appeared, a gushing, shy eighteen-year-old stumbling to find the right words to convey my admiration and curiosity. I like to think that today's equivalent would react with the same generosity of spirit and kindness that he showed, for he sat with me for a good twenty minutes explaining how the three of them had conceived and put together their routine. We were joined by Denis Wilson who, as well as being a fine pianist, was one of the foremost arrangers of the day. I asked him how he went about giving a piece of music a twist by substituting chords. He pulled out a sheet of manuscript and started to pen a new chord sequence for "Happy Birthday", showing me how one chord led into another. I must have looked out of my depth because he soon gave me a wonderful smile and told me not to worry, it would all become clear in time. I believed him. And he was right.

What I remember most about that day was feeling completely at home in this environment. As we walked back to the Television Centre, I thanked Johnny Stewart for a marvellous day, for his time and his kindness. He looked me in the eye and said "You ought to come and work here, you've got a feel for it." I thanked him for the compliment, wished him all the best for his project and said I would certainly follow his advice and apply for a job. He told me to stick at it. "You'll get there", he said. He certainly got there with TOTP. The first one was transmitted on New Year's Eve in 1964 and it went on to be the longest running TV music show of all time, still running in 2006.

The following day I wrote a second letter to the head of light entertainment explaining how much I had enjoyed the day and that I would really like to work for the BBC. This time I attached my (very short) CV. The reply came back promptly saying that my letter had been passed on to the engineering department in view of my pending A-level results in Physics, Maths and Chemistry. Some weeks later I attended an interview at Langham Place in front of a panel of four stern looking executives who asked me a series of questions including where would I put the cameras if I was running an outside broadcast of a football match. I replied that I would put them all on one side of the ground so that the viewer would not be confused by the constant changing of the direction of the game. This answer seemed to cause my interrogators some consternation as they then spent several seconds discussing it in hushed voices amongst themselves. They then asked me a couple of simple questions about Ohm's Law which, disconcerted by their reaction to my last answer, I fluffed. The letter of rejection came a week or so later - in hindsight, probably the best outcome all round.

It was to be thirty years before I produced my first television series. I offered it to the BBC and they turned that down, too. Fortunately, ITV snatched it up and it became one of the most successful comedy drama series of all time. But, more of that later.

Some things are just not meant to be...

Claude Cavalotti

I liked Claude Cavalotti. He was an impressive man, at that time in his late fifties, who looked more like a prosperous Italian restaurateur than a bandleader with his mane of silver hair, great charm and elegant bearing. Compared to Syd Lipton he was less formal and more approachable with an easy, relaxed manner, which only infrequently gave way to displays of high emotion attributable no doubt to his Tuscan roots. He was also more of a working musician than Syd who, apart from the obligatory violin solo, was essentially a front man. By contrast, Claude would not hesitate to pick up his ever-ready alto and join the sax section. Also, whilst Syd believed in maintaining a distance between himself and the 'boys' in his band, there was nothing Claude enjoyed more than a casual chat over dinner. Which did not mean he was respected any the less.

Of course, Claude knew all about the Semitones and had often booked us through Syd for cabaret performances. He also knew that I was successfully leading small bands. One day he told me he had a proposition, namely, if I was prepared to form a four-piece group performing current 'pop' material, he would promote us and act as our agent. However, rather than simply being a band within a band as had been the case with Syd, he wanted this group to have it's own name, it's own repertoire and its own identity. This would mean some expenditure on presentation and he would not only help us with this but also guarantee us some regular bookings straightaway. The only concession he asked for in return was that we would only work for him. I was excited by the idea and knew immediately who I wanted for the other three players. I promised to put together a forty-five minute programme and suggest a name. Claude immediately gave us a series of six trial bookings where we would play one or two sets alternating with his ten-piece dance band. We settled on the name "The Nightimers" and, unsurprisingly, these first few jobs were to be at Claude's flagship venue, the Hilton. I was lucky to get the three guys I wanted, all semi-pros like me and excellent contemporary players - Tony Gold on guitar, Dave Edwards on bass and my great friend Arthur Lecomber on drums. We went to Carnaby Street and bought ourselves some tight black trousers, frilly yellow shirts and dark brown velvet jackets with matching bow ties. The first performance was a great success and soon Claude was offering us more work than we could handle.

By now it was becoming clear that whilst audiences were still enjoying the big band sound, especially as traditional ballroom dancing was still popular, once the dance band had left the stage to us with our youthful presentation and heavily amplified sound - not to mention the rock n'roll with vocals on every number – the floor was packed in seconds. In fact, it could be embarrassing when the big band returned to a less than enthusiastic welcome three quarters of an hour later. Still it worked, made for a great evening and "The Nightimers" under Claude's exclusive management were soon in great demand.

Far from being perplexed by my Jekyll and Hyde existence (by this time with a wife and new baby I was taking my fledgling publishing and design company pretty seriously), Claude took an active interest in all this and would sometimes take me to one side to chat about his own commercial problems, something he did not feel he could do with his other musicians. So much so, that on a couple of occasions we met socially for dinner with our wives. Eventually, he hinted that he intended to retire in the not too distant future and go back to Italy. By now I was working out of some rather charming Mews offices in Kensington and he suggested that he would like to come over, take a look at my operation and buy me lunch. I was pleased to accept and a week or so later, intrigued to know what he wanted to talk about, we met up at his local Italian. Following a few pleasantries, it transpired that he wanted me to take over his business believing that I was in a good position to build it up and - clearly of great importance to him - make sure that, when he departed the West End music scene, his band would stay together and his loyal musicians would not suffer.

I was greatly flattered and told him I would think it over very carefully but would need some financial details first. He seemed a little non-plussed, seeming to think that I should be able to work all that out for myself. When I explained that I had no idea how many bookings he was taking or how much he was charging and, therefore, what his turnover and profitability was likely to be, he said he would let me have some figures over the next few days - however, I should take comfort from the fact that he enjoyed a very good lifestyle, a West End flat and a new Jaguar every year. I asked him what he thought was the value of the business and he replied that he would settle for a percentage of the profits for the following five years. This seemed reasonable enough and we shook hands after a brandy and a very convivial lunch.

Despite several reminders, the information never materialised and the idea went no further. I think he must have realised that by divulging the figures I'd asked for, I would know what he had been paying himself. And to Claude, a proud Italian, that was a bridge too far.

The Ken Macintosh Band playing at the Odeon, Leicester Sqvare

The Dance Hall

I was never keen on working in dance halls - although a number of famous bands were still in residence at places like the Odeon, Leicester Square, the Lyceum in the Strand and at Hammersmith. Joe Loss and Ken Mackintosh, and later Ray McVay, had all built up their reputations playing the Mecca circuit, at that time run by Eric Morley of 'Miss World' fame (of whom more later). Eventually, nearly all of these famous 'Palais' establishments were turned over to bingo but for many years had been important and popular dance venues where some serious reputations had been established.

Some of them, including Leicester Square, were constructed below ground with a cinema above. I can't remember why or how but I once found myself playing there for several nights with Ken Mackintosh and his band. This was outside my usual line of work with the keyboard already set up and the entire repertoire neatly assembled in playing order in a large book. Most of the arrangements had been done specially for the band, which, as a result, had its own distinctive sound. We were also required to wear costumes.

The band was pretty much a traditional line-up with a rhythm section, two trumpets and four saxes, but with the addition of two male and two female singers. I was greeted by one of these, a long-haired, white faced, pimply youth, plump and short of stature with a monosyllabic Tyne and Wear delivery.

I learned a lesson that night. As I was putting on my band costume - shiny grey jacket, frilly white shirt and blue tie, coupled with my own black trousers, this lad had stripped down to his socks and underpants and was struggling to get into a tight fitting, one piece outfit, frankly better suited to a male ice skater. This was not a pretty sight as he squeezed his squat, unhealthy looking, pudgy body into this shiny nylon garment.

Once inside, he set about hair and make-up. Suffice to say that ten minutes later when we took to the stage, he appeared with a glossy mane of blonde hair and a sun-tanned face looking very much the part. He was also a great mover, had a good voice and made a thoroughly professional contribution fronting a top-class band.

Of course, at the end of the evening the process was reversed and, like Cinderella, our sexy, dynamic pop singer was transformed back to his alter ego. There was always a queue of female fans outside the stage door and a number of scribbled notes made their way into the dressing room addressed to individual performers, nearly always the singers. He would get his share but always slipped away via front of house, unrecognised by his fans. I imagine he had learnt the hard way that meeting them was certain to be a disappointing experience all round and I often wonder how many other singers and lead artists suffered in this way as a consequence of having their stage persona so far removed from who they really are.

Another reason that dance halls were hard work was the sheer level of noise the band created. Quite literally, not only could you not hear what you were playing yourself, neither could you hear anyone else nor the sound the band was making as a whole. All sense of relative levels was lost and you quickly developed a ringing sound in your ears, which lasted for hours afterwards.

Things worsened as the night wore on and the band got louder and louder. This became a major problem at Leicester Square. Beyond a certain level of decibels the music from the dancehall below began to interfere with the audiences' enjoyment of the film in the cinema above.

Now I'm sure the management had tried countless times to explain this to the bandleaders, clearly to no avail. The eventual solution was crude but highly effective. At the opposite end of the hall to the stage was a set of traffic lights connected to a sound sensor - green being acceptable, orange dangerously loud and red, too loud. So long as the bandleader stayed with green and orange all was well, but if he allowed the noise level to creep up to red the entire electrical supply to the stage was cut off. One moment the band and singers were in full flight, the next the dancers were prancing around to the reedy, unamplified sound of a brass and sax section playing on their own!

Once again I had discovered that any sort of residency was not for me.

Learning to Play

TWO figures influenced me enormously in my early days playing piano and guitar.

The first was Bert Weedon who, as well as being an accomplished guitarist in his own right, had just written probably the most famous musical teach yourself book of all time aimed at would-be guitar players – and in the 60's that meant almost every hot-blooded young male under twenty.

Bert began learning classical guitar at the age of twelve and decided to become a professional musician. In his teens during the 1930s, he led groups such as the Blue Cumberland Rhythm Boys, and Bert Weedon and His Harlem Hotshots, before making his first solo appearance at East Ham town hall in 1939. He worked with leading performers including the great jazz violinist Stephane Grappelli and legendary pianist George Shearing, and performed with various big bands and orchestras, including those of Ted Heath and Mantovani.

He joined the BBC Show Band directed by Cyril Stapleton in the 1950s, when he began to be featured as a soloist. He also worked as a session musician on many early British rock and roll and other records for artists such as Adam Faith, Billy Fury and Tommy Steele and worked as an accompanist to visiting American singers such as

Frank Sinatra, Judy Garland and Nat King Cole. It is estimated that he performed on over five thousand BBC radio broadcasts. He was also seen regularly on British television in the 1950s, including some of the most popular children's television programmes.

In 1959 he was asked by Top Rank Records to make a record as a solo guitarist. This was a turning point for him. He became the first British guitarist in the UK Singles Chart, with 'Guitar Boogie Shuffle' in 1959 and was cited as an influence by many later stars, including Eric Clapton, Brian May, Paul McCartney, George Harrison, John Lennon and Pete Townshend. McCartney once said: "George and I went through the Bert Weedon books and learned D and A together."

Although committed to the piano as my first instrument, many hours stuck behind a keyboard with others getting all the attention upfront had convinced me that the guitar was the 'cool' choice of instrument. So, I went down to Potters Music shop in Croydon's South End and bought myself a second hand Hofner President and a copy of Bert's book 'Play in a Day'.

As soon as I got home I understood why Bert had written the book. Anyone who thinks the guitar is an easy instrument is wrong - at least, not if you want to play it properly. To put it simplistically, unlike a keyboard the notes on a guitar are not in a nice easy sequence, you have to dodge around all six strings to find the notes you want and, of course, you also have to know how to play a large variety of chords. Surprisingly, most budding guitar players find that learning chords is easier that playing melody lines - although, of course, proper guitarists can do both.

Although Bert never claimed to have invented chord charts (little drawings that show the position of the fingers on the strings you need to produce certain chords) nonetheless, Bert's great skill and understanding of his instrument enabled him to organize them in an easy to understand, contemporary way. It was this that quite literally enabled the keen student to master just a few chords quickly and 'play in a day'.

Well, I was hooked. It helped, of course, to have a pianist's understanding of music in general, for example, being able read notation in the first place, and it wasn't long before I had learned to 'strum' a large number of songs by putting together chord sequences using Bert's charts. In fact, I soon found that playing guitar helped me understand how music went together, and thus accelerated my improvisational and composing skills on the piano, too.

Years later I met Bert socially, together with his gorgeous wife, Maggie and got to know him well. By this time he was in his seventies and, although he would not admit to retirement, his performing days were largely over. He was a charming man, full of gratitude for the great success he had never expected and an enthusiastic supporter of charities including the Water Rats and Variety Club. He was always anxious to give something back.

1999 was the fiftieth anniversary of Variety Club and I was privileged to have been asked to serve as Chief Barker during that milestone year. I wanted to kick it off in style with, if possible, an unforgettable 50th Birthday Celebration. I arranged for it to be held at the ITV Studios on the South Bank and invited Prince and

Princess Michael of Kent to be my guests of honour, together with all the surviving Chief Barkers who had preceded me. I also wanted to put on a first-class show for this distinguished audience and asked Bert if he would play. He did and was the star of the evening.

Bert died in 2012 and many of you reading this will recall the enormous media coverage the event received. Eric Clapton said: "I wouldn't have felt the urge to press on without the tips and encouragement Bert's book gave me. I've never met a player of any consequence who doesn't say the same thing." Brian May agreed: "There's not a guitarist in Britain from my generation who doesn't owe him a great debt of gratitude."

Well, speaking as a guitarist of no consequence at all, so do I. Thank you, Bert.

The other figure who influenced me greatly was the dashing and good-looking pianist, Russ Conway. Russ was born Trevor Herbert Stanford in Bristol and was largely self-taught on piano as he whiled away hours as a youngster during a three-year term in Borstal. His father then encouraged him to go to sea.

He served in the Merchant Navy from 1942 to 1948, and was awarded the Distinguished Service Medal as a signalman in a minesweeping flotilla "for distinguished service, efficiency and zeal" in clearance of mines in the Aegean and operations during the relief of Greece 1944-45. During his Navy service, he famously lost the tip of the 3rd finger of his right hand.

In the fifties and early sixties, Russ amassed an incredible twenty UK chart hits, achieving a cumulative total of 83 weeks on the UK

Singles Chart in 1959 alone. This included two self-penned number one instrumentals, "*Side Saddle*" and "*Roulette*", the latter deposing Elvis Presley's "*A Fool Such As I*". He was a fixture on TV shows and radio for many years, appearing several times at the London Palladium and becoming a regular on the Billy Cotton Band Show.

That's when I became fascinated with his style of playing. Essentially, he had adopted the same 'stride' left-hand method as many great popular pianists who had gone before him - Art Tatum, Fats Waller and the popular English pianist Winifred Atwell, plus countless others. This gave his accompanying left-hand great depth and rhythm, which impressed me no end. I remember clearly as a fourteen-year-old sitting for hours at the piano trying to replicate his style discovering happily in the process that I could also stretch an octave and a third with my left hand! Before long I had '*Side Saddle*' and '*Roulette*' off to a tee!

I met Russ on two occasions, the first at a concert at the Fairfield Halls in Croydon many years later, sometime in the middle 1990's. By then he was in his late sixties and had been seriously ill with stomach cancer. His first line of the evening was: "I know what you are all thinking - hasn't he put on weight!" He was right, of course, and this self-deprecating remark relaxed the audience who went on to enjoy a thoroughly enjoyable performance including a more than half-decent rendering of Gershwin's '*Rhapsody in Blue*'. Afterwards, I went round to his dressing room not wanting to miss the opportunity to thank him for being such an inspiration to me all those years ago. Of course, he didn't know me from Adam but seemed genuinely pleased that I had taken the trouble to say 'thank-you'.

The next time I saw him was in 1999 at a Variety Club Lunch in Bournemouth, ironically in honour of Bert Weedon. I was Chief Barker at the time and my job was to host the event and make the speech in praise of Bert. Sitting at the top table, Christine and I found ourselves next to Brian May who made a great speech happily reciting his own recollections of the great man and how he owed his career as a guitar player to Bert's "Play in a Day".

During Brian's address and with mine yet to follow, I cast my eye around the packed room and spied a familiar figure sitting in a corner. It was Russ. He had suffered a relapse of the cancer and was looking old and frail. When it was my turn to speak I covered all the ground in praise of Bert and then, knowing Bert well enough to be sure he wouldn't mind sharing the limelight, referred to the fact that there was someone else in the room to whom I owed a musical debt. I gestured towards Russ and asked him to stand so that people knew he was there. He did and was greeted by a tremendous ovation. I have seldom seen such a transformation. The years fell off him and there he was, beaming with that wonderful, charismatic smile that had made him so loved in his prime, forty years earlier. It was a moving and emotional moment. Sadly, he died within the year and I have always been glad that I was able to do that for him.

Russ' career had been blighted by ill health, including a nervous breakdown and a stroke, which prevented him from performing between 1968 and 1971. At times he drank heavily and smoked up to eighty cigarettes a day. Despite his sunny TV persona, he was clearly a troubled man, had been on anti-depressants and had periods of severe self-doubt. But he kept going. Having been diagnosed with cancer in the late eighties, he founded the Russ Conway Cancer Fund with his friend, writer and broadcaster Richard Hope-Hawkins, and they staged charity galas in major theatres that raised thousands of pounds for cancer charities. He never married.

Reading this you might think that Bert and Russ were pretty lightweight musical heroes and, perhaps, I should have set my sights higher. Well, later I did. But during those tender years you don't choose your icons, they choose you. Both of them were enjoying enormous popularity and were there, right in front of you whenever you switched on a radio or TV, or (as we did in those days) pop down to the shops to buy a record.

Make no mistake, these two were gifted artists. Bert had started life playing classical guitar and Russ had begun his musical career by winning a scholarship to the Bristol Cathedral Church Choir. As is so often the case with very accomplished people who make it big time, what we see is only a fraction of what they have to give - but it's that fraction which appeals to millions of viewers, listeners and (in those days) record buyers.

The Royal Family

OVER the years and in various capacities I have found myself rubbing shoulders with members of the Royal family. 'Rubbing shoulders' is probably not the appropriate term but in this context it is intended as a compliment – for, given the opportunity, they really do seem to relish something approaching normal conversation and can be great fun.

As I mentioned earlier, at the Variety Club's 50th Anniversary Party at the London Studios on the South Bank in 1999, I spent the evening dining and dancing with Princess Michael of Kent. An interesting lady.

She was born in 1945, in Karlsbad, at the time a German populated area now in the Czech Republic, near the family estates of her Austrian maternal grandmother, Princess Hedwig von Windisch-Graetz. Through her mother, the Princess is a descendant of Diane de Poitiers, mistress of Henry II of France and also of painter Peter Paul Rubens. So, a very old royal line indeed.

Her first husband was the English banker Thomas Troubridge, the younger brother of Sir Peter Troubridge, 6th Baronet, who she met during a boar hunt in Germany. They were married on 14 September 1971, at Chelsea Old Church, London. They separated in 1973, were divorced in 1977, and the marriage was formally annulled by the Roman Catholic Church in May 1978 for undisclosed reasons.

One month after the annulment, in June 1978, she married Prince Michael of Kent, a first cousin of the Queen, in a civil ceremony in

Austria. Upon marriage, she assumed the style and title of HRH Princess Michael of Kent, the female equivalent to her husband's title; because she was not born a princess, she is not entitled to be styled Princess Marie Christine. After receiving Pope John Paul II's permission, the couple later married in a Roman Catholic ceremony in 1983, at the Archbishop's House, London.

Now, like everyone else, I had read all about 'Princess Pushy' in the media and was curious to see how she measured up in real life. Accompanied by Prince Michael, she arrived perfectly on time and, I must say, looking like a million dollars, complete with tiara. Once greeted by our small reception committee, the Royal couple preceded us upstairs to a spectacular room with floor to ceiling windows overlooking the Thames. For the next twenty minutes or so over a glass or two of champagne I introduced them to as many of our guests as possible, including all the Past Chief Barkers present who I had invited especially for this unique anniversary event. After that Christine and I took them down to dinner in the largest of the LWT studios, which had been set up for the banquet and the entertainment that was to follow. The whole event was being recorded for subsequent transmission and, as was customary, the

Princess was seated next to me whilst Chistine's job was to keep Prince Michael entertained. The free-flowing conversation that followed was as unexpected as it was fascinating. It would, of course, be both injudicious and impolite to disclose every detail of what she told me during the course of the evening but, on the assumption that my main concern was to make sure she relaxed and enjoyed herself, I must have succeeded on both counts.

I discovered, for example, that as a young woman and member of the Austrian Royal Family, she was anything but pleased to hear of her proposed marriage into the English Royal Family whom she had been brought up to regard as upstarts when compared to her own family's much longer lineage. Nevertheless, she had agreed to meet the dashing young Prince although the only impression she could recall from that first meeting was thinking how much he looked like the Tzar. In all other respects she was unmoved. The Prince, on the other hand, was smitten by the beautiful and haughty young blonde and clearly intended to press his suit. For political reasons both families were strongly in favour of the match and eventually she agreed, whilst still believing that she was marrying a man she didn't love and who was beneath her station.

She went on to say that her parents had told her that it was a good marriage and they liked the Prince very much. He was a fine man, they said, and even if she didn't love him at the outset, she would come to love him as time went by. This, she told me, casting a fond eye in her husband's direction, was precisely what happened. She had, of course, come to England, learned the language (so well, in fact, that she has subsequently written a number of acclaimed books) and attempted to settle down. This had not been easy, she explained, partly because she always felt as if she were living in a foreign country - which, of course, she was - and secondly, because certain members of our Royal family, who had so successfully buried their own central European origins, never really accepted her. Add to this the fact that she and Prince Michael were expected to keep up a 'royal' way of life sustained by very little money from the Queen or the public purse, she had never felt truly welcome.

During the rest of the evening she told me many other things - as I said, some of them far too intimate to mention! At the end, I was left with the impression that she was very much a central European who, in characteristic fashion, wore her heart on her sleeve rather than keeping her feelings and emotions in check; what we rather 'grandly' refer to as the 'stiff upper lip'. Consequently, she was the antithesis of our idea of a Royal and, at the end of the day, had never 'fitted in'. Thus she found herself uniquely positioned amongst our other 'junior' Royals as easy fodder for the tabloids.

Maybe she *had* been outspoken, indiscreet - even 'pushy' on occasions. Speaking from the position of 'take as you find' I can only say that she seemed to me highly intelligent, charming and captivatingly good company. Whilst there were no doubt two sides to her story, it was difficult not to empathise with her and Prince Michael as they struggled for years to find a place within the 'firm' to which neither of them were naturally suited.

There was an interesting rider to the evening. Accompanying Princess Michael was her lady-in-waiting, Emma Joy Kitchener (a great niece of Lord Kitchener), a particularly striking young woman with a cascade of red hair tumbling, Rapunzel like, down to her waist. A step behind her was her husband, a shortish, rather plump and jolly young man called Julian who introduced himself to me in what I thought were rather affected tones, saying he was an out-of-work actor. He was clearly aware of the recent success of 'Darling Buds' and 'A Touch of Frost' and asked me to bear him in mind for any parts that might come up that would suit him.

It transpired that his surname was Fellowes and I don't suppose he is looking around for many parts now.

* * *

The other Royal who I had the privilege of meeting more than once is the Duke of Edinburgh.

The story goes that it was he who brought the idea of setting up a branch of Variety Club in the UK back from the States soon after the war. In 1992 the Duke was seventy and, as a Gold Card member of Variety Club, the charity decided to hold a banquet in his honour. The Chief Barker at the time delegated this job to me.

The first thing was to find a suitable venue as, somehow, our regular Park Lane haunts such as the Hilton and the Dorchester didn't seem to fit the bill. A Royal palace would have been ideal, but not easy to find! In the end, we secured the Banqueting House in Whitehall, which, if not exactly a palace itself, was at least opposite one! A couple of visits, one of them with the caterer who protested he would have to set up his own kitchen from scratch, convinced me that the Great Hall was perfect. Complete with a glorious and historic painted ceiling and a Minstrel's Gallery, it reeked of grandness and tradition. Just what was needed for our royal event.

I laid on some special ingredients for the occasion, including the trumpeters of the Coldstream Guards of whom the Duke was Commander-in-Chief at the time. Not only that, but I managed to persuade their Director of Music to compose a special fanfare in his honour. I have a copy of that fanfare, suitably framed, on my wall at home to this day. I couldn't persuade the Duke to sign it, though!

The other rather inspired idea was to book the lovely young Scottish singer, Marie McLaughlin, to sing after dinner. This turned out to be a stroke of genius since, as the Duke was unaccompanied that night (his wife presumably, being otherwise occupied), we needed a lady to sit next to him. Marie was happy to oblige and our guest of honour clearly relished her chirpy company throughout the meal, as well as her fine performance afterwards.

Also, sitting at the top table was my friend, the actor Robert Powell, who had agreed to propose the birthday toast in honour of Prince Philip. Robert and I spent hours working out the detail of what he would say. I even telephoned another old friend, the late Lance Percival, who alongside his other talents was a gifted and sought after speechwriter, to see if he would let us have one or two of his best new after-dinner jokes. He gave me a couple of crackers that Robert delivered, of course, with exemplary timing.

Quite rightly, Robert's speech had been full of praise for the Duke who, in his response said that he had heard of 'laying it on with a trowel, but felt that tonight it had been laid on with a Powell', which, I thought was pretty good off the cuff.

I had produced a souvenir programme for the event and, in the course of compiling it, learnt quite a lot about this extraordinary man who, for most of his life and for obvious reasons, has been obliged to hide his own considerable talents under a bushel.

Some years later I met him again, this time at the Sports Awards Dinner at the Hilton in Park Lane. I was hosting the event and Prince Philip was seated next to me for the meal. In my opening remarks, aimed at the large number of sporting personalities amongst the five hundred strong audience, I said that we welcomed them because: 'if show business personalities are our icons, you are our heroes.' This drew an appreciative round of applause and I noticed the Duke clapping, too. When I sat down he whispered to me: 'Liked the bit about the icons and the heroes'.

Again, during dinner, I found him to be friendly and thoroughly good value, so much so, that I summoned up the courage to ask him a 'real' question. At the time some of the younger royals had been in for a bit of drubbing by the tabloids for not the best of reasons and I asked him whether this was difficult for him and Her Majesty to cope with. He thought for a moment before replying. 'They are extraordinary people.' 'Who, the journalists?' I enquired. 'No,' he said, 'my children.' Another insight into the Royal mind.

The next time I saw him was twenty years later at a daytime function at St James Palace when he was handing over the Presidency of another charity to his daughter, Princess Anne. By now he was nearly ninety - although, for the life of me, I couldn't see much difference in his appearance.

Everyone was standing; the hundred or so guests and the two Royals who both made witty and brief speeches. It was then the turn of the Chief Executive of the charity to briefly thank them both for coming and express the appreciation of all those present. This she duly did and we all presumed the event to be over. Not so. She then went on to say that for the benefit of those who weren't familiar with the work of the charity, she would give a brief explanation. Forty-five minutes later she was still going - and we were still standing.

It was mid-summer, the room was hot and airless and people were dropping like flies. Footmen were bringing in chairs from adjacent rooms, other guests were leaving and yet, throughout this inappropriate, interminable drivel, the ninety-old Duke stood calmly at ease on one side of the oblivious CEO whilst the Princess Royal did the same on the other. Not for a moment did either of them falter or flinch or give any sign of wanting to sit down. It was a remarkable display of thoughtlessness on the one hand and fortitude on the other and I am certain that as the hapless CEO bid them farewell, she had no idea what she had done or how lucky she had been. I wonder whether the next generation of Royals will have it them.

We have seen so many similar signs over the years of what an extraordinary man he is and yet I still ponder how much he is valued and appreciated. We British have a habit of taking people for granted and only saying 'thank-you' when it is too late. It would be nice if we could do rather better in his case.

Tony Hatch

IN the year 2000 it was the turn of Variety Club in the UK to host the International Convention. In those days it was thought to be an honour to be the host country as delegates came from all over the world to exchange ideas and experience in the worldwide quest to raise money for underprivileged and disabled children. The Chief Barker that year was Tony Hatch.

I first met Tony when he turned up to a Variety Club Crew Meeting a year or so previously. Although we all knew he had been involved in the charity for a long time, until then he had been based in Australia with his ex-wife and collaborator, the singer Jackie Trent, which had rather kept him away from his native England. Their divorce had been a long and acrimonious affair. After thirty years of marriage they separated in 1995 but did not divorce until 2002. One can only imagine the nightmare of sorting out the financial implications of the many hit songs they had written together, including the theme from the TV series 'Neighbours' - to name but one. By the time I met him he had settled down with his new wife, Maggie, in Minorca and had started travelling regularly to London.

When I was approaching the end of my term as Chief Barker, I telephoned Tony to see whether there was any possibility he might take over from me. He had already been Chief Barker of the Australian Variety Club and was prominent in the whole Variety International movement. It seemed unlikely that he would take on the UK as well. But, much to my and everyone else's delight, he did. Needless to say his international connections guaranteed the success of the 2000 Convention over which he and Maggie presided flawlessly.

Tony must go down as one of the great names in popular music this century, not only as a songwriter but also as a producer, performer and broadcaster in his own right.

He was born in Pinner in North London. Encouraged by his musical abilities, his mother - also a pianist - enrolled him in the London Choir School in Bexley, Kent when he was ten. After that, he could have gone on to the Royal Academy of Music but instead left school at fifteen and found a job in London's Tin Pan Alley.

Before long, he was writing songs and making a name for himself working for Top Rank Records. When he was called up for national service his musical skills led him to join the band of the Coldstream Guards (the shortest man ever to wear a busby, he'll say!) and, on his return in 1959, he began his own recording career in earnest with a cover version, ironically, of Russ Conway's piano instrumental *"Side Saddle"*.

In 1960, a recording of his composition *"Look For A Star"*, featured in the film 'Circus of Horrors', became a Top Ten hit in the UK. In 1961 he moved on to a part-time job with Pye Records, where he assisted his new mentor, Alan A. Freeman, with the recording of *"Sailor"*, a number one hit for Petula Clark, thus launching one of the most successful and famous partnerships ever in popular music.

Tony continued writing songs, sometimes under the pseudonym Mark Anthony and, in 1963, US teen idol Bobby Rydell hit the charts with *"Forget Him"* which Tony wrote and produced. This led to him producing, arranging and writing for other American stars such as Connie Francis and Pat Boone. In 1964 he wrote, under the pseudonym Fred Nightingale, the Searchers' number one hit *"Sugar and Spice"*. He went on to produce The Searchers, David Bowie and The Montanas, amongst many other stars - including, of course, Petula Clark.

In the same year he made his first trip to New York in search of new material for her. The visit inspired him to write *"Downtown"*, originally with The Drifters in mind but, when Petula heard the still unfinished tune, she told him that if he could write lyrics to match the quality of the music, she would record the song as her next single. Its release transformed her into a huge international star, topping charts globally and introducing her to the US market. That year also yielded the remarkable series of hits *"I Know a Place"*, *"You'd Better Come Home"*, and *"Round Every Corner"* for Petula. Tony also wrote her 1967 hits *"Don't Sleep In The Subway"* and *"The Other Man's Grass Is Always Greener"* written with his wife, Jackie Trent. With this string of huge successes behind them, it wasn't long before Tony Hatch and Petula Clark became established as the British equivalent of Burt Bacharach and Dionne Warwick,

During the 1970s Tony became familiar to television viewers as a regular panellist on 'New Faces' where his blunt style of assessing the contestants earned him the nickname 'The Hatchet Man'. This, of course, proved to be the forerunner of later similar series - including, most recently, Simon Cowell's 'Britain's Got Talent'.

All of this adds up to a stellar career and yet a more modest, approachable, quietly spoken man you couldn't wish to meet.

In 2009 I had a call from our friend Vikki Smith. Vikki is a great hostess and I had happily helped her organise the entertainment for a series of spectacular parties at her beautiful home in Guernsey. Her husband, Jim, was about to celebrate his seventieth birthday and she wanted to do something special, and could I help. It turned out that she had booked The Compleat Angler at Marlowe, a particularly nice hotel overlooking the Thames. She was inviting about a hundred people, many of whom were arriving from far afield and were staying overnight, and she wanted to give them a great time. Plus, Jim shouldn't know anything about it. I told her that I would think it over and come back to her with some ideas.

The following day I rang her to ask whether Jim had a favourite artist, someone who had given him particular pleasure over the years. Vikki said she would find out. She soon called back and said: "Petula Clark - Jim has been a big fan of hers for years." I said I would see what I could do - and that's when I rang Tony Hatch in Menorca!

As always Tony was incredibly helpful. I suggested that if the idea was feasible at all, I would like him to do twenty minutes on his own and then, as he went into the introduction to '*Downtown*' Petula would appear from nowhere and take over from him. Tony said he could do the date in question and would fly in the night before but he would have to ascertain Petula's schedule to see whether the idea might work logistically.

As it transpired, Petula was flying back the day before the event from Canada where she had been performing to sell-out houses. He had asked her about the gig at the Compleat Angler and she was calling him back. I waited with bated breath for Tony's next communication. It came the following day; yes, she would do it, a private party would make a change from the big venues she had been playing on tour and it would be fun to work with Tony again.

And that is exactly what happened. As it transpired the two of them hadn't performed as a duo for many years and in this small, relaxed environment, the years rolled away and, with no rehearsal, they sang and played along together as if it was yesterday. Needless to say, the audience was not only taken aback but enthralled to see these two musical legends performing for them at a private birthday party! I should perhaps add that the quality of their performance was outstanding. Both were doing material they knew like the back of their hands and the years had been kind to Ms Clark's voice: if anything it sounded better, more rounded and had greater depth than in her prime.

But it didn't stop there. After the show both Petula and Tony were in no hurry to leave and chatted away happily with anyone and everyone, behaving more like fellow guests than the international stars they were. The following morning those who had travelled from the Channel Islands – if not from further afield – agreed it was great value and more than worth the trip.

Finally – and most importantly – there was the reaction of James, the birthday boy. Well, he was over the moon, realising, of course, that he had enjoyed witnessing a quite remarkable reunion that would have been unlikely in other circumstances. He did, however, confide to me that although Vikki had managed to keep the secret for the best part of two months, a rather conscientious employee of the hotel had rushed up to him the night before to ask whether he thought the suite she had reserved as a dressing room for Ms Petula Clark was suitable! Eternal gentleman that he is, Jim, of course, behaved as if it was all a total surprise.

I have enjoyed many other happy times with Tony, often after dinners or on occasions when some impromptu entertainment was required. In more recent times Tony has turned his immense talents to composing humorous little songs that he performs from the piano. When I first heard a couple of these - *'I Think a Lot of You'* and *'Senior Moments'* - I asked if he would mind me borrowing them as I am often asked to do the same sort of thing. Within days he had sent me the manuscript, accompanied with a CD. I quickly learnt them and have since performed them countless times along with others in the same genre written by Richard Stilgoe and Peter Skellern and Flanders and Swann, as well as some of my own efforts. This particular style of entertaining at the piano is a dying art and people are always pleased to hear it revived, especially when the songs are as clever and witty as Tony's.

One evening at the Institute of Directors, Tony and I were doing a spot of impromptu light entertainment after dinner and, thinking that we both knew the number (me because I had sung it many times and Tony because he wrote it *and* had sung it many times!), I struck up the introduction to *'Senior Moments'*. Now, as the title suggests, the song is about those embarrassing lapses of memory that occur with increasing frequency as we get older. Inevitably and ironically what should have been its first rendition as a duet, deteriorated into a complete shambles as we discovered that neither of us could remember the words. Fortunately, our friendly audience saw the funny side as we drew the song to a hasty conclusion.

I have often said that I would like to have had Tony's career and written all those fabulous songs – not to mention working with the greatest musicians and entertainers of a generation. Like so many supremely talented and creative people, Tony Hatch has no need to adopt airs and graces of any kind. What you see is what you get.

Anita Harris and Mike Margolis

DURING the 60's and 70's a beautiful young elfin-faced star with huge brown eyes enjoyed a series of hits and was always popping up on television and film both as an actress (most memorably in the 'Carry On' films) and, of course, a singer. Anita Harris was, in fact, a major artist who appeared in several Royal Variety performances as well as being surprised by Eamonn Andrews one evening at the 'Talk of the Town' for her own episode of 'This is Your Life'. She was also alleged to be one of the highest paid cabaret performers in the world.

The first time I saw the name Mike Margolis was on an envelope. Over the years that followed their two names were destined to crop up for me in many different circumstances and guises.

Soon after I had joined up in business with my old school friend, Alan Cowing, we were effectively evicted from our premises off Fleet Street where our newly combined publishing, design and advertising business had been located. After searching high and low we eventually found a charming mews property in Kensington, which we thought might suit our operation.

When the estate agent opened the front door we were confronted with the usual pile of unopened mail addressed to the previous tenant. The name Margolis was on pretty much every envelope – and, on one or two of them, 'Miss Anita Harris, c/o Mike Margolis). Whilst this was mildly intriguing we had other things on our minds, namely, whether this rather quaint suite of offices might work for us. It didn't take us long to agree that it would and soon we were back at the estate agent's offices signing up.

After many a late night painting and decorating (and building a few stud walls and partitions) we had 2a, Drayson Mews in a state we thought was suitably fashionable and 'cool' to present our small, creative 'hot-shop' in the right light. Luckily it did just that. It suited us very well and, undoubtedly, our business – now expanded into sales promotion thanks to Alan's experience and skills – benefited from the move.

It transpired that our predecessors at No 2a had been a firm in a similar business to ours. In fact, Lane-Margolis was one of the first so-called 'hot-shops'. In the early eighties the advertising world was structured quite differently to now with a dozen or so full-service advertising agencies serving pretty well all the major clients. Yes, there were a number of smaller outfits around, many of them thriving on the crumbs from the rich men's table - but the big agencies really had it sewn up.

Being full service, the large firms like J.Walter Thompson, FCB, Young & Rubicam, Lintas and so on all had their own creative departments - but many of them were happy to draw on the skills of outsiders to boost the efforts of their own team when required. This was particularly useful when pitching for new business. A number of freelance creative people, many of whom had served their term with the large outfits, had seen the opportunity to strike out on their own, charging substantial fees for injecting their creative ideas into the

mix. Indeed, it wasn't long before we were doing the same thing working on a number of campaigns for larger agencies as well as directly for their clients.

As I mentioned, Lane-Margolis was one of the first to enter this field and Mike was its leading creative mind. In fact, some years later I was to discover what a brilliant artist he was.

It has been a repeating pattern for me to meet up with the same people, sometimes after long lapses of time, in totally different social and business contexts. So, although I had encountered the name Mike Margolis (and, of course, Anita), it was to be another fifteen years before I met them in the flesh. It was only then that I learned they were man and wife – an apparently unlikely match in many ways: Anita, tall, elegant and decidedly beautiful and Mike, short, plumpish and dapper. But their total devotion to each other was obvious.

By then Anita's career had moved on and she had become much in demand as a musical theatre star, particularly after her great success following Elaine Paige as Grizelda in Andrew Lloyd-Webber's 'Cats'. Her performance had also inspired Mike to produce a fabulous painting of her in the role. He went on to develop a series depicting all the other characters in 'Cats' as limited edition prints and postcards.

Christine and I were introduced to them at a dinner party when I lost no time in reminding Mike of our mutual connection with 2a Drayson Mews. He found this very amusing and told me that not long after he had moved from Drayson Mews, he had left Lane-Margolis to devote himself full-time to managing Anita's career. I also told Mike how brilliant I thought his 'Cats' pictures were – in fact, if ever he decided to sell the original of Anita as Grizelda, would he please give me first option. He responded by saying that the original was far too valuable for him to sell, but he would be pleased to let me have a signed print. We left it at that.

Not long afterwards he rang to ask if I would meet up with him to discuss an idea for a new television drama series. We had a London flat at the time and I arranged to see him there the following week. When the time arrived I was surprised and pleased when Anita turned up as well.

It turned out Mike had been working on an idea based around a female detective set in Victorian London. He had the plot all sorted out and presented me with a stylish treatment and a CD. Glancing through it, I quickly realised that, far from a TV series, he had come up with a concept for a stage musical with, not surprisingly, the lead part Verity providing a starring vehicle for Anita. Despite the totally professional approach they had adopted – including the demo CD which contained a number of fully orchestrated songs which must have cost a small fortune to record – the project had one major flaw which would have been as obvious to any theatre producer as it was to me. Anita was thirty years too old for the part!

With Anita sitting there, curled up on the floor by my sofa looking lovely with her dancer's body and knees tucked under her chin, I didn't have the heart to state the obvious so, instead, expanded on why it was so difficult to get such ambitious projects off the ground. As hardened pros they had heard all this often before and were used to disregarding negative thoughts (quite rightly otherwise nothing new would ever happen in showbusiness). I also explained that as a television producer I had little experience in the world of theatre. Thus the meeting came to a natural end but I promised to call Mike within a day or so with any further thoughts I might have.

Working on the assumption that I could say things to Mike that I would have found difficult to say in front of Anita, I telephoned him the following day to explain that if he wanted to get his musical off the ground – not to mention some return on his considerable personal investment - he would need to present the whole thing with a different, much younger star attached. The industry was even more notorious then for not employing older experienced artists than it is now. To say his response was lukewarm would be an understatement. He was simply not interested in even contemplating the possibility. That was when I realised for the first time that Mike and Anita might have an uphill battle ahead. However, they were lovely, talented people joined at the hip and it felt right to do everything possible to help them.

Verity Lake, the character Mike had created, had great merit. She was a plucky, well-born, educated girl, who combined her love of the music hall with a fascination for magic and crime detection. Set in the murky world of Victorian London, the story involved multiple murders and political intrigue, with a side cast of famous, real-life characters peppered along the way. All good stuff. I suggested to Mike that as a first step to developing the project further, he write the story in book form.

It didn't take him long. Within a few weeks he'd given me the manuscript for book one, complete with little illustrations for the chapter headings. He'd also written the synopses for the next five! The series was to be called 'The Verity Lake Casebook'. But there was a problem. Although the story was well structured and plotted and the characters well drawn, the writing style was, to say the least, idiosyncratic. Having assumed, perhaps optimistically, that the material would be immediately acceptable, my plan had been to send it on to a well-known literary agent I knew with a view to finding a publisher. It was obvious, however, that it would need some drastic editing.

I put this to Mike who quite accepted that his writing style was highly individual; nevertheless, he had no intention of changing it. That was when I found myself offering to edit the whole book, a self-imposed task that I knew would take several weeks. He agreed and, eventually, I was able to send him the fully revised and edited manuscript for book one, in a state where I believed it would be taken it seriously. Following his approval of the revised version, he asked that I submit it to my agent friend.

During the next week or so, I heard nothing from Mike and began to wonder whether he was keen for the project to go any further. After a while the agent called me to say that he thought the idea had great merit and he would like to meet the author. At that point I decided to bow out and put the two of them directly in touch.

Despite all the effort that had gone into to this, I never heard any more, nor did I make any further enquiries of either party. On reflection, I could only assume that since the project no longer involved Anita, Mike had no real interest it. On the other hand, he might have simply had other things on his mind.

A year or so later, we decided to have a big party at home and invite a number of celebrity acquaintances as well as long standing friends, neighbours and family. It was close to Christmas and I had prepared a selection of festive songs for everyone to join in. I telephoned Anita to ask if she would lead the singing, fully expecting a 'no'. To my delight she accepted with enthusiasm and, on the night, was an absolute joy and greatly appreciated by the fifty or so guests who had gathered around our Christmas tree. The Verity project was not mentioned.

We had a few more social encounters over the next four years. By now Anita was appearing up and down the country in various touring stage productions including a season in Dickie Harris' 'Stepping Out', which included a run at the Theatre Royal in Brighton. This was fairly close for us, so I rang Mike to tell him we would be coming down. He told us how good the production and that he and Anita would look forward to seeing us. When we arrived, he was in the foyer to greet us, saying that Anita would have a bottle of champagne open in her dressing room after the show.

Richard 'Dickie' Harris had written some scripts for 'Darling Buds' and 'A Touch of Frost' so, whilst I would not claim to have known him well, I was well versed in his work. 'Stepping Out' had been one of his greatest successes, both onstage and subsequently as a film starring Liza Minelli. It was a great show.

This particular touring version had clearly done well elsewhere and certainly was well supported in Brighton. As we took our seats, we did so in a mood of optimistic anticipation. We were not disappointed; Anita's performance and those of the rest of the cast were enjoyable, the direction excellent and the play, of course, virtually foolproof.

We had no hesitation in accepting Mike's invitation to go backstage, safe in the knowledge that we would be able praise the show and the performers with sincerity (although in true theatrical tradition we would have done so anyway!)

When we arrived backstage her dressing room was full of people, with Anita, still in costume, dispensing champagne to one and all. We were welcomed like long lost friends and ushered in to join the party. I noticed that sitting quietly in a corner was a familiar, elegant, elderly lady who we quickly recognised as Dame Vera Lynn.

We stayed for maybe half an hour soaking up the backstage atmosphere with its carefully observed conversational rituals, before making our way homewards. We could not have been made to feel more at home.

Other than the odd meeting at various charity events, the next time we really heard from them was when we received a formal invitation to an exhibition and sale of Mike's paintings at a Bond Street art and antiques gallery. The guests of honour for the evening were to be Prince and Princess Michael of Kent. Apart from wanting to support Mike, this seemed like too good an occasion to miss.

It was indeed a splendid evening, well attended and with Mike, the flamboyant artist, floating around in his huge fedora and sunglasses with the beautifully groomed Anita on his arm. I fully intended to buy a picture, in fact I had in mind the painting of Anita as Grizelda the Cat - until I saw the prices. As we looked around at the two or three dozen paintings for sale, there wasn't one under £5,000 with the most expensive – and I'm sure I don't need to identify which one it was – marked up at £25,000! Overhearing the conversations around us, we were obviously not the only guests who considered the pictures to be over priced and that, despite the universal admiration of Mike's work, very few (if any) red stickers appeared on the works that night.

The following day an extraordinary story appeared in the media. As soon as the gallery opened, bailiffs had raided the premises and confiscated all Mike's work, reportedly in settlement of the couple's debts. Mike and Anita ended up making nothing from their brave attempt to salvage their financial affairs.

A lot of negative press appeared over the following weeks: how all of Anita's early wealth had been lost through bad investments (although Mike later described this as the collapse of a Swiss bank), how they had apparently been living for some time in a friend's upstairs room, how Anita's earnings over the last few years, touring in poorly paid provincial rep, had added up to very little and how Mike, despite his creative brilliance, had been lacking as a businessman. All of this was now distressingly revealed in the full gaze of the public.

It is not surprising that after these revelations this lovely and talented couple chose to retreat from public life - and I don't blame them. The effort of keeping up appearances whilst knowing one is on the verge of ruin would subject anyone to intolerable strain. And yet, they would have known that without this pretence the chance, however remote, of Anita landing one last starring role and thus saving them from financial ruin would have been impossible. There is something heart-rending about a fallen star. At the time she was recorded as bravely saying: "If I've made any mistakes on our behalf it's to keep up an image that's expected of me. I don't want to disappoint. It's very difficult to say you're up against it. It's part of the profession to be on top."

I like and admire Anita and Mike immensely and their persistence and optimism during those impossibly difficult times was both courageous and touching. But that is not the end of the story.

Nothing is forever and, more recently, we were pleased to see Anita give an excellent performance at a charity performance of Stephen Sondheim's work at the Theatre Royal, Covent Garden. Many of those in the audience came from the world of showbusiness and were well aware of recent chapters in her life. Her appearance was greeted with huge enthusiasm, warmth and affection. Since then she has been back at work in a touring version of her own one-woman show, appearing in pantomime and endless radio programmes. What a trouper!

Will she regain her early fame and fortune? Now in her middle seventies, but looking at least twenty years younger, probably not. Will she secure her reputation as a thoroughly professional artist and legend? Almost certainly, yes. We wish her well.

Roger Hargreaves and the Mr Men

DURING our time at Drayson Mews we often worked for other agencies, coming up with additional creative ideas for major campaigns or, sometimes, dealing with smaller pieces of business; either where we had some particular additional expertise or, more often, simply because they didn't have the time themselves.

One such agency we worked for regularly was David Macaulay Advertising located in rather swish offices overlooking Marble Arch. They were a medium sized full service agency who worked for a number of quite prestigious clients including Timex Watches, Lindt Chocolate, Berlei Bras and a company called Lovell & Christmas, part of the Fitch Lovell Group (since taken over by Bookers). In the eighties the company was a major player in the manufacture and distribution of food products of all kinds.

For example, we had done a huge job for them re-designing the whole of their Newforge canned goods range which included just about every fruit and vegetable product imaginable as well as tinned meats. In fact, there must have been a hundred different products, all contained in cans of different shapes and sizes. Not only did they want us to give the range a new, updated look, but we had to arrange for photography and finished artwork for each and every label as well as oversee all the printing.

The project took several months to complete and many late nights at the office - sustained in my case by eating the contents of the sample cans sent down to us for the job. As most were unlabelled, when I opened the tin I never knew whether I was in for mandarin oranges or Irish stew. It also led to us designing new labels for other Fitch Lovell products with different brand names, including De Haan Ox Tongue, which required a trip to their factory in Wigan -

of which the less said the better. Suffice to say that my ideas about the food industry suffered an abrupt reality check.

Anyway, both agency and client were very happy with everything we did, especially when they were able to report that sales of Newforge products had soared by 30% following the appearance of the new packaging on the retailers' shelves!

Another major brand manufactured and distributed by Fitch Lovell was the famous canned pork product, Spam. The subject of many jokes and jibes since its invention in the States in 1937 - not least by the Monty Python team who cemented its immortality with their spoof musical 'Spamalot' - the product has always sold well worldwide with little advertising support. Nevertheless, Macaulays had been asked to try a new tack in the UK by promoting sales of the product through butcher's shops. This was a typically small promotional exercise by their standards, with a correspondingly small budget, which they were more than happy to put out to us.

We took the brief from the agency's creative director, a tall, dark haired, handsome man in his middle thirties, immaculately dressed in a suit and tie (very unusual for a 'creative' man at that time, most of whom sported 't'-shirts and leather jackets) who was obviously well-educated and spoke beautifully. He was rather disdainful of our little job and I don't suppose we discussed it for more than fifteen minutes; it really was a case of 'over to you'. It was 1971 and this was my first encounter with the suave Roger Hargreaves.

I took the job back to the office realising that for the money on offer all we could really do was a poster to go in Butcher's shop windows and, maybe, a recipe leaflet showing what could be done with Spam other than eating it straight out of the can. As always with small budget jobs, the trick is to make the promotion even more eye-catching and appealing so that a little money is made go a long way.

Unfortunately, a tin of Spam, whilst highly recognisable, is not the most attractive item to feature on a poster so it occurred to us that we would have to come up with something unique for this promotion. When I took the job back to the studio the idea had already formed itself - a colourful, cartoon-style little butcher character who would become the face of our mini-promotion. I set one of our designers to work and before long we had him - a childishly drawn, black outlined, boldly coloured butcher in a straw boater and striped apron with a big moustache and fancy lace-up shoes. We called him Mr Spam.

We already had a food hygienist working on some recipes and, within the week, I was back in Roger's office together with the Fitch Lovell account executive presenting the work. They were pleased and, with a few minor modifications, we were up and running.

Shortly afterwards I had a call from Roger asking if I could go in again, this time to talk about some work for another of his clients, the well-known chocolate brand, Lindt. When his secretary showed me into his office I was staggered by what I saw - pretty well every square inch of wall space was covered with A3 magic marker drawings of what looked like a whole family of Mr Spams! Several of them even had the fancy, Italian looking lace-up shoes. Roger must have seen my jaw drop and asked me what I thought.

"What are they?" I replied.

"Children's books," he answered as if it was the most obvious thing in the world. "I'm going to call them Mr Men, all sorts of characters with different stories. Simple - text on the left, drawings on the right. What do you think?"

"They look like Mr Spam," I found myself saying.

"That's where I got the idea," he replied, "And that's why I'm going to offer you the publishing."

Do you remember when Decca turned down the Beatles? Or the BBC turned down 'The Darling Buds of May'? Well, this was my moment to do the same thing, and it is why I've never blamed the guys at Decca or the BBC. For the simple reason that, at such an early stage - not much more than the germ of an idea in someone's head - it is almost impossible to envisage what might lie ahead.

"Thanks, Rog," I replied, "but, frankly, children's books aren't my thing. But, good luck, I am sure they will be a great success."

"Are you certain?" he asked.

"Yes, not my bag, really, sorry." And that was that.

The next few times I saw Roger he was clearly spending very little time working for his employer and an awful lot on his children's book idea. There were even more sheets of layout paper strewn around his office, as well as printer's proofs and promotional material. Roger drew with Magic Marker pens and his trademark bold lines masked the fact that his colour spread across the page in the days before bleedproof paper. He told me he often drew the smile in last because he loved to come down in the morning and fill it in. He said it was the smile that brought his characters alive. Lovely.

After my turndown, he'd been to see a printer/publisher friend called Jack Thurman, who was only too pleased to take on the job. Before long the first series of books were out and had started to appear in bookshops. Not long afterwards I was at Macaulays picking up another job and popped in to see him.

"We're on TV," he reported. "Arthur Lowe is doing the narration." Within a few weeks Roger had resigned from Macaulays (or been politely asked to leave, I never quite knew which).

His dream paid off. And how. With the TV series running on the BBC, his first book, Mr Tickle, became an instant success and five more quickly followed. Within three years, Roger had sold a million copies and ultimately became so wealthy he moved to Guernsey as a tax exile. But in 1988 the dream came to an abrupt halt when he suffered a stroke while walking down to breakfast. He was taken to hospital but died later that day, aged just 53. Tragic.

Of course, he left behind a huge fortune (and legacy) and was fortunate to have a son, Adam, who was happy to take up his inheritance - in both respects. As it transpired the Mr Men empire was in good hands and in 2004, Adam and his family made the decision to sell the intellectual property rights to the entertainment group Chorion, which also owned the copyright to the works of Enid Blyton and Agatha Christie, for a cool 24 million pounds.

I never asked Jack Thurman how well he did out of the Mr Men, nor did I ever have any regrets about turning Roger down. I felt that he had more than fulfilled any moral obligation by offering me the opportunity first. I also have no doubt that if I had accepted I would have made a great deal of money. But I didn't and that wasn't his fault.

Besides which the Mr Men have given huge pleasure to millions of children and their parents. Including mine. Maybe one day someone might re-discover Mr Spam.

Wally Stott and Angela Morley

THIS is an extraordinary story. When I was in my mid-twenties and playing the piano for a significant part of my livelihood, I tried hard to get onto the 'session' scene, basically another name for making recordings. The money was much better - a day's work in the studio would pay as much as a week of live gigs - and, generally, your reputation as a player would be enhanced; session musicians were definitely considered the 'crème de la crème'. But the 'dead man's shoes' principle applied and, unlike violin players, for example, there was only one keyboard player on a session.

Still, I did get the chance on one or two occasions, simply as a result of someone dropping out or there being a shortage of keyboard players available on a certain day. The one I remember most clearly, however, was at the Lansdowne Studios in Holland Park. The musical director was the very well known and highly respected arranger/MD, Wally Stott.

Wally Stott was born in Leeds in 1924, where he lived with his parents above their jewellery shop. As a young boy, he was intrigued by their collection of dance records which he recognised by their labels before he could read. (Funnily enough, my parents always said that I could do that, too). He had piano lessons, but they stopped when his father died in 1933. His mother returned to her hometown of Rotherham and there he taught himself to play the alto saxophone, playing in a dance band when he was 15.

When the war started, many dance band musicians joined the forces. This enabled the young Stott to find professional work, mostly in the north of England. In the early '40's, he joined the widely known Oscar Rabin Band, and then Geraldo, possibly the best-known bandleader of the time and certainly the busiest. They were featured on numerous BBC radio shows and they could play swing or symphonies. Bob Adams, who played saxophone alongside Stott, remarked, "Wally played the alto beautifully. It is the sexiest of instruments and there was a beautiful effeminacy about the way Wally played."

Remember that observation as you read on.

Stott studied Geraldo's orchestrations, particularly those written by Robert Farnon, and started lessons in harmony and composition. In 1953, Wally became the musical director for a new British label, Philips. The label had a relatively small staff and Stott's job was to assist Johnny Franz in selecting material for the artists and then to arrange and conduct the recording session, which Franz produced. Although many British artists were covering American hit songs in the late 50's and early 60's, Stott determined to make his records as distinctive as possible. Frankie Vaughan's personality was showcased in *"Green Door"* and he also arranged the explosive *"Tower of Strength"*, an early Burt Bacharach and Hal David song, which topped the UK charts. The same principle held for Shirley Bassey with hits including *"The Banana Boat Song"*, *"As I Love You"* and *"Kiss Me Honey Honey Kiss Me"*.

He went on to score, arrange and orchestrate the music for several films as well as albums for international artists such as Marlene Dietrich and Mel Torme. "Wally Stott was at the top of the range," said his fellow arranger, Tony Osborne. "We all looked up to Wally because we knew that he was second only to Robert Farnon, and it was a pretty close run thing at that!"

Despite this huge workload, Wally also worked for the BBC and when another composer, Stanley Black, became ill in 1954, he was

assigned to write the music for a new comedy series 'Hancock's Half Hour'. He wrote a cantankerous signature tune, played on a tuba by Jim Powell. Although Wally had never met him, it conveyed Hancock's personality perfectly. When they did meet, Hancock congratulated him on his work. He also wrote a parody of The Archers signature tune for Hancock by playing its theme, "Barwick Green", backwards.

Had his many creative friends and colleagues known about Wally's private life, they might have been tempted to write about it. His first marriage, to the choral arranger Beryl Stott, had ended in divorce, and he had recently remarried. However, when he returned from a holiday in Scandinavia in 1972, everyone was astonished to find him dressed as a woman. He had undergone a sex change operation, causing Harry Secombe, to remark that, "I've heard of leaving your heart in San Francisco, but this is ridiculous." What's more, he had settled on a new name, Angela Morley.

Musicians can be coarse and blunt, and a few months after the session I was on, he was back in the studio as MD, this time as Angela Morley. I can only tell this story second hand as I heard it from a friend after the event. This was the first time that the tightly knit group of session players had encountered Wally in his female persona and the atmosphere in the studio was somewhat tense. Wally/Angela said, quite firmly: "Well, gentlemen - yes, it's me, but from now on you will address me as Angela. Does anyone have a problem with that?" There was a lot of shuffling and nervous coughing before one of the trombone players blurted out: "I suppose a f...'s out of the question?" At which point everyone fell about and the matter was never referred to again. Or, so the story goes.

In fact, the resumption of normal service was made very much easier as, remarkably, Christine Parker, Wally's second wife, decided to remain with her.

Angela went on to receive Oscar nominations for the scores of Frederick Loewe and Alan Jay Lerner's music for *The Little Prince* (1974) and for Robert and Richard Sherman's musical version of Cinderella, *The Slipper and the Rose* (1978) which I subsequently adapted for the stage in 1980. By that time Angela had moved to America.

Settling in Los Angeles with Christine, she worked on several TV series including *Dallas, Dynasty, Cagney and Lacey*, and *Wonder Woman*, and won three Emmys for her work. She assisted John Williams in arranging his gargantuan scores *for Star Wars* and *Superman* (1978) and *The Empire Strikes Back* (1980) as well as many other film scores that she either arranged or conducted.

In 1994, after being close to an earthquake, the couple moved to Scottsdale, Arizona, where Angela continued to work until her death in January 2009. She left a son and daughter.

Every time I listen to her superb arrangements of the Sherman's delightful music for '*The Slipper and the Rose*' I marvel at their sheer beauty. The arranger's skill is often underestimated with the bouquets normally being heaped on the composer. And yet all the famous contemporary light music composers from Andrew Lloyd-Webber to John Williams know and acknowledge the enormous contribution that their arrangers have made to their success.

Make no mistake, Wally/Angela's career was based on pure skill, artistry, plus enormous talent and hard work which nothing, least of all a change of sex, was going to stop.

The Slipper and the Rose

IT was a Sunday afternoon not long before Christmas and we were sitting down at home 'en famille' watching the film *'The Slipper and the Rose'* on television. At that time, in the early eighties, the BBC was showing it several times a year so we had all seen it before. We always enjoyed it. Not only was the 'Cinderella' story enhanced by the film's treatment, there was beautiful music, wonderful acting, romance, humour, magic - well, everything you could wish for in a fairy tale, really. The children really loved it.

But this time it occurred to me how theatrical it was. Conceived by David Frost and directed by Bryan Forbes with a glorious score by the Sherman brothers, famous for *'Mary Poppins'*, *'Chitty Chitty Bang Bang'*, *'The Jungle Book'* and a host of other Disney musicals, the film proceeded at a leisurely pace, with long scenes, plenty of dialogue and some wonderful set pieces, not least the big ensemble numbers. It was almost like stage show that someone had captured on film. Made at Pinewood with some luscious location work in Austria, and with a cast of England's finest, this was an attempt by the producers to out-Disney Disney.

That's when I thought it might be worth pursuing the idea of turning it into a stage musical. What followed was quite an adventure.

As always with projects like this, the first thing was to establish the various rights and who owned what. Rights in musicals are notoriously complicated due to the number of differing talents involved - writers, composers, choreographers, directors, producers, etc, - and this was no exception. It soon transpired that the position was anything but straightforward. The idea for the film belonged to David Frost who apparently had thought of it at 35,000 feet on his way to Los Angeles. He then met up with the Sherman brothers, Richard and Bob, who agreed not only to write the score but also the book and lyrics.

With their name attached to the project, all he needed was to find the £3m or so it would cost to make the film. This led him to the door of Naim Attalah who, at the time, was chairman of Aspreys the jewellers and who, not surprisingly, was well acquainted with a number of extremely wealthy individuals. It was one of these, rumoured to have been the Sultan of Oman, who Naim persuaded to put up the necessary funding.

Now off the starting blocks, and with David Frost and Naim as joint executive producers, they set out to find a director who would add further marquee value to the title and who would be able to attract some serious stars. Legendary British director Bryan Forbes agreed to take it on - which is when things started to get complicated.

When Bryan was presented with the Shermans' script he threw it out insisting on a complete re-write, which he would undertake. Somewhat reluctantly, but anxious to keep their director on board, Messrs Frost and Attallah agreed - much to the chagrin of the

Shermans who still maintained that the original concept owed much to their contribution. Nevertheless, peace prevailed and the project went ahead. All of this I pieced together afterwards.

So, as the story unfolded, I concluded that the principle rights were owned by Paradine Productions, with Messrs Frost and Attallah as directors and shareholders, the rights to the music and lyrics were owned predominantly by the Sherman Brothers, who also owned a share of the book and script with Bryan Forbes. In fact, had I realised then how this would all come back to haunt me, I would probably have left things well alone at the outset. But I didn't. The project appealed and by now I was already halfway through the adaptation. I knew I would have to meet up with Paradine at some point and by then I wanted a new script, finished, in my briefcase.

Turning a film into a stage show is not as easy as it sounds. Unlike a film where the director has the facility to cut in and out of scenes at will, onstage you have to see each scene through to completion. Nor does the theatre director have close-ups at his disposal, nor the flexibility to assemble different groups of musicians for different songs. And, of course, you can forget those lovely sweeping landscapes shot in the Austrian Alps. Another feature of this particular show was the magic content; massive transformation scenes as well as much prestidigitation and legerdemain along the way - all perfectly simple on film, but devilishly difficult to do onstage in real time. What you do have in the theatre, however, is the intimacy of a live audience - which is a great help, especially when it comes to comedy.

Having successfully overcome these obstacles (I thought), three months later I had my script and was on my way to see Mr Attallah. At the time, as well as his other activities, he ran a book publishing business in Soho and it was to these offices that I was summoned. He obviously liked to employ posh young ladies as there were a number floating around - including, as he was quick to point out, the young Nigella Lawson, daughter of the then Chancellor of the Exchequer, Nigel Lawson.

I was quickly ushered into Naim's inner sanctum. In his early fifties, with pronounced Arab features, I later discovered he was a Palestinian who had settled here and made something of a name for himself by publishing a journal called The Literary Review. I also discovered that this had been a venture more to provide him with a literary reputation than make money. The latter he had achieved by publishing one remarkably successful book - *"My Secret Garden"* by Nancy Friday, a study of women's sexual fantasies. After that, he had gained a reputation for publishing 'women's books', justified, he said, by "his great love of the female sex".

Still he seemed very enthusiastic about my project and said that he would pass the script around the other interested parties and get back to me. This happened quite quickly and within a week or so he had arranged a meeting with Bryan Forbes, Stuart Lyons, who had been line producer on the movie and, finally, a charming man called John Hargreaves who was running Cinderella Theatrical Promotions Ltd, yet another company which had been set up to deal with the task of exploiting and promoting the film following its release. It transpired that I would have a lot of pleasant dealings with John later on.

The meeting was conducted by Naim in typically flamboyant style and, at that stage, it was only Bryan Forbes who had anything to say. He told me he had enjoyed reading the script and was pleased to see that I had mostly stuck to his dialogue. This was quite true although he seemed to miss the point that whole chunks of the original screenplay had been re-structured and, in some cases, entirely re-written. I had also added considerably to the comic content. Still, he was happy and that was the main thing.

We agreed that we couldn't do much more without the Shermans' consent and it was left for me to send them a script accompanied by an up-date on the current position, and await the outcome. Again, this was not long coming - literally, in fact, as a handwritten reply from Dick and Richard confirmed that they would be flying to London the following week to meet me! Would I care to join them for lunch at the Royal Garden Hotel where they would be staying? I responded by telephone to say that I would be delighted and should I arrange for any of the others to be present? "No, no," said Richard on the 'phone, "just you, if that's okay".

As it happened, the Royal Garden was just down the road from my offices in Kensington, so the whole assignation could not have been more convenient. Dick and Bob were there in the foyer to warmly greet me and we were soon sitting across a table enjoying a light LA style lunch (or as close to it as the RG could get), chatting about this and that. They were both great Anglophiles and Dick said he planned to move to London permanently within the next year or so whilst Bob would remain in LA. The two brothers were delightful, gentle people, obviously inspired by a great joy of doing their job and the pleasure they had been able to give two generations of children and their families. The subject of money, nor the great fortune they had obviously amassed from their hugely successful career, never arose and they explained how that 'side of things' would all be dealt with by their agent Mike Connor in due course.

However, as lunch progressed it became clear that they had been deeply hurt by the treatment they had received regarding their original script. So much so that, whilst they were keen to lend their support to the project, they did not wish to become involved with the rest of the team - something that would not be too difficult given the co-ordinates of the Atlantic Ocean. They also asked, somewhat anxiously, whether I had any plans to appoint Mr Forbes as the producer of the theatrical version? I explained that we had not got as far as that yet but I thought it unlikely as, to my knowledge, he had no theatrical experience. Their relief was palpable.

So, we parted on good terms and I was left with the impression that they were largely relying on me to make sure that their interests would be looked after. They were such likeable people that I could see no reason why I should not do just that.

Meanwhile Naim had been applying his entrepreneurial mind to the project and informed me that he had set up a meeting with a man called Howard Panter, at the time of writing CEO of the immensely successful Apollo Theatre Group, but, in those days, running a small theatrical management company somewhere off the Strand.

This time we were joined by David Frost and John Asprey (Chairman of Aspreys and also credited as a production co-ordinator on the original film). At Naim's invitation I outlined the project for Howard's benefit, glad to keep it short as I was finding it hard to breathe as the room rapidly filled up with the smoke from D.Frost's cigar. Howard said that he could see no reason why the project should not be viable, although it would require the appointment of a first-class stage director to add to its credibility in order to obtain the necessary investment. Naim asked whether he had anyone in mind and Howard suggested he would approach Martin Charnin, the American writer/director who had enjoyed huge success with the musical *'Annie'* all over the world - onstage and as a film. It was left that Howard would get in touch with Mr Charnin.

As soon as got back to my office I did some work researching Martin Charnin (remember this was before the days of the Internet!) and discovered that he was a heavyweight showbusiness figure indeed, very much a member of the Broadway 'aristocracy'. Not only was he a writer and director, he was also a successful composer and cabaret producer as well as having masterminded and directed successful shows and series on television and stage. In the early seventies he had created, written the lyrics for and directed the musical *'Annie'* which ran for 2,327 performances, becoming one of the twenty-five longest running musicals in Broadway history. I agreed with Howard that if this man was prepared to direct "The Slipper and the Rose" in London, then we had every chance of success.

Imagine my surprise, therefore, when I had a call from Howard saying that Mr Charnin was indeed interested and would I go to New York to see him!

So, that's what I did - took the plane and flew to NY to meet with one of the great Broadway producers of our time. Fancy that.

I met Martin at the Waldorf. He was extremely pleasant but explained that although he thought "The Slipper and the Rose" onstage was a great idea, he had to confess that he had not really enjoyed the original very much and, basically, the whole thing needed to be re-written including most of the songs. This was obviously a bad start. Probably what I *should* have said there and then was: "Well, it's a pity you didn't tell Howard that on the 'phone, because I wouldn't have bothered to come." What I *actually* said was: "Oh, in what way do you think it needs changing?" On reflection, I think he probably wanted the job of going back to scratch and starting with a new story and new script which, of course, he would write - much in the way that Bryan Forbes had 'usurped' the Shermans. But I didn't spot that at the time and felt that my responsibility to the 'team' was to deliver Martin Charnin to the project. I had booked in to my hotel for a couple of days and had nothing else to do so I asked him whether it would be helpful if I were to come up with some new story lines and a different structure for the show. He said, yes, that would be very useful indeed and we agreed to meet again the following day.

I worked pretty much all night and by the time I went to bed had a new treatment typed up with a number of different options as to where the story might go. If anything the new version was more 'grown-up' than the film, which itself was, of course, merely a re-working and extension of the original Grimm Brothers fairytale. I signed the new treatment off with 'Philip Burley, 1987'.

When we met the next morning over coffee, Mr Charnin read the document attentively. I waited with bated breath wondering what on earth he would make of my ideas and was relieved when he said he quite liked quite a lot of them, particularly the Lord Chamberlain and Fairy Godmother rediscovering each other as long-lost lovers. He also liked the more masculine version of the Prince, who I had re-drawn as a soldier returning from the war (which, historically, is probably what he would have been). In fact, I had modernised the whole story somewhat, made it less of a fairytale, more of a fable. He also approved of my cuts - for example, I had left out some of the more humpty-tumpty songs, which he clearly hated. He then asked me to add his name to the bottom of the document and let him know what the rest of the team back in London thought. With that we shook hands and I left to do some quick sight-seeing before my flight home the following morning.

When I reported back to the rest of the team, Bryan Forbes in particular was less than enthusiastic about Mr Charnin's approach. There were also grave concerns about the re-invention of the Shermans' score, which had generally been praised as a minor masterpiece. Plus, I got the strong impression that no-one round the table wanted to yield any more points to a new creative input. A further complication was that the Shermans had sent over some new songs for the stage version which were distinctly 'humpty-tumpty! Naim immediately 'phoned Howard Panter and told him we wanted a director not a new adaptor.

And that was that. We heard no more from Howard Panter and the whole idea of a West End production fizzled out.

I was reluctant to wave goodbye to the project after all that effort. Because I had done some work in the amateur theatre I knew that there was a steady stream of income available from societies all over the country who were always looking for new shows. With its established reputation and familiar subject matter I guessed that 'The Slipper and the Rose' might appeal to this market. However, I also knew only too well that all we had was a script plus a video of the film. My version of the show had never been performed! Before I could go any further I needed consent from Paradine. Fortunately, Naim was happy with this development and, with the help of John Hargreaves, we were able to come up with a short agreement confirming that the amateur rights would be vested in my company Excelsior. Now I had to bring the script to life.

My idea was to produce a pilot version of the show with a specially assembled amateur cast and director. In this I was fortunate to obtain the enthusiastic assistance of a lady called Margaret Hunter, an old friend who had produced many shows locally including several in which I had been involved in one capacity or another, including several Shakespeare productions for the National Trust at Polesden Lacey during the time I was Artistic Director. I had the highest regard for Margaret's talents and knew she would do a great job. So, whilst Margaret took on the job of setting things up, securing a venue and assembling a cast, I busied myself with the practicalities of sorting out the show itself - the biggest problem being that we had no orchestral parts and no score to work from.

It would have been relatively easy to do the show with a piano accompaniment but then Angela Morley's beautiful arrangements would have been lost and, with them, much of the charm and romance of the show. I wondered whether there might be another way of going about it. In the days when the film was made, the usual way of handling the songs was for the orchestra to record the backing tracks and then the vocals would be added later. If this was the case with 'Slipper' then the original twelve track tapes would have been stored somewhere - probably, I guessed, at Pinewood. John Hargreaves was based there so I picked up the 'phone and asked him. Within days a mountain of blue and white boxes arrived at my house containing fifty or more one-inch tapes. All I had to do was transpose them onto quarter inch. This was easier said than done because the old twelve track machines were by now few and far between.

I telephoned the friendliest studio buff I knew: John Hiseman, the brilliant drummer with Coloseum and husband of legendary saxophonist and composer Barbara Thompson who had worked with us on the music for 'A Touch of Frost'. As luck would have it John had an old Ampex twelve-track machine, which he promised he would get up and running for me. Within a couple of weeks I had my backing tracks.

While all this was going on Margaret had begun to assemble her cast and had created a new company for the purpose to be named the Ad Hoc Theatre Company. She had also secured a venue, a large hall with a decent sized stage. We were ready to start rehearsals. It became clear to me very soon that she had everything well under control. The cast were quickly getting used to the idea of rehearsing with the backing tracks and were soon able to sing without the help of a conductor! Hearing the piece come to life for the first time was thrilling and I went off to start putting together some ideas for the set.

Technically, the biggest problem was the magic - particularly the scene where Cinderella is transformed from her rags into a beautiful gown ready to go to the ball. We had already decided not to bother with the coach and the pumpkin! The solution we came up was ingenious. The transformation occurs at the end of act one during the song '*Suddenly It Happened*' sung firstly by the Fairy Godmother and then, following her transformation into a princess, by Cinderella. This is how we managed it - in quite spectacular fashion.

The secret was in the kitchen fireplace and the Fairy Godmother's cloak. As she cast her spell, she spread the cloak with both arms completely masking the actress playing Cinderella. At precisely that moment, again hidden from the audience's view, the fireplace swung inwards where a second actress fully made up, masked and be-wigged, in a ballgown, was waiting to take her place. The switch took seconds. When FG dropped her cloak everything was back as before - except there was a bewildered Cinders transformed into a princess! To complete the illusion, the dialogue and subsequent singing continued with the voice of the first actress pre-recorded and the second actress miming. Whilst all this was happening on one side of the stage, an entire piece of scenery was distracting the audience as it rotated on the other to reveal a red-carpeted flight of steps, leading to the doors of the Prince's palace. As the doors were opened by a couple of red-coated valets, Cinderella entered the palace and the music climaxed. End of act one. I have since seen this done a dozen or more times in various productions all over this country and abroad and it still amazes me how effective it is. The voice provides the continuity and, amidst everything else that's going on, the audience never spots it. Now, I've spoilt it for you.

It was soon time for the opening night and I was pleased to see that both Naim and Bryan Forbes had accepted my invitation to attend. Okay, it wasn't the West End but it was still a premiere! They both thoroughly enjoyed it and Bryan even went round the back to talk happily to the cast after the show.

After that, I sent the script and score - together with an accompanying video - to NODA, or the National Operatic and Dramatic Association to give them their full title. On the basis that I would be supplying them with orchestrations and band parts, they expressed enthusiasm for the project and were keen to take on the licensing of the show to amateur companies.

Of course, the scoring of the show and supplying the orchestral parts was a formidable task! Yes, we had the original orchestrations (released from the Pinewood vaults along with the tapes) but these had been arranged by Angela Morley on a song-by-song basis for whatever group of instruments were required. For a stage show we needed everything arranged for the same orchestral line-up. Plus, the way all the scenes had fallen into place for the stage version was quite different to the film and consequently much of the incidental music had to be re-arranged. Still, I had the backing tapes from our 'world premiere', which would at least give our new arranger a musical model to work from.

In the event the job was marvellously well done by an old colleague of mine, Chris Norton, who I had also worked with on "The Darling Buds of May". Chris and his small team worked diligently for eight weeks and delivered everything we needed for an 18-piece orchestra. There was only one thing missing - the overture. Early in the day Chris had pointed out that we had the original arrangements for all the songs but the overture was missing. Now, I must say that the overture to "The Slipper and the Rose" is probably one of the most haunting and evocative pieces of musical theatre scoring of all time, a true example of the arranger's genius. And, musically, quite complex in its genre. And all I had was a vinyl record! With heartfelt apologies, I posted the LP to Chris and told him that I could see little alternative but to transcribe it as best he could from that. Two weeks later the parts for the overture arrived together with the conductor's marked up score. Brilliant. Job done.

I was nervous about releasing all this musical material to NODA unheard. Regardless of Chris' skill there were countless opportunities for error and I didn't want to find this out from the hapless musical director of an amateur operatic group performing the show for the first time. In order to iron out any problems in advance, I approached another local amateur group (who I knew had a first-class MD) to see whether they would like to perform the first production with a full orchestra. I also offered to direct. Fortunately, they snapped up the offer and so our second stage production was on the road.

After three months of rehearsing the cast, it was time to hear the orchestra run through the score for the first time. We had hired a room at the Epsom Playhouse and I sat down waiting for them to get ready full of apprehension. Finally they were all set and the conductor raised his baton. Chris had come down from Leeds and we were about to hear the result of many weeks work for the first time. As soon as I heard the first notes of that familiar overture, I relaxed to enjoy the result of Chris' work. It was beautiful and indistinguishable from the original. Again, the show went on to much critical acclaim and, with the few inevitable gremlins corrected in the score, I was ready to release everything to NODA.

Since that time there have been literally hundreds of productions, not only in this country but in the States, Australia, Canada and in English-speaking countries elsewhere. One of these was in Salt Lake City, which, to my surprise, Christine and I received an invitation to attend. We decided to go and I am glad we did. We were treated and entertained like royalty and were thrilled to witness an original and highly crafted production, brimming full of new ideas and production values. Ironically, they had pre-recorded all the music and used backing tracks for the entire production - in their small theatre in the round, there was no way they could accommodate a live orchestra! If they had asked I could have sent them my tapes!

Of course, being Salt Lake City, everyone was of the Mormon faith and, as is their custom, we were treated to a number of trips into the city centre to learn about their religion and culture. So, when we saw *"The Book of Mormon"* musical in London quite recently, we probably watched this hugely entertaining satire with a more enlightened eye than most of the audience!

Over the years I have had a number of enquiries from professional stage producers keen to investigate the potential of the show. All have fallen by the wayside, in every case due to the complexity of the rights, with so many parties vying for percentages. These little sorties took up an enormous amount of time involving meetings with the late Sir David Frost, the Shermans, Naim Attallah, the late Bryan Forbes, not to mention their agents and advisors. Frankly, I don't see it happening until someone, probably long after all the original participants are dead and gone, is prepared to put all the eggs into one basket and share and share alike. Not likely to happen for a few years yet.

There have been a number of pleasant epitaphs to this long, drawn out project, one of which was undoubtedly the trip to Salt Lake City. Another was a chance meeting with Dick Sherman. For some years I had the job of producing the Variety Club Showbusiness Awards, televised each year by the BBC. In 2002 we held the event at the Dorchester in Park Lane and the show that had won in the Best Musical category was the West End version of the Sherman's musical 'Chitty, Chitty Bang Bang', starring Michael Ball. As part of the show Michael performed the song *'Hushabye Mountain'* with a small group of children. It was a delightful performance and I noticed Dick Sherman sitting at a nearby table enjoying the show with members of the production team. Afterwards, I went to say hello and introduced him to my daughter Georgina, who was nineteen at the time and a great fan. She was thrilled to meet the great Dick Sherman who, good as his word, had moved to London and was now living in an apartment in Park Lane right next door to the Dorchester. He seemed equally delighted to be admired by this lovely young lady. The two of them got chatting and I left them to it.

When Georgie got back to our table she had some interesting news - she had a date! Mr Sherman had offered to take her to see the show at the Palladium as his guest. She was a little uncertain as to whether or not to accept but Dick would have been in his seventies at the time and I was sure he had no dishonourable intentions! We encouraged her to take up this very unique opportunity.

After the event she told us she had enjoyed a magical evening. He had her collected from her flat, bought her dinner preceded by champagne, they had watched the show together from his private box and chatted at length about it during the interval and afterwards. It had been a very special experience and one she would never forget.

As always, it is the people with real God-given talent who are the best company.

Diana Rigg - A Brief Encounter

I don't know anyone of my generation who wasn't at some time fascinated by the actress Diana Rigg. Quite apart from being very beautiful, sexy and a fine actress she had been cast in a series of parts guaranteed to enhance her allure and aura of mystique – not least as Emma Peele in the iconic TV series 'The Avengers' and, of course, the only woman who James Bond had ever wanted to marry, killed in the last scene of 'On Her Majesty's Secret Service'. However disappointed you may have been with George Lazenby's sole excursion as Mr Bond, I defy you not to remember that scene and his reaction when he realised she was dead in his arms. And, credit to the largely discredited George, there wasn't a great deal that Ms Rigg with all her skill and talent could have contributed to that scene!

Shortly after that film was released I was travelling back to Brighton by train from Victoria late one winter night. In those days we still had trains with individual compartments and, on my own and lost in some office paperwork, I hardly noticed a rather elegant young woman enter the compartment just before we pulled away from the platform. In fact, we were well beyond Clapham Junction by the time I took any interest in her and noticed that she was mouthing lines, a script alternately face down and face up on her lap. That was when I realised I was sharing the compartment with an international star, Diana Rigg.

After that I couldn't take my eyes off her – however much common courtesy dictated I shouldn't stare, I simply couldn't help it. Of course, she must have known exactly what was going on for, after fifteen minutes or so of this, she looked me straight in the eye, offered me the script and said: "I'm learning some lines, would you like to help me?"

There are times in one's life when it feels as if some teenage fantasy has come true – even if it hasn't really. This was one of them.

"I'm doing 'Brief Encounter' in Worthing," she went on to kindly explain, "and we have a couple of days rehearsal, that's all. We open on Friday. So it helps to go in word perfect. Perhaps you'd read Ralph for me?"

And so I did, relishing every moment. Needless to say it was I who was stumbling over the lines. Ms Rigg was word perfect.

When we got to Hove where my car was parked, I clumsily offered her a lift for the relatively short journey on to Worthing, under some pretext or another, such as 'it might be hard for you to pick up a cab so late at night'. Or something. This she politely declined thanking me for my assistance. "You were very professional," she said.

And with those words of inestimable praise ringing in my ears I drove home. Even now, thirty years later, I can remember every detail of that journey. I don't suppose Dame Diana Rigg recalls it at all.

Syd Dean

WHEN Christine and I first met, I had already acquired a little two-bedroom cottage in Brighton, not far from the seafront in Cross Street. It was in the part of Brighton made famous by Dickie Attenborough in his first starring role as the young hero in the film 'Brighton Rock'. By the time I alighted there, it had become rather genteel – 'bijou' was the word at the time. On one side of us we had two of the once famous Kaye Sisters - not a bad copy of the much more widely acclaimed Beverley Sisters (of whom more later) - and on the other a rather nice young man in his thirties who was a BBC radio producer but never seemed to go to work.

True, we had a massage parlour opposite and next to that a rather good fish and chip shop, whose owner would occasionally get drunk and throw things at his wife. In fact, as they lived in the flat above the shop it was not unusual for us to be woken in the early hours of the morning as a kettle came crashing through the shattered window landing noisily on the pavement. Still, these disturbances were relatively few and far between and, generally, it was a good first home. Like other residents in the little street I had virtually demolished the place and turned it into a rather chic, albeit sparse, bachelor pad and, later, with Christine's help, into a fully furnished home. You could say that Cross Street was in a process of transmogrification – slowly shaking off its shady past and emerging as a 'smart' place to live.

Anyway, we quickly settled in to life in Brighton. Transport was good; I could be in my office in Kensington in an hour and a half (having done a good deal of work on the train) and back again in the same time. The problem arose if I was playing in the West End after work - which involved driving up in the morning with my keyboard and assorted equipment in the back and, of course, driving home again in the early hours of the morning. Following a couple of journeys where I had all but fallen asleep at the wheel, it seemed like a very good idea to try to find some musical employment locally.

It didn't take me long to locate the Brighton bandleader par excellence, a man called Syd Dean who had been running highly successful public dances at the King Alfred Centre in Hove for many years and before that at the old Regent Ballroom near the clock tower (long since defunct). In fact, Syd was quite the local celebrity. In his time he had been an excellent pianist and, throughout his many years as a bandleader had been a prolific broadcaster. In his later years, just as Ken Tapper had the Croydon scene sewn up, so Syd Dean was the 'guvner' in Brighton and Hove – except, of course, his was a much larger parish with more musical activity going on. I telephoned him, outlined my experience and credentials, and within a week I was playing with his band at the King Alfred. What happened to my predecessor I never discovered.

Mr Dean's line up was typical at the time; a rhythm section comprising piano, bass and drums, four saxes, two trumpets and a trombone. He also had a singer, Rebecca, who shared the fronting with the dapper but ageing Syd, providing a little glamour to what otherwise would have been a rather middle-aged line-up. It wasn't long before Syd discovered I could sing, too, which initially, rather put her nose out of joint. However, she soon got accustomed to the idea, realising that I was always going to be singing from the piano and not competing with her for the limelight. In fact, as time went by, and as the two youngest members of the band by some years, we became good friends. She was a good singer, too.

So, that was Saturday nights taken care of. Needless to say the pay didn't compare with the West End, but taking into account the cost of travelling, it probably evened out. I soon learnt that Syd paid exactly the Musicians Union rate for every job, not a penny more, not a penny less.

Like the other bandleaders I worked for, Syd used to provide bands for other events in the locality including the two big Brighton hotels, the Grand and the Metropole - as well as the relatively new Brighton Convention Centre where the political parties were increasingly holding their annual conferences. When the Conservatives held theirs at the Convention Centre in 1978, with Margaret Thatcher at the peak of her powers if not popularity, Syd got booked for the end of conference ball. That's when the unthinkable happened. Just as Syd was about to count us in for a rousing opening number, a young man approached the stage and caught his attention. Some brief words were exchanged and Syd turned to us with a dismayed expression. "Does anyone know a tune called 'A Town in Singapore'?" - and this from a man who until then had always seemed to know every dance tune ever written. We all shook our heads; none of us knew it. To make matters worse, Margaret and Dennis were making their way to the centre of the floor to generous applause from a delighted audience. While Margaret smiled demurely at her followers, Denis looked up at Syd expectantly. Syd turned to me, a desperate expression on his face. "A quickstep", he said, "anything!" In a panic I played a four bar introduction, and went into the first tune that flashed into my mind, at the same time signalling the key to the bass player.

It could indeed have been 'anything' but turned out to be *'Pick*

Yourself Up, Dust Yourself Down and Start All Over Again' which, to my relief, the alto player and the rest of the band quickly picked up.

Much to my surprise, the applause started again, this time growing in volume until the whole audience was on its feet. We busked our way through, somehow managing to round it up with a big ending, until the Prime Minister and her husband finished dancing with a final twirl, graciously acknowledging the wild enthusiasm surrounding them. Syd turned to me and beamed. "What happened?" I mouthed.

He shrugged as he spotted the Thatchers approaching the stage. Margaret was clearly thrilled and spent a minute or two chatting to Syd. She then turned back to her admirers, gave them a final wave and was led back to her table by Dennis. Syd announced the next dance, the floor filled and we went back to the pad and, quite literally, started all over again. We had to wait until the interval to hear from Syd what had occurred.

Syd related his conversation with the Iron Lady with a mixture of glee and disbelief. Firstly, she had thanked him for playing Denis' request - although Denis had muttered to her that it was a bit quicker than he had remembered! For her part, she thought Denis had been very clever to have chosen such an appropriate tune, bearing in mind the recent slump in her popularity ratings which had been all over the papers before and during the conference. "Pick Yourself Up" was precisely the message she and the party needed. Very clever of Dennis and a big 'thank-you' to Mr Dean for being so professional.

It was my habit in those days when I got home to check out any request that I didn't know. I presume Denis' original request must have been the old Harry James number *'On A Little Street in Singapore'* which, in truth, I couldn't have played by ear anyway. But we didn't know that at the time. Nor, I suspect, did Mrs T, then or later. I doubt whether Denis owned up either.

On another occasion, the TUC chose to hold their conference in Brighton. This time Syd booked me to play solo piano at a private dinner for top union officials at the Old Ship Hotel. It sounded like a rather exclusive and intimate affair. I was booked to play during dinner starting at 7.30pm, take a half hour break at around 8.30 when they would provide me with a meal and then play again after they had finished eating, possibly for a sing-song, until 11pm. Quite a long evening, but all very clear and, as usual, meticulously set out in writing by Syd. I think the pay was about £25 – equivalent nowadays to nearer £100 – which I had come to expect was precisely the MU rate for the hours and the venue. What Syd was charging the client I had no idea.

When I arrived in black tie (as instructed) the room was already filling up. The first thing I noticed was that they were all wearing lounge suits, some even sports jackets. There was a long top table and several sprigs and I estimated there were fifty to sixty men present. I would have imagined there must have been some fairly heavyweight lady officials at the conference but, if so, they were not invited. This was strictly stag.

Some of the faces making their way to the top table were instantly recognisable – Arthur Scargill, Len Murray and Jack Jones, to name but three. All prominent media celebrities in their time. The atmosphere was jovial, if a little rowdy, with large jugs of beer on every table. No-one bothered to greet me so, as it was nearly 7.30pm I sat down at the old upright provided and started to play. Nobody took a blind bit of notice, which was fine, particularly as the piano was painfully out of tune - not for the first nor last time.

The meal continued free of incident although with the stimulus of considerable quantities of beer, there was a great deal of noise and shouting. Having played continuously for an hour and a half, I stopped at 9pm and left the room. I passed the head waiter at the door and asked where I should go for my meal (another MU requirement if a musician was employed for more than two hours). Well, there was no meal and, clearly, nothing had been arranged. Eventually, the banqueting manager kindly provided some sandwiches, which, he explained, were 'on the house'. "Nothing unusual," he added resignedly, "we've had this all week."

At 9.30 I was back in the room, playing again, this time a selection of well-known tunes from the musicals. There was a lot of coming and going, mostly to the gents, but I noticed that the familiar tunes had caught the ear of some of my audience, who had turned their chairs around and were starting to sing along. Before long the room had filled up again and we were treated to some impromptu, largely irrelevant, not to say incomprehensible speeches. One of the delegates got up and told some terrible jokes as his colleagues sunk lower into their padded chairs. One or two had already fallen asleep.

While this was going on I had another opportunity to scan the faces of those present and thought I recognised the bearded features of John Morton, General Secretary of the Musicians Union, a face I had seen a hundred times on communications from the MU head office.

It must have been half past ten before the endless ramblings, anecdotes and crude jokes had run their course and I thought the time might be right to wind things up with a 'singalong' selection. Off I went into *'On Mother Kelly's Doorstep'*, *'If You Knew Susie'*, *'Daisy, Daisy'*, etc, and, rather to my surprise, the evening came back to life as more and more of them joined in. After fifteen minutes of this I finished the first batch of songs. They were clearly enjoying themselves and started shouting 'more!' straightaway. I realised that with more of the same I might just get through to 11pm.

Off I went again with *'My Old Man Said Follow the Van'* and a dozen others, determined to go on until the end of the evening. Bang on 11pm I finished the second sing-along selection to much hearty and generous applause - mostly directed at themselves, no doubt, but mildly rewarding for me just the same. With that I got up and started collecting my bits and pieces together, frankly pleased to have finished on a high note and relieved that I was about to get away from what had been a dull and tedious evening. Frankly, I was looking forward to getting home. Just then a small man of about forty came rushing up.

"What are you doing?" he said angrily, "You're not finished yet!"

I looked at my watch and replied as coolly as I could: "I was booked til 11pm and its now two minutes past, so I have finished for the night. I hope you enjoyed the dinner."

"Don't be daft," he said (or words to that effect), "the night's just getting going! Carry on, we'll tell you when we've had enough."

"Alright," I said, "but you'll have to pay for the overtime. It's £12.50 an hour."

"Overtime? Don't be ridiculous! We're not paying overtime! Now, my son, get back on that Joanna and start playing."

His attitude and threatening demeanour was the straw that broke the camel's back. I had no intention of being bullied. I looked him in the eye. "Listen, my friend," I said calmly, "it may not have occurred to you that I am member of a trade union, too, and I get paid the rate for the job. If you want me to do another hour – which, incidentally, I am not obliged to do - you'll have to pay the going rate, and that's another £12.50."

"You're making it up!" he scoffed turning to a small group of cronies who had gathered. "Hear that, brothers? This twerp is saying he won't play no more unless we pay him extra!" Grunts of disapproval all round. I felt very lonely.

"Well, as a matter of fact, you can check what I am telling you very easily as my union is represented here tonight." I pointed to a table in a corner where the plump, bearded secretary of the MU appeared to be keeping himself very much to himself. "Over there," I said, "that's John Morton, general secretary of the Musicians Union," I searched around in my inside pocket. " - and this is my MU membership card. Why don't you go and negotiate with him? Here, I'll introduce you."

I led the officious little man over to John's table. "Hi, John," I said, "we've not met but my name is Pip Burley and I've been a fully paid up member of the MU for eleven years. Your colleague here wants me to play on after my allotted time without paying overtime. Can you set him straight on our rates, please?"

John looked as though he would have preferred the Old Ship to have sprung a leak and sunk to the bottom of the ocean.

"Could we have a quiet word, Pip?" he said, steering me away from the table. Once out of earshot, he went on: "Look, can't you just go on for another half hour or so? It's embarrassing for me, don't you see? These chaps are my peers, after all."

"But, I'm your member, John, aren't you supposed to be looking after my interests?"

"Yes, but extenuating circumstances, I'm sure you'd agree, eh, old chap?" He gave me a lop-sided smile.

"Not really, John, no. Any way, regardless, I'm going home now. If anyone has a complaint, I'm sure they will register it formally with Mr Dean in the morning."

And with that I left, accompanied by some muted boos and catcalls.

The following day Syd rang to ask how it all went. I recounted the story, blow by blow, just as it had happened, warning him that he might get a letter of complaint from the TUC.

"I hope you got their money upfront," I asked.

"Of course," he said. "I'm not stupid. They were lucky to get you. No-one else would do it."

He never received a letter of complaint.

I carried on working with Syd for a couple of happy years until one night at the King Alfred he fell off the stage. He was bobbing around quite happily in front of us as usual when suddenly in the middle of a number he wasn't there. Although I didn't see the fall it would have been a pretty bad one – the stage was at least five feet above the dance floor and I don't suppose that any of the pre-occupied dancers would have broken it. Syd was back onstage like a flash, looking pale and shaken and managed to see the evening through to a close when he limped off, clearly in great pain. The audience showed their appreciation of his fortitude. He carried on working after that but never seemed quite the same to me.

Eventually, the council decided not to carry on with Saturday night public dances at the King Alfred and, together with the general decline in demand for big bands, his work dried up. I hope he went on to enjoy a happy retirement.

As for me, we were about to move house and start a family. So, my mind was on other things.

Syd died in 1993 at the age of 86.

Two Guitarists Called Steele

OVER the years I had the privilege of working with some fine musicians and some great characters. Among them were two guitar players, both different in style, both successful and both interesting men.

Bob Steele was born in Manchester and had fallen in love with the guitar as a child. By the time I got to know him, he had played with most of the big bands of the era including, most notably, Joe Loss. He had featured on most if not all of Joe's many LP's and had an unequalled technique for playing his instrument in a swinging rhythm section. In fact, on the many late night visits to his house – with his long-suffering wife fast asleep upstairs (although not necessarily for long once we had turned up) - he would take repeated pleasure in playing me these records and pointing out his work. Apart from the occasional solo when he took the melody, he was mainly in the background except for one track where there was a four-bar bridge with just the four-piece rhythm section swinging away between full-blown brass and sax passages. "Listen, Pip," he would say, "that really swings great, doesn't it?" then he would lift the needle off the vinyl and replace it at the beginning of the same four bars over and over again. He loved that bit so much that you could hear the scratched surface of the LP on that section when the rest of the record had none at all! And he was right - it really did swing.

He had done well since he came south in his early twenties with his young wife, also from Manchester. When I knew them they were living in a very pleasant semi-detached three bedroom house in

Isleworth and, as far as I could tell, were very happy.

There was only one problem – and, believe me, this was pretty general at the time amongst musicians – Bob liked a drink. In fact, in the late 60's and early 70's, if you were a musician and could confine yourself to alcohol you were doing pretty well. But, unlike me, Bob didn't like going home straight after a job. High on adrenalin, he preferred to go on somewhere for a few drinks after a job, meaning he would not arrive home until three or four o'clock in the morning. This was clearly a bone of contention between Bob and his wife.

He told me the story of how he had once driven home blind drunk and let himself into his old house. The new owners had not bothered to change the locks and were somewhat alarmed when he appeared in their bedroom in the early hours of the morning in full evening dress. Fortunately, they recognised him and took matters no further.

On another occasion he got home sometime after 4am, staggered out of the car leaving the driver's door open (in today's world the mind boggles) and found himself standing at his front door attempting to locate the key in the lock. At this point, with the exaggerated sense of logic and supreme will power that comes with a total lack of sobriety, he became aware of the necessity not to wake his wife – and, no doubt, risk the tirade of abuse that would inevitably ensue.

As you do, with intense concentration, he managed to insert the key in the lock and open the front door without making a sound. With a similar superhuman effort he closed it silently behind him. The next task was to get up the stairs. When your balance is to say the least challenged, this formidable task required every ounce of patience and determination he could muster. Still, encouraged by his success thus far, and holding on with both hands, he managed to negotiate every tread without an audible footstep or creak and now found himself on the landing outside a closed bedroom door. His recalled that it must have been at least twenty minutes since he had parked the car in the drive.

Sweating with concentration, millimetre by millimetre, he turned the handle and let himself in. He could hear the sound of steady breathing. So far, so good. Removing his dress suit piece by piece and slipping out of his shoes in close proximity to the sleeping form nearby was excruciatingly hard but, eventually, there he was standing unsteadily by the bed in his stockinged feet. Bending down to take them off was out of the question – who knew what might happen if he subjected his swimming mind to such a manoeuvre. There was no chair in the room and so, with no other option, he sat on the edge of the bed.

A murmur came from under the sheets: "Is that you, Bob, what time is it?"

Now, it may have been that the last thirty minutes of supreme self-control had him done for or, quite simply, that blind panic – never far from the front of the drunkard's mind - set in, but the best Bob could come up with was:

"It's all right, darling, I've got to be up early. Don't let me disturb you, I'll get dressed as quietly as I can."

With which he proceeded to put all his clothes back on, retrace his steps and let himself out of the house. What he did for the rest of the day he couldn't remember.

I have never been much of a drinker myself and, in fact, over the years have often felt left out of things as a result. Equally, I have seldom found those tales of past drunken escapades, so thoroughly enjoyed by many, remotely amusing. But, that is not to say I haven't faked a laugh on many occasions. One doesn't want to be a total party-pooper after all. But I did think Bob's story was a classic.

* * *

Another guitar player I greatly admired was Laurie Steele who had made a name for himself with the Oscar Rabin Band on 'Go Man Go', one of the BBC's flagship lunchtime shows during the late

1950s and early 1960s.

I first met him at the Grosvenor House when Sydney Lipton had two functions going on at the same time. I had been playing in the Ballroom and had come down to the Great Room to say hello to my other mates during the break. So, for once, I was watching the band instead of playing in it.

Right at the front of the stage was this good-looking, charismatic guy in his thirties with long flowing blonde hair, perched on a high stool, singing and playing away with the crowd in the palm of his hand. I thought what an excellent performer he was. When the number was finished it was time for the interval and, after a minute or two, he got down from his stool. It was only then that I realised he was badly deformed and was less than five feet tall.

Later, when I got to know him better, he told me something about himself. He had been born quadriplegic with severe curvature of the spine and several internal organs misplaced. By the time he was eighteen, he had spent the equivalent of ten years in hospital undergoing a series of operations, which, effectively, had enabled him to remain alive whilst his body grew into adulthood. Fortunately, he was keen to point out, he had no physical problems below the waist, which had enabled him to enjoy many of the pleasures associated with young adulthood, plus, he could walk.

His musical talent had emerged at an early age and, since his education had been consistently disrupted by long spells in hospital, he had been able to indulge his passion for music to his heart's content. Nevertheless, in his early twenties he had studied and qualified as an accountant. But, it was his musical career that had taken off and, by the time I knew him, he was firmly established as a composer with a number of TV scores to his credit and as an accomplished guitar player always in demand.

What Laurie lacked in physical stature he more than made up for through sheer charm and force of personality - plus, as I learned later and got to know him better, an extraordinarily philosophical view of life and his own condition. He also possessed great intelligence.

On one occasion we went back to his house after a gig and he invited me in for a coffee. He lived in a beautifully furnished bungalow in a leafy Surrey crescent with a shiny Volvo estate parked in the drive. He shared all this with a stunning Scandinavian girl who obviously adored him.

I felt thoroughly welcome although it was probably around 1am when we turned up. I stayed for a long time that morning, chatting but mainly listening to Laurie. I was struck by his astonishingly positive outlook. The longer-term prognosis was not good, he explained, and as he got older the corrective surgery that had sustained his body so far would become progressively less viable. He knew he was dying but then, hey, so was everyone else!

Looking around, I commented, perhaps rather tactlessly, that he appeared to have done very well for himself. Was there anything he still wanted to achieve?

"No," he replied. "Everything I could possibly have wanted, I've had. Not necessarily in real life but in my mind. All those years lying in a hospital bed, unable to move, gave me the chance to imagine and enjoy every experience a human being could dream of. I don't need ambition. I've been there."

I worked with Laurie many times during the next ten years and always enjoyed his humour, talent and zest for life. He was such good news. I lost touch with him after I got married and moved to Brighton but heard word of him from time to time. It would have been in the early eighties that I was told he was ill. He was still on the old telephone number and was quick to answer when I called. He would have been in his late forties by then. He sounded just the same, cheerful, positive and delighted to hear from me. He explained that he was now confined to a wheelchair and couldn't play or perform anymore. However, he was doing some music teaching and spending much of his time working on some proposed designs for improving the functionality of wheelchairs for people in his condition.

He died soon afterwards and I went to his funeral. There must have been a hundred people there, nearly all musicians, gathered to pay tribute to this remarkable man. His Scandinavian girlfriend was there til the end and, eventually, made her way around to speak to me. I commented on the extraordinary turnout.

"He only wanted a quiet funeral, Pip," she said, "not all these people. He would never have imagined this."

I'm not so sure about that.

Sir Fitzroy Maclean

WHEN I was a teenager my father gave me a book called 'Eastern Approaches' by Fitzroy Maclean which he told me was one of the best books he had ever read. It describes the adventures of a young man in his early twenties (Fitzroy) who had travelled across Russia mainly by train to visit the exotically named extremities of the Russian empire, Turkestan and Samarkand. This was in the 1930's when such a journey would have been considered treacherous, if not impossible. In those days hardly anyone had travelled to those places - the main reason, no doubt, why Fitzroy Maclean was determined to do so.

To give him his full title Sir Fitzroy Hew Royle Maclean, 1st Baronet, KT, CBE was a Scottish soldier, writer and politician. He was a Unionist Member of Parliament from 1941 to 1974 and was one of only two men who at the outset of the Second World War enlisted as a private and rose to the rank of Brigadier, the other being his future fellow Conservative MP, Enoch Powell.

As well as his travels in Russia, 'Eastern Approaches' describes Fitzroy's military career in the early part of World War Two, particularly in Yugoslavia, where he was parachuted into the mountains by Churchill to establish contact with the rebel leader, Tito. It is probably worth mentioning that before he was thirty, Fitzroy was already a Brigadier!

In his later writings he often referred to the 'spirit of contradiction', a facet of his personality which he believed had been a constant factor in his extraordinary life, at university, in the army, as a politician and, throughout it all, as a writer. But, more of this later.

Not long after the great success of the first series of 'The Darling Buds of May' I re-read 'Eastern Approaches' and wondered whether it might make a series for television. My partner Richard Bates agreed and suggested that the well-known Scottish dramatist Ian Curteis who, at the time, was married to the novelist Joanna Trollope, would be the ideal choice for adapting the book into a six-part series. Ian, who had become well known for his work on 'Crown Court' and 'The Onedin Line' was thrilled at the prospect and it was left to me to locate and contact Sir Fitzroy.

This was not too difficult. Fitzroy was now in his eighties and still divided his time between his main home in Scotland where he lived with his wife Veronica and a flat not far from the Carlton Tower. Following a brief letter explaining our intentions, a meeting was arranged at his suggestion, the first of several, and I went up to see him to determine the lie of the land.

The flat was easy enough to locate and Sir Fitzroy was there at the door to greet me. It would not be honest to say that he didn't look his age and I noticed that he walked with a pronounced limp, but, once seated, he was keen to talk about the project and full of impish enthusiasm. In truth, our conversation went far beyond my remit which was simply to make sure the idea was practical and straightforward. After that, it was Ian's job to put the flesh on the bones. But the great man (for I was beginning to realise that this is what he was) chose to talk at length about how the story might split into episodes and how there was quite a lot of entertaining material that was not in the book.

"That might be useful when it comes to your early love life," I mentioned.

He chuckled. "Yes, I suppose we'll need that for television, some strong female characters. Not much in the book, I'm afraid. I was engaged at the time, you understand?"

I couldn't help noticing that on the mantelshelf of the sparsely furnished flat were a number of formal invitations, including one from the Queen Mother, amongst those from high ranking military leaders and the inevitable prominent politicians. Fitzroy was clearly still very much in demand and, I suspected, did not have many spare evenings during his weeks in town.

I spent an enthralling couple of hours with him during which he told me how his involvement with Tito had come about. Although he touches on it in the book, to hear the events described by the man himself brought history very much to life.

Although very young, Fitzroy had clearly been favoured by Churchill and was part of his inner sanctum of military advisers. On this occasion Churchill had summoned his war cabinet down to Chartwell to discuss the situation in central Europe. The resistance movement in Yugoslavia played an important role in World War Two. Yugoslavia fell to Hitler in 1941 and after this, two resistance movements had developed. The first was the royalist Mihailovic with his Cetnics who had expressed support for the Allies and was well established. But he had a problem in his own backyard in the shape of the rebel communist Josef Tito and his 'Partisan Army' who had retreated to the mountains where they were expanding their forces. To all intents and purposes, the two resistance groups were at war with each other.

"Which side is Tito on?" Churchill asked his assembled advisers. Apparently nobody knew, except that he was a communist and obviously against his rival Mihailovic.

"This is a tribal country," Churchill went on. I'm not interested in their domestic squabbles. Our job is to defeat Hitler! So, politically, militarily, what do we do? Who do we trust?"

Fitzroy described how the discussion went round in circles with the unanimous conclusion that there was no alternative but to go with the well-established Mihailovic and hope that he remained steadfastly on the side of the allies.

As the youngest there by ten or more years, Fitzroy had not contributed to the discussion thus far and was suddenly cast into the spotlight when Winston turned to him and asked him what he thought. All eyes turned to the young brigadier. Fitzroy describes how this moment prompted his 'spirit of contradiction'. Something was telling him that such a unanimous decision should be challenged.

"I think we should consider supporting Tito," he said. "If we help him overcome Mihailovic, then we make it a condition that he helps us oust Hitler from Belgrade."

Gradually, one by one, the generals were persuaded by the sense of this argument and the whole tilt of the debate had shifted. They had no such leverage over Mihailovic and if Tito could muster 60-70,000 rebel troops to help the Allies kick out Hitler, then they could worry about the ramifications of a potential communist government in Yugoslavia later.

Churchill was also impressed by young Fitzroy's courageous if somewhat perverse plan.

"Right then, Fitzroy, you'd better get out there, track him down and see what you can make of it."

Within a day or two Fitzroy had been parachuted into the Yugoslavian mountains. He found Tito agreeable to the plan and the rest is history. It was not long before the 'Partisan Army' had marched triumphantly into Belgrade with Tito at its head and Fitzroy at his side.

Such tales of derring-do abide in 'Eastern Approaches' and, with

Fitzroy's help and Ian's treatment we were able to take the project to ITV in Scotland. They were hugely enthusiastic and were keen to give it the green light. That's when world events overtook us. Until his death in 1980 Tito and his totalitarian regime had successfully kept the ethnic tensions in his country at bay for forty years. However, this wasn't to last for very long. By the early nineties the whole country was breaking up into separate states again and chaos had again erupted in central Europe. With history again in the making, the events described in 'Eastern Approaches' became of less interest and ITV lost its nerve.

I was left with three things: firstly, an enormous sense of privilege that I had met and shared some remarkable conversations with truly great man; second a collection of cassette tapes recording our meetings and, lastly, my father's forty year old copy of 'Eastern Approaches' finally signed by its author.

Hubert Gregg

IN 1989 I had a phone call from Sydney Lipton's office to ask if I was free to play the piano at the famous Quaglino's for an after-show reception. I asked which show but no-one seemed to know - only that they had been told by the organisers there would be a lot of well-known stars present. The job didn't start until 11pm and was due to go on into the early hours. My guess was that none of Syd's more regular pianists were available or, more likely, didn't want to do it. It sounded a bit of a thankless task but I needed the money, which in this case was very good. Plus, I was quite attracted to playing for (and meeting) some well-known theatrical folk.

I was quite familiar with Quaglinos, which, before it was transformed by Terence Conran in the 1980's, had a largish downstairs ballroom which was a favourite haunt for private parties and dances. I had played there many times and always enjoyed the place. The chef was friendly and welcoming and we enjoyed many excellent meals in his kitchen amidst all the shouting and mayhem as he and his staff prepared and served food for three or four hundred people. In fact, so friendly was he that for some months I bought meat from him. He always had the very best and was happy to pass on a steak or two or even a whole rib of beef at a most advantageous price (which, I suspect, went straight into his back pocket).

On this occasion, however, the reception was in a much smaller room that would probably only accommodate forty or fifty people. I was quite excited about the evening and, as always, made sure I was there in good time, well before the guests arrived. This gave me the chance to take a look at the piano, which in this case was an oldish upright on a small raised dais in the corner. Upright pianos are a pain for the simple reason that the performer can't see his audience, nor they him, plus the fact that they are usually set up with their unattractive back against a wall. This was the case here. Experience had taught me to re-position the instrument sideways on to the audience so that at least I could look over my shoulder and maintain eye contact with the people I was playing for.

With this in mind I approached the restaurant manager and asked if he would give me a hand to shift it through ninety degrees. I could have done it myself but again I'd learnt the hard way that this is not the best way to go about things! Anyway, by the time a couple of waiters had moved it into an acceptable position the guests had started to arrive - at which point I hastily began to play. That's when to my horror I discovered the old upright was seriously out of tune.

By this time the room was filling up and there was a definite air of expectation amongst those already assembled. I sensed that the show's star was due to arrive any minute but I still didn't know who it was and, frankly, didn't like to ask. I felt I should have known. Meanwhile I was playing as little as possible. There is nothing worse than playing an out-of-tune piano - it sounds terrible and, needless to say, it is the player who gets the blame rather than the instrument. Sometimes, if it is just the odd note or three, you can get away with it by avoiding those particular strings but, in this case, I doubt whether the instrument had been played for over a year, let alone tuned. Frankly, it was disgraceful. Still, the inescapable truth was that I was stuck there condemned to play this thing for another two hours. Gritting my teeth I ploughed into a medley of, as I thought, sophisticated Latin American numbers. I was dying inside but, to my surprise, no-one seemed in the least perturbed.

Anyway, my concerns were consigned to the back burner as, judging by the commotion, our star had arrived. From my elevated position on the raised platform I could make out the unmistakable figure of Eartha Kitt, beaming triumphantly at her assembled friends and admirers. I later discovered that she had just performed at the first night of a series of concerts at the Shaftsbury Theatre (later released on a CD called "Live in London"). She would have been in her sixties at the time but looked wonderfully youthful and radiant. This was the woman once described by Orson Welles as "the Most Exciting Woman in the World" and looking every inch the international star that she was.

Her entrance was accompanied by a round of enthusiastic applause and I noticed that one or two people turned to look at me, clearly expecting some suitable musical tribute. Realising how badly I had been prepared for the job - and promising myself that I would complain to the office the following day - I vaguely recalled that she had famously recorded the song *'C'est Si Bon'* and hovered between this and an improvised 'fanfare'. With little time to think I launched into *'C'est Si Bon'* as best I could from memory. Fortunately, the crowd recognised the opening bars and the rest was drowned out by another wave of clapping and cheering.

I was now sweating profusely and feeling vulnerable. I realised, of course, that the obvious thing to have done would have been to reel off a number of Eartha Kitt hits, but that presumed that I knew them and could play them! I also realised that to inadvertently play well-known songs associated with other artists would be inappropriate. I was caught between a rock and hard place with nowhere to go - not to mention a discordant piano that would defeat me whatever I did. Disaster.

As I ploughed into a piece of Chopin I was surprised to hear a beautifully modulated male voice at my shoulder.

"Stop," the voice said, "you can't win. I know, I've been there."

I turned to find a handsome man with silver hair, impeccably dressed, smiling at me. He was holding two glasses of champagne and offered me one.

"Listen," he said, "I'm truly sorry for you. No-one should have to play that thing, it's shameful for a place like this". I took the champagne gratefully and downed a mouthful.

"Thank you," I replied, "but the problem is I'm booked until the party finishes, so I suppose I'll just have to make the best of it." I took another gulp.

"Good, isn't it? Dom Perignon; only the best for Eartha. Listen, if I were in your shoes, I'd do one of two things, one, get blind drunk and carry on or, two, give up and go home. Personally, I'd advise the latter."

His face was very familiar and I realised this was Hubert Gregg the broadcaster to whom I had listened many times on radio.

"There's nothing I'd like more," I said, "I feel ashamed that I can't do the job properly. But I can't just walk out."

"Just what I would expect you to say. Leave it to me," he said, "Can you play some London songs, honky-tonk style? Maybe a few World War songs, too."

"Yes, of course," I replied.

"Good, and can you finish with *"Maybe It's Because I'm a Londoner"*? Do you know it?"

"Of course," I replied, "the song made famous by Bud Flanagan?"

"That's the one - I wrote it, you know. In F, alright? By the way, what's your name?" I told him and he walked off.

So, I went into my 'pub selection' and, of course, it was a brilliant idea. All those tunes were *supposed* to be played on out-of-tune pianos! It sounded okay and I noticed one or two of the audience turning towards the piano and starting to sing along. After a few minutes of this I glanced over at Mr Gregg who was chatting away to Eartha.

He gave me an imperceptible nod of the head. I transposed into the key of F and slowed down the tempo. Within seconds he was alongside me singing his great hit. At the end of the first chorus he walked back to his group and returned with a smiling Eartha on his arm. I carried on playing whilst he said to her:

"Eartha, dear, I know you were born on a cotton plantation in South Carolina but you are a great star and after your triumph tonight we'd like to adopt you as a Londoner. So this song is dedicated to you."

With that he sang it all again, slowly, to her, almost like a ballad. Ms Kitt was transfixed and, at the end, thanked him with a kiss. Mr Gregg then went on to announce: "Ladies and gentleman could you also show your appreciation for our pianist, Pip, who has done a splendid job tonight against difficult odds and who I don't think we need detain any longer." Another generous round of applause. I stood up and took a bow.

"That's it," said my new friend. "Go home young man and reflect on a job well done." I did, most gladly, and that was the last I heard of it. I'd done less than two hours work and the office paid me in full with no questions asked the following week.

Whether or not Hubert Gregg had planned that little performance in advance or whether he had staged it spontaneously inspired by my plight I never found out, but either way, I was impressed and grateful. I determined to find out more about him. What I discovered was quite remarkable.

Born in London 1914, he had studied at St Dunstan's College, in south-east London, and the Webber-Douglas Academy of Dramatic Art. He first got noticed as a Shakespearean actor and was barely out of his teens when he appeared at Regent's Park and the Old Vic. In 1937, he crossed the Atlantic to play Kit Neilan in Terence Rattigan's *French Without Tears* on Broadway, which he later reprised in London (in all, he reckoned he played the part some 650 times). But his success in this and other notable stage roles was curtailed with the onset of war. Starting as a private in the Lincolnshire Regiment, he soon became an officer in the 60th Rifles. Two years after that, he was in the Political Warfare Executive, where his command of German equipped him to broadcast in the enemy's language, to the annoyance of Nazi propaganda minister Joseph Goebbels. However, he still managed to maintain his contacts in the theatre.

After the war he appeared regularly in the West End but his desire to direct found an outlet in Agatha Christie's 'The Hollow' - her first stage success. In 1952 her phenomenon, 'The Mousetrap', still running today, opened, with Gregg overseeing its emergence as one of the greatest theatrical successes of all time. After that he went on to direct an array of plays, mostly London-based, but also in America.

His film appearances included 'In Which We Serve', 'The Root Of All Evil', 'Once Upon A Dream' and 'Doctor At Sea', for which he also wrote the music and lyrics, including the song *'Je Ne Sais Pas'*, mimed to by Brigitte Bardot.

He was a talented pianist and brilliant songwriter and, by the '70s, had branched out into performing one-man shows. *'Maybe It's Because I'm A Londoner'*, was composed in 1944, and was included in The Crazy Gang show of three years later. His first published song, *'I'm Going To Get Lit Up When The Lights Go Up In London'*, written in 1940, and initially performed by Gregg in an army concert, aroused considerable criticism, not least in the House of Commons where Churchill commented characteristically: "we shall celebrate in a manner befitting". Nevertheless, the song was broadcast in 1944 as a radio signal to the resistance that D-Day was imminent.

He was also an author and playwright and, like Noel Coward, whose career he mirrored in many ways, he frequently appeared in his own plays. He wrote two novels 'April Gentlemen' and 'A Day's Loving' as well as a collection of biographies, 'Thanks For The Memory', drawn from his radio scripts.

It was as a consummate broadcaster that most of us remember

him. His first radio appearance came in 1933 but it is his later radio shows, with the emphasis on nostalgia, that will probably stay longest in the memory - 'I Call It Genius', 'Hubert Gregg Remembers', 'I Remember It Well', 'Now And Then', and, on and off from 1972 till the end of his life, his best known show 'Thanks For The Memory'. In 1993, he celebrated sixty years of broadcasting with 'Sounds And Sweet Airs', which he wrote and presented - followed the next year by 'Hubert Gregg And The 40s', commemorating the 50th anniversary of D-Day.

In the fifties and sixties he was chairman of BBC television's 'Brains Trust' and presenter of 'Youth Wants To Know' on ITV. He wrote the music and lyrics for the radio adaptation of Jerome K Jerome's 'Three Men In A Boat', in which he starred alongside Kenneth Horne and Leslie Phillips, and devised, wrote and presented a 40-week radio series on London theatres.

All this dynamism, creativity and confidence was wrapped in a personality of great charm. As I discovered, he always appeared elegant and sophisticated, even when the pressure was on. He was active to the end, and, many years after our brief encounter, he gained a BA through the Open University at the age of 83.

Actor, director, composer, lyric writer, author, playwright and broadcaster, this remarkable and brilliant man died aged 89 in 2004.

The Language of Music

ONE of the pleasures of living in Brighton and Hove was my daily train journey to and from London. In those days I had a first-class season ticket and the trip to Victoria took less than an hour.

I'd acquired the habit of getting into the same compartment - in the days when trains had individual compartments - and got to know my travelling companions pretty well.

One of the quieter ones, a man called Adrian Cooper, turned out to be a television producer and director working for Thames, who had just been commissioned by their schools department to make a series about music for non-committed students. Let me explain.

At this time both the BBC and ITV were required by law to produce a significant output of educational programming as an aid for teachers in the classroom. Broadly speaking, this had to span the whole syllabus, some of it aimed at children who were already specializing in certain subjects, the rest to encourage an interest in a particular subject amongst all children. *'Musicround'*, the proposed title of the series Adrian had been asked to put together, fell into the latter category.

He explained to me that he was not finding this easy. Trying to explain and unravel the intricacies of what music was and how it all went together when your audience had no inkling about the subject nor, it had to be assumed, any interest in finding out, made it tricky even to find a starting point.

Perhaps because I recalled my own musical education (or lack of it) so clearly, I found myself fascinated by the subject and, over the next few train journeys, a pattern of how I thought he might tackle the series began to emerge.

It was to start with an episode called 'What is Music?' which would attempt to deal with the three components of music - rhythm, melody and harmony – first separately and then together. The second programme would then deal with 'The Language of Music', how a piece of music starts life as an idea in a composer's head and then develops into an arrangement for an orchestra, with the notation and 'language' required to capture it on paper for musicians to play. Thereafter, subsequent episodes would deal with different types of instruments, whether struck, bowed or blown and the sub categories within those groups. A separate programme would deal with music written for film and television, the focus throughout being on accessibility for the 'disinterested' child. All of this was by way of conversation and after a day or so of this, Adrian asked if I wouldn't mind writing it all down. Which I did.

A day or so later I handed him my proposal – with one important new ingredient we hadn't previously touched on. Who would present the series? It had occurred to me whilst writing the treatment that, although the idea was to present music in all its aspects in the simplest and most stripped-down way, it might still seem very dry to our young viewers. The answer might be to dress it all up with some well-known, celebrity presenters.

Although somewhat surprised at this suggestion (the practice had generally been to use 'teacher-type' presenters for such programmes), nevertheless, he liked the idea of a more entertainment-based approach but said that he would present the whole package to his boss at Thames and see how it went down. Of course, at this point there had been no discussion at all about any formal involvement for myself, but I was happy to work with Adrian, whom I had come to like.

The following week we met again on the train and, with some excitement, he told me that not only had the Head of the Schools

Department been interested in the idea, he had given Adrian the go-ahead to commission the scripts and that he would like me to write them. I took this as a great compliment and was excited by the task ahead. There was only one problem, he went on to explain, namely, that the inclusion of celebrity presenters was going to increase the budget considerably and this had to be sanctioned by a higher level on management. However, whilst waiting for their decision we could crack ahead with the scripts.

Episode one was the key to it all. 'What is Music' needed to set the tone for the rest of the series. My idea had been to separate the three elements of music - rhythm, melody and harmony - and thus to distinguish music from noise. Of course, there had to be an element of generalisation since, arguably, in certain contexts the creation of noise might be considered musical. Still, I took the view that with the wider aim of explaining music to the uninitiated younger mind the niceties of these points were not helpful. What I needed was an approach that simplified the subject rather than complicated it. So, some basic explanation was required at the outset and I needed a setting and a person who could make this interesting.

What better place, I thought, than a recording studio. After all, the studio was the factory where music became immortalised and, in the process, was broken down into its constituent parts.

As for a presenter, who should I choose? Not a musician, surely, as this would immediately emphasize the divide between viewer and subject. What we wanted was a familiar figure, well-known to our young audience, who would command their attention and explain things in his own style and language. I threw this idea back at Adrian who promised to come up with some suggestions. I also needed a composer who could demonstrate how a piece of music was put together from start to finish.

After much consideration we settled on two familiar figures, Rolf Harris and Mike Batt. Rolf's already well-established career traversed all age groups and, although he had enjoyed top ten hits, he

was certainly as well-known as an artist and presenter of kid's programmes. Mike Batt, then in his late twenties, had enjoyed huge success with 'Watership Down' and his music for 'The Wombles' which was current at the time. What's more, Adrian had secured the budget to book them!

We decided on Abbey Road Studios as our location and I polished off the script for episode one, together with detailed treatments for the other five episodes in the series. A pre-production meeting was arranged at Mike's house in Surbiton and I met Rolf and Mike for the first time. By now they had both read the script and were enthusiastic about what we were trying to do. During the meeting I noticed Rolf scribbling away and assumed he was taking notes of what we were saying. An hour later, as we drew to a close, he presented me with a pencil cartoon captioned 'What is Music – What Indeed' which he signed and I have to this day. I wonder if today, languishing in jail, Mr Harris ever reflects on some of his less well-known appearances and works of art.

We filmed the first programme in a couple of days the following week. It went extremely well, both Rolf and Mike lived up to our expectations and, on the strength of a very positive response from Thames, we got the green light to move ahead at all possible speed with the following five episodes. The tiles were: 'The Language of Music', 'Strings', 'The Keyboard', 'Film Music' and 'The History of Music'.

Following the principle of employing entertainers, Jo Brown and the Bruvvers acted as frontmen for 'Strings' (the guitar being a stringed instrument, to state the not so obvious) alongside a group of string players from the LPO. My old friend, Paul Lewis, a fine composer of film and TV music, featured in 'Film Music' and I personally featured in two episodes – as the composer/conductor in 'The Language of Music' and as the pianist in 'The Keyboard'.

For 'The Keyboard' we featured the harpsichord, the pipe organ, the piano and the synthesizer (quite a novelty at the time). I presented the programme and Adrian commissioned Paul Lewis to write a classical piece for the four featured keyboard instruments. I had been so busy with the rest of the programme that I hadn't had time to think about playing my part in his piece. A day or so before the recording Paul telephoned to ask me whether I would like to have a look at the piano part in advance. I said 'yes' and he put it in the post. It arrived the day before the recording.

As soon as I looked at it I knew I was in trouble. The piece was very fast and contained passages that, quite frankly, I was not sufficiently adept technically to play. After all, I wasn't a classically trained pianist and my skills, such as they were, lay in other areas. However much I practiced the night before, I went to bed having not once managed to get through one eight bar section without fluffing it. As I drove to the school in Ealing where, for some reason, there was a newly installed pipe organ (the reason for choosing it as a location), all I could think about was that damned piano part.

Still, I had the rest of the programme to get through first - although, as the time approached to record Paul's piece, I was becoming increasingly apprehensive!

By now I had been introduced to the other three players, a well-known and distinguished organist, a harpsichord player from the Royal Philharmonic and a long-haired young man who was taking on the synthesizer part. We all sat at our instruments, Paul raised his baton and we ran it through. If anything he was taking it at an even quicker pace than I had imagined. Needless to say, when it came to my troublesome eight bars I fluffed it as before and ploughed on through the rest of the piece in a complete sweat waiting for the inevitable reprimand. It never came. Instead, Paul went over to the synthesizer player who, when I looked over, was in a worse state than me. Paul then went over to chat with the organist and then, as he returned to his rostrum, he merely gave me a wink. "Okay," he said, "let's go for it." His baton came down, we got to my dreaded eight bars and I played them perfectly!

I have watched that recording many times since and have never been able to understand how I managed it. Not only that, but I have attempted to play it subsequently – and still can't! Adrenalin, I suppose, just one of the several mysterious ingredients which can cause a performer to excel himself 'on the night'. Audience reaction being another.

Within its somewhat limited remit, the 'Musicround' series was considered a big success, was sold to schools all over the world and remained in the Thames catalogue pretty much until the company finally lost its franchise in the early nineties – in my view a gross political error and an irrecoverable loss to ITV.

It also led to me doing a number of other jobs for Thames, including the theme tune for a series called 'Database' about the digital revolution, also produced by Adrian, and some work on a series called 'Potty Time' created and performed by that brilliant and remarkable man, Michael Bentine. I set several of his Potty songs to music and was always astonished at how he could pick up the vocal part, run it through once and record it error-free straightaway.

Many years later when we moved to Walton-on-the-Hill in Surrey, Michael Bentine became a neighbour. I occasionally bumped into him in the local fishmongers where he would regale anyone lucky enough to be present with his jests and stories.

I remained in touch with Adrian Cooper for many years following our brief professional association, soon after which he had retired to help his wife run a drama studio in Guildford. He had occasionally spoken of his great interest in wine but it was only later that I found out that he was quite an authority and lectured widely on the subject.

Talking about wine, it was said that Michael Bentine could turn water into wine. He was a genius - so I wouldn't be surprised.

Richard Burton & Suzy Hunt

LET me make it clear I never worked with Richard Burton. But I did once exchange a couple of words with him under memorable - if rather humiliating - circumstances.

It was a hot summer's evening and I had just arrived to play at the Hilton having driven up in my old Simca estate. Now, this was no ordinary vehicle. Firstly, it had a picnic table in the floor of the boot, secondly it was big enough to accommodate my rather bulky musical equipment and still carry a couple of passengers and, thirdly, well, nobody else that I knew had one. And when you are in your early twenties that matters.

In fact, I loved that car so much that, soon after the incident I am about to relate, I had a new engine fitted. Not a Simca engine, but a Ford Cortina engine - this considerable feat of engineering being carried out by the main Ford dealer in Croydon called Dees. Yes, they actually took the old engine out and replaced it with one of their's. The logic was quite simple: I loved the car, the original engine had died and I wanted to keep the car with a passion - but with a different, more reliable engine. Simple as that. Can you imagine any high street dealer taking on such a job today?

Anyway, as I was saying, one of the incidents that led to all this happened on a beautiful, hot summer's evening just a few steps from the Hilton Hotel in Park Lane. I was in full black tie ready for the gig and the Simca had been overheating for the last half hour. In fact, by the time I got to Park Lane, there was steam coming from under the bonnet and fellow motorists were hooting and gesticulating at me.

I knew that if I left the car in the Hilton's underground car park, I might never get out again. So I stopped on a little road between the hotel and Park Lane, switched off the ignition and propped up the bonnet. I had to step back sharply in order to avoid being engulfed in a cloud of greasy steam. Dave the bass player was with me - not to mention all our equipment in the back. I asked him to go up to the ballroom and tell the other two what had happened - perhaps they would come down and at least get the instruments to where they needed to be. Also, could he ask the hotel for some water.

We had three quarters of an hour or so before we were due to play and it was beginning to dawn on me that, unless I was able to sort out the Simca, I probably wouldn't get home after the job.

It was only a few minutes before Tony and Arthur turned up.

"Where's Dave?" I asked.

"Getting some water," came the response.

Just then Dave appeared around the corner carrying bottles of water in his hands, pockets - any other part of him that could convey a water bottle.

"Best they could do," he said breathlessly, "there's more inside.

"Surely they have some sort of container?" I asked. Apparently not.

Soon the four of us were standing around the Simca, jackets off in the hot sun, with a couple of dozen bottles of water strewn all over the pavement - I don't suppose they contained more than a few pints between them. The engine had cooled down sufficiently to remove the radiator cap and I was patiently pouring water in, a bottle at a time, passing the empties to Dave. That is when we noticed a steady trickle of water appear from under the car.

Arthur - who by profession was a gas engineer - was quick on the uptake.

"That could be good news," he said cheerfully. "If it's just a faulty connection I can fix it. On the other hand, if the radiator is cracked, that's another matter."

"How can we tell?" I asked. He passed me his DJ and peered under the bonnet.

"Nothing I can see from here, I'll have to get underneath," he said.

"You'll get filthy," I protested and then remembered I had a raincoat in the back. "Here, put this on, it will protect you from the worst.

"Don't worry, it's dry under there. Shouldn't be too bad." And with that he disappeared with great agility, his lower body, complete with shiny patent shoes, sticking out into the road.

Now, picture the scene. Three young men standing round a car with the bonnet up, in full evening dress, dishevelled, jackets off, perspiring profusely in the heat, a fourth with only his feet on view and the pavement littered with half full and empty bottles.

It was at that moment that I saw four people walking towards us.

Two of them I didn't recognise, the other couple were a different matter. It was Richard Burton and, on his arm, his newly acquired girlfriend, Suzy Hunt, the super-model and ex-wife of racing driver James Hunt. They were dressed to the nines, clearly on their way to an important function, I guessed at the Dorchester a short stroll further up Park Lane, where, presumably, they had opted to stay.

The two of them were very much in the news at the time. Their relationship had caused a sensation and it had been suggested that Burton had "bought" fashion model Suzy for a million dollars from her racing driver husband, James. It was also rumoured that he had agreed to pay off the Hunts' divorce settlement so he could be with her.

It was at the end of 1975, just fourteen months into their marriage, that Hunt and Suzy had gone skiing in Switzerland for Christmas with friends. Burton and Elizabeth Taylor, then the most famous actors in the world, were staying at the same resort. They had been married since 1964 but, after a tempestuous decade together, had divorced, only to remarry a year later. But it was not to last long.

It was at the resort in Gstaad that Burton first bumped into Suzy Hunt. He was 50 and she was 26. By this time, Hunt, a voracious womaniser, had left to compete in the opening race of the 1976 Brazilian Grand Prix. Within hours of his departure Burton and Suzy Hunt had met at a party and struck up a friendship.

By the end of the year, the divorces of Taylor and Burton and James and Suzy Hunt were formalized, and Suzy Hunt and Burton were married. Eight years later Burton died of a brain haemorrhage. Suzy Hunt later went on to marry millionaire Jack Cawood and settled in the US.

This was the stunning apparition that appeared before us that evening outside the Hilton. Towering above Burton, Suzy looked every inch the glamorous model she was and he the consummate, beautifully turned out film idol.

As they picked their way through the empty bottles strewn across their path and took in the sorry state of the four of us, Richard Burton stopped for a moment, looked me straight in the eye, and said: "Good evening. Sorry I can't help, but I don't know much about motor cars". I always wondered whether that remark was directed at me or to the ex-Mrs Hunt.

And then they'd gone.

Mr Muzak

NOT far from where we lived in Kingswood, Surrey, there was a house, set well back and hidden, with maybe an acre of park-like garden in front to screen it from the road. It was called 'Kerchesters', the name carved discreetly on a piece of wood displayed outside the front gates. I had driven past it a hundred times and had no reason to wonder what might be at the end of the drive.

This changed when it came to looking for some library music for a series we were making at the time. 'Library' music is the name given to music that has already been composed and recorded with a particular genre of programme in mind. It is, if you like, music for hire, avoiding the necessity to employ a composer especially to write and record a score for your programme. It also offers the advantage of being free of copyright, to the extent that all the recording costs have already been absorbed and the residuals are low or, even in some circumstances, covered by a set fee payable in advance. The only drawback is that you don't 'own' the music for your programme - it could turn up elsewhere at any time.

There have always been a number of firms who specialise in supplying library music, one of the most famous being de Wolfe, whose immense catalogue stretches back more that a hundred years. Another smaller company, but with an equally good reputation, was called Amphonic Music. I knew that they were likely to have the sort of music we were looking for. What I didn't know was that its founder, Syd Dale, lived in that house called 'Kerchesters'.

Once contact had been established and they discovered that I lived just down the road, an invitation to visit 'Kerchesters' was quickly forthcoming, which was how I first came across this kind-hearted and brilliant man - and was fortunate enough to get to know him.

By that time Syd was one of the country's foremost composers and arrangers, but his first job was far removed from the world of music. In fact, he started as an apprentice engineer at the confectionery giant Rowntrees, working in their chocolate factory, spending three years designing machines that fitted chocolates into boxes. He was enthralled by the big band sounds that were popular at the time and, once he had decided to make music his career, spent as much time as possible studying arrangements and listening closely to the big bands of the time. Thus, after the war he left Rowntrees and became a member of various local bands including 'The Squadronaires' where his role was pianist and arranger.

Syd founded Amphonic in the '70's to provide the TV, film, radio and advertising industry with music that covered all bases, produced to the highest possible standards. Its success was helped in no small way by Syd's contributions as composer/arranger.

His catalogue highlighted the qualities that would come to define Syd's 'sound': intricate arrangements, an emphasis on melody and harmony, crystal clear recordings and first class musicianship. He had a rich, colourful style of orchestration that gave his music a unique and distinctive sound. Whether he was writing a hard-hitting theme for a detective or documentary series, a delicate underscore for a romantic interlude, a period piece or a humorous 'throwaway' number, the common factor uniting them all were his lavish, flamboyant arrangements.

This musical attitude was reflected in the work of the leading British composers and arrangers Syd invited to write for his company, amongst them my old friend Tony Hatch.

From its original base in Mortimer Street in London's West End, Syd moved the company to Kent and then on to 'Kerchesters' in Kingswood - which, of course, brings us full circle. But I knew little of all this when I first made my way up that long winding drive to meet him for the first time. What I encountered was much as I expected; a large, red-brick Edwardian-style house, similar to many others in Kingswood, with some impressive steps leading to the front door. What I didn't expect was to be re-directed to the back of the property, apparently to the 'offices'. For there in all its contemporary glory was the headquarters of Amphonic, a large car park and single storey suite of offices complete with (as I soon found out) a fully-fledged and beautifully equipped recording studio, large enough to house a full orchestra! How Syd had ever got planning permission for all this remained a mystery, but it was most impressive.

Although surrounded by staff, Syd wasted no time in welcoming me personally and we were soon chatting away like old friends. Of course, he had no reason to think I was a musician and, when I told him, hurriedly adding that I was not in his league, this helped create a quick bond between us. The business of the day was soon dispensed with and I was invited into the house to meet his wife, Audrey, who, unsurprisingly, was equally delightful.

Over the next year or so our paths crossed many times. On one occasion I was producing a little show at the Village Hall and had worked out a piano medley of well-known classical tunes set to a modern beat. With some trepidation I asked Syd if he could arrange and record an orchestral backing for me that I could play along with. He was instantly on the case and within a week I had my track, which sounded like the Royal Philharmonic. In fact, he had done it all himself using what we would now consider to be a very primitive early synthesizer.

Syd was also very generous with his party invitations. No family or festive occasion went by without Syd inviting his musical chums to join him at 'Kerchesters' - and, once we had met, Christine and I always received an invitation. We would move heaven and earth to be there. It probably goes without saying that Syd's chums included the musical legends of the day - Max Harris, Kenny Baker and Don Lusher to name but three - and it wasn't long before these guys were jamming away in Syd's front room. But, a funny thing always happened. For example, at Christmas, when all this great creative energy had been expended, Syd would turn to me and say: "How about a few Christmas songs, Pip?" or at Audrey's birthday parties,: "Can you play 'Happy Birthday' when the cake comes in?" or "What about 'A Nightingale Sang in Berkeley Square', it's her favourite song?" Whilst only too pleased to oblige, I never understood why he asked me to play these simple pieces - maybe he thought he'd give me the easy jobs! In fact, I think it was something quite different, namely, that he was acknowledging my experience as a 'live' performer when all the others, brilliant as they were, were studio players with limited personal repertoires. Funny, but I think that was it.

Syd was a pioneer. Not only in terms of his music but also as a businessman. Unfortunately, his facility to compose, arrange and record vast quantities of music in a very short time led to him becoming known as 'Mr Muzak' and it is true that the lion's share of the background music we all heard at that time in supermarkets, pubs, clubs, factories, leisure centres, hairdressers and airports flowed from Syd's pen. But the nickname didn't do him justice.

Syd passed away in the 1990s, but the recent resurgence of interest in 1960s and 1970s library music has meant that his musical legacy has been discovered by a new generation of listeners, eager to hear the beautifully realised sounds produced by Syd and his chums during that golden era.

About Beadle

WHAT conundrums showbusiness people can be. And what mistaken assumptions we can make about them. Jeremy Beadle was a case in point.

He was an impish, lovely, flickering, annoying, infuriating, brilliant, well-read, intellectual man, much, much more than the shallow prankster portrayed by the media.

When he died in 2008 the newspapers ran headlines about Jeremy as the man the nation loved to hate, the man who humiliated unsuspecting members of the public on shows like 'Game For a Laugh', 'Beadle's About' and 'You've Been Framed'. Yet how many entertainers in the last four decades would get - and deserve - double-page spreads in the tabloids and half-page obituaries in The Daily Telegraph, The Guardian and others like them, whose television critics over the years were less than generous to him? In reality, Jeremy understood very well the public image he had created and was long since reconciled to living with the consequences.

The real Jeremy Beadle couldn't have been more different. He was just about the most literate and well-read person I have known. To share a taxi with him was to be educated, sometimes needlessly: he was a true fount of knowledge and a joyful master of useless facts. I never minded, for example, as we drove over a level crossing, being told where the first one had been built. And who wants to know when you're having your lunch that Beadle knows who invented the paperclip!

There was the other side to his appetite for facts and figures: he was almost maniacally curious. Whenever he thought he'd informed you enough, you'd then get the questions: about your school, where you'd been on holiday, about your business. Where you'd been, who you'd met, what were they like? He wanted to know everything: facts, figures, information. Anything that was new, no matter how trivial, was what he loved.

I first met him in 2003 when he was conducting the auction at a charity event at the Grosvenor House. We hit it off straightaway and it wasn't long before we were back in touch. I had been looking for a new fundraising event for Variety Club that would be based around comedy. I mentioned this to him and he told me that he had just the thing - all he needed to do was find the treatment, dust it down and post it to me. I gave him my address, not really expecting to hear any more. Within a couple of days there it was in front of me.

What he had sent me was a format for a proposed annual televised event which he had called 'The Jokers' Awards' to be broadcast every year on April Fools' Day. The accompanying note explained that he had tried it on all the broadcasters, none of whom had seen its potential. Would Variety Club be interested in staging it as a live event with himself as master-of-ceremonies? Needless to say, I jumped at the idea and suggested that we get together as soon as possible to discuss it further. He invited me to meet him at his home in Hadley Wood the following week.

I was met by his lovely wife, Sue, who told me that Jeremy had three meetings going on at the same time that morning - which, she added, was quite normal! However, he knew I was there and he would be out immediately. Within seconds there he was, expansive and larger than life, explaining that he had several teams of people working on different formats for TV shows and other projects but, not to worry, they could get on quite happily without him. He then showed me into his famous library. I had read somewhere that Jeremy had 22,000 books, all housed in this huge extension at the back of the house. It was a unique experience to be led between row after row of bookshelves, each section meticulously labeled and catalogued. Eventually, we arrived at the far end of the room where he had left a clear area flooded with natural light for his desk and small seating space.

During the next hour or so we planned the event between us and I was impressed by his grasp of every aspect of the project. He wasn't the least dogmatic or possessive about his original idea, fully prepared to adapt and change it to suit the occasion and happy to embrace my input as we went along.

As our conversation inevitably drifted away from business over a sandwich lunch, we discovered that we shared a mutual friend, someone we both knew very well indeed. That friend was a certain Dr Alex Williams, a close neighbour of ours in Kingswood, whose family we had known very well for many years. Apparently Jeremy and Alex had shared a flat in their bachelor days when both were struggling to establish their respective careers. A few months later we arranged for our three families to get together at 'Heathwoods', our home in Walton-on-the-Hill. It was a beautiful summer's afternoon and we all had great fun, adults and children alike.

Meanwhile Jeremy had been working on 'The Joker's Awards' and had made considerable progress. He had decided that although he would produce and appear during the evening, he had arranged for Chris Tarrant, (who he modestly and generously suggested was a more current 'name') to compère and present the evening. This was great for the charity, of course, as we now had two big names to hang the evening on. But he hadn't stopped there - Nicholas Parsons and the lovely Bonnie Langford, together with Bernard Cribbins and Rula Lenske were to form the panel of judges and he was now contacting the comedians who would compete for the award.

The date for the event had been set for April Fools Day 2003 at the Dorchester and the ballroom was packed to overflowing. The whole evening was hilarious and went on well past 11pm, but nobody minded. Stan Boardman eventually won the 'Best Joke' category with a rambling and irreverent joke about Terry Waite and an Islamic radiator whilst veteran comic, Charlie Smithers, got a Lifetime Achievement Award. Largely thanks to Jeremy, the evening was a huge success.

I bumped into him many times after that and couldn't help but notice how his general demeanour seemed to be deteriorating. Of course, he had never been entirely well having been born with the comparatively rare Poland Syndrome, the reason for the stunted growth of his left hand. In fact, by the age of two he had already undergone surgery for the condition. He had also suffered from leukemia.

He died only a few years later in 2008 due to severe pneumonia. He was 59. His headstone in Highgate Cemetery bears the inscription "Writer, Presenter, Curator of Oddities". Shortly afterwards a television tribute was broadcast, 'An Audience Without Jeremy Beadle', hosted by Chris Tarrant with contributions from Sir Alan Sugar, Henry Kelly, Ken Campbell, Anneka Rice and others. An obituary in The Daily Telegraph said that he was "the most avidly watched presenter on television". In 2010, he was the subject of a documentary, 'The Unforgettable Jeremy Beadle'.

Jeremy changed the momentum of British television, probably without knowing it. His invention, intellect and capacity to spot the twist at the end of a story were unique. He was the pulse and heartbeat of the Saturday night schedules for more than twenty years.

His friend and co-presenter on *Game for a Laugh*, Henry Kelly, said at the time: "musicians will admit - some reluctantly - that the key to an orchestra, a jazz band, a pop group, is the drummer: he sets the rhythm and the pace. Beadle was the drummer." A nice analogy.

One final thing: Jeremy Beadle, quietly, with little or no fanfare, television cameras, newspapers or radio, did something else which has literally changed the lives of countless people: through his sheer hard work and energy he helped to raise more than £100 million for the charities with which he was associated.

Prankster? Yes! Practical joker? Yes! Good man and great friend? That's how I remember him. Yes!

Bobby's Girl

ONE of the most memorable hits of the 1960's was recorded by a rather lovely young brunette singer from County Durham. The song was called *"Bobby's Girl"* and it propelled her well and truly into stardom and a glittering, if relatively short-lived, career on TV and on the live concert circuit. So, imagine my surprise when, one day in 1980, who should turn up to buy our house in Brighton but Susan Maughan.

We were selling for one simple reason, I was finding the daily journey up to town tiresome and time-consuming, especially now that we had two young daughters who I was hardly seeing. A move northwards appeared to be the answer.

In fact, we had already found a place on the other side of the downs and put in an offer. It was called 'Woodsmill' and was located in the charming little village of Henfield. I had calculated that by travelling up from Haywards Heath instead of Hove I would save at least an hour on the train every day. There was another factor. Although in need of extensive renovation, 'Woodsmill' was a beautiful property. It stood in its own grounds of nearly five acres and, much to Christine's amusement, had its own cricket pitch where the local club team was based. The current occupier was a man in his forties, living alone, who clearly wanted out - and quickly. He told us that he had been badly messed around by another buyer who had been dragging his feet. I could tell that his patience had been tested to breaking point and maybe there was an opportunity to move quickly and buy the property from under the other buyer's nose. So, I had made him a very low offer, conditional upon us being able to exchange and complete within a couple of weeks which, fortunately at the time we were able to do.

It came as a bit of a shock to get a call from the estate agents the following day reporting that he had accepted our offer. After a brief conference we decided to go ahead and, within the month we were the proud owners of 'Woodsmill' and the occupier had moved out. We immediately called in an architect who started to draw up plans for the renovations and some tree surgeons to sort out a number of arboreal issues. The only problem was - we hadn't sold our house in Hove! This was when Ms Maughan turned up with her new husband, a rather unimpressive man who, quite frankly, looked a bit washed up. Still, that was none of our business. Anyway, it was clear that she was making the running and, I assumed, more than able to afford to buy the property.

There followed a couple more visits and several telephone conversations during the course of which a rather different story emerged. I had naturally assumed (forgetting the golden rule – never assume anything about showbusiness people), that Ms Maughan was a wealthy woman. *'Bobby's Girl'* alone, which had remained popular long after the original release and had become something of a classic, must have netted her a small fortune, apart from the money she had earned from television, live appearances and subsequent recordings for many years afterwards.

As it happened I had some business interests in the Caribbean at the time and during the course of one of our conversations, not long after I had returned from a trip to Barbados, I mentioned a restaurant on the west coast which I had very much enjoyed called

'Greensleeves'. Her face fell. "That was set up and financed with the money I made from *'Bobby's Girl'*", she explained. I lost every penny." Well, of course, this explained a lot. I had wondered, for example, why she was driving a ten-year old Volvo two-door coupe (the same *Volvo* P1800 from the 1960s that Roger Moore drove in 'The Saint'). It also explained why she had married the sad, defeated looking businessman who, I later discovered, had been something in the fashion business until he had gone bankrupt. In short, Ms Maughan and her new partner were skint and there was as much chance of her buying our beautiful Regency house than having another number one hit. Having said that, she was a nice lady and I felt sorry for her. So much so, that when she had told us she was appearing at Littlehampton with Freddie Starr, we had gone down to see her. That was a pretty sad experience, too.

Some years later when I was working for the National Trust at the Polesden Lacey Festival, I thought it might be a good idea to run a 60's night. The lead act was Gerry and the Pacemakers who I'd booked to do the whole of the second half. So, I needed a few acts to comprise the first half. Naturally, I invited my old mate, Jess Conrad, and thought that Susan might be a good bet on an otherwise all-male bill. Well, she turned up, strutted her stuff and, in fairness, although the voice had lost some of its strength, did a good job. The last I heard was that she had married the manager of the Fairfield Halls in Croydon and was working in pantos and on the retro circuit. Her birth date is always quoted as 1942 but is probably a bit earlier so, at the time of writing, she would be in her early 70's. Good luck to her. She's a trooper and I admire that.

Anyway, back to our domestic arrangements. As I said, the purchase of 'Woodsmill' had gone through very quickly indeed and, we had, in fact, bought it at a very advantageous price. But that was not the end of the story. One night a few weeks later, we had gone to bed when the telephone rang. It must have been well after eleven, so I thought it must be a matter of some importance. I picked up the receiver and said 'hello'. The male voice at the other end sounded peeved to say the least.

"Mr Burley?" came the opening remark in an accusing tone, "you've just bought my house."

This came as a bit of a surprise. It didn't sound like the man from whom we had recently bought Woodsmill so I asked him who I was speaking to.

"My name is Tugwell," came the reply. You've bought Woodsmill from under my nose and my wife has made the curtains!"

As this late-night conversation continued, it appeared that Mr Tugwell was the other purchaser, the man, who in the words of the vendor, had been 'messing him about'. I explained this to him, pointing out that the house had certainly still been on the market when we'd viewed it and we would hardly have been able to buy it had the vendor not wanted us to! Still, I could tell he felt cheated.

After this Mr Tugwell seemed to calm down and asked what would I want for the property should he wish to make me an offer. I explained that we were delighted with our purchase and had no wish to sell; we had architects working on plans for a total re-furbishment and a firm of tree surgeons looking at the forestry. Moreover, it was nearly midnight and I really didn't want to engage in a protracted conversation at this time of night. With that, my first (but not last) conversation with Mr Tugwell came to an end.

Whilst this extraordinary exchange had been going on, I couldn't help thinking that the name Tugwell sounded vaguely familiar. But, try as I might, I couldn't place it.

The following day we took a trip out to Henfield with the children. It had been raining all night and it was pouring down when we arrived. We were glad to get indoors and, armed with the architect's initial thoughts, applied ourselves to the task of imagining how it would work out in practice. Our intention was to preserve Woodsmill's traditional country house elegance whilst creating a more contemporary allocation of the space. To achieve this we needed to sacrifice a bedroom and extend the kitchen/family area. All of this appeared feasible and the early designs looked promising. It was while we were upstairs that Christine looked out of the window, gasped, and called me over.

I have to say I was disturbed by what I saw. The back lawn and what we could see of the cricket field were practically under water! It hadn't occurred to us that there might have been some significance in the name 'Woodsmill' – maybe at one time there had indeed been a mill there with the possibility of a stream running through the property. Even it had been re-routed since, there was still the likelihood that the water table beneath this low-lying ground in the lee of the downs was unusually high. In hindsight we realized that perhaps in our hurry to secure the house, we had omitted to look sufficiently into such things. Still, we reassured ourselves, this was unlikely to be a regular occurrence and the rain had been particularly heavy after all. We locked up, returned to the car and drove back to Hove.

That evening we had another call from Mr Tugwell who admitted that he was under considerable pressure from his wife. They had made plans, he explained. Not only had she bought the fabric and nearly finished the curtains, she had been looking at furniture and fittings. For his part he had been planning to fence off some of the land and keep sheep – which prompted me to ask him if he was a farmer. No, he replied, he was butcher.

That was it! The penny dropped and I remembered that in our previous house in Brighton, there had been a very good butcher's shop on the opposite corner called Tugwells, which, in fact, sold very good meat. We shopped there all the time. Was this his shop I asked him? Indeed, he replied, one of three that he owned in the area. I told him we were great supporters of his branch in Cross Street, which seemed to relieve some of the tension between us.

He admitted that, with hindsight, he had tried to be too clever, believing that by playing a waiting game, he would save himself a few thousand pounds off the purchase price – which, he presumed, is what we paid. In fact, we had paid fifteen thousand or so less than the asking price in exchange for moving very fast; but I was not about to disclose that to Mr T.

He was not going to make the same mistake twice, he declared. If I was prepared to sell him 'Woodsmill' straightaway, he would pay me the original asking price plus five thousand pounds. Again, I told him we were not even contemplating selling, but I would bear his offer in mind should circumstances change.

The following day British Rail announced that they were reducing their service from Haywards Heath. Most of the fast trains from Brighton and Hove would no longer be stopping there. Not long afterwards we received a horrendous estimate from the tree surgeons. Apparently, half the trees within the grounds were dead, rotting or dying and we had a major job on our hands to sort it out. I was beginning to think things were moving in Mr Tugwell's direction. If he wanted Woodsmill that badly - maybe he could have it.

Something else occurred to me. He was a businessman who had had no qualms about giving the original seller a hard time – so, even though it had backfired on him, I didn't need to feel sorry for him or, for that matter, give him an easy time myself. So, I decided to wait until he called again.

He was on the 'phone within the week and this time he sounded as if he was about to throw himself off Beachey Head.

"Alright", I said, "you can have Woodsmill but, to make it worth our while, I want a premium of twenty thousand pounds above the original asking price."

I guessed, rightly, that he would come straight back with an offer of fifteen and told him it was simply not enticing enough to prise us out, bearing in mind we had already incurred architect's and surveyor's fees. Not to mention that we were planning to live there for the next twenty years. He needed to come up with the extra five thousand.

I couldn't actually hear him tearing his hair out but I could certainly make out Mrs Tugwell berating him in the background. It was in those few seconds that I came up with a stroke of genius. I consulted briefly with Christine who nodded enthusiastically.

"Okay, Mr Tugwell," I said, "here's the deal. You can make up the difference in meat for as long as it takes for us to eat it." There was a stunned silence at the other end. "Wholesale or retail?" he asked. "Wholesale," I replied. There was a pause. "Alright then, I'll have it delivered to you monthly."

So, the deal was done. He had got Woodsmill, we had made a handsome profit and secured enough beef, lamb and sausages to feed us for the next three years.

There was a curious codicil to this story. With the extra money we'd made out of Woodsmill – where we had never spent a single night - we were eventually able to move to a lovely house in Kingswood, much closer to our family, parents and many of our old friends; and much further from Mr Tugwell who, in fairness, continued to deliver our meat. But, in the meantime, we carried on living in Hove.

So, it was just as well Ms Maughan didn't buy that house.

The Man who Made Bricks

WE have owned six houses during the course of a long marriage and in every case there has been some sort of twist in the tale. But, as with Woodsmill, some of the strangest things have cropped up with properties we have failed to buy or never lived in. In fact, although I have no real interest in property as such, my dealings with estate agents, buyers and sellers, have nearly always been amusing.

One such was the case of 'Smuggler's Ridge'. At the time I sold the publishing and advertising business, we were ready to move from our lovely home in Kingswood. Two things had prompted this: firstly, the great storm of 1987 which had caused us to lose two magnificent lime trees amongst other damage and, secondly, a huge construction project which the Legal & General had undertaken almost opposite us resulting in a procession of hgv's and other construction traffic rumbling relentlessly past our house every day. This was due to go on for a further three years and, frankly, the two things combined made us feel that the house we were living in was no longer the one we had fallen in love with fifteen years earlier.

As the children were now in their teens, and with my elderly father to consider, we were looking for a fairly substantial house, ideally, with some separate accommodation if required. We had no wish to move away from Kingswood where we had made many friends and established an active and rewarding social life. Properties of the type we wanted did not abound, however, and I was excited one day to get a call from a friendly local agent saying that one such might be about to come onto the market. The name of the owner was a Colonel Young. I telephoned him immediately and he agreed that we should go round and take a look.

Harold Carter was married to Nancy and had two daughters. The Carter family and Alec Young had found and purchased 'Smugglers Ridge' together, deciding to share the magnificent seven-bedroom house, each with their own designated areas. No doubt this arrangement had suited them well over the years, enabling the two men to entertain business associates and other influential contacts in some style with Mrs Carter always on hand to act as the charming hostess. In fact, it was to last until well after both men retired.

Forty years or so earlier, Colonel Young, a chartered accountant, had been working for a small brick-making company based in Reigate called Redland, eventually being appointed Chairman, a role he occupied until 1970 when he was succeeded by Lord Beeching. One day, he had received a telephone call from the managing director of an equally small engineering company who requested a meeting to discuss a new idea. That meeting led to an extraordinary collaboration which not only netted both firms (and presumably their directors) a substantial fortune but was to become the platform for Redland's rapid growth worldwide, eventually, becoming one of the UK's top 100 companies. The engineer who had developed the idea was a Mr Carter and he and Col Young had become close personal friends as well as business partners.

Mr Carter's idea was to manufacture roof tiles out of concrete rather than clay. What's more, he had developed the machinery to do it. Redland had the distribution network to market the new tiles and Col Young was quick to take up the idea and shrewd enough to lock Mr Carter in by offering him a directorship and a position on the board of Redland.

Not only that but, later, when Mr Carter decided to marry in 1953, Col Young had offered the newly weds temporary accommodation at 'Smuggler's Ridge' whilst they looked for a house of their own. Presumably, the colonel had been living in the seven-bedroom house alone and, although presumably entertaining in some style, may have even welcomed his friend and business partner moving in with his young wife.

Anyway, for whatever reason, the arrangement must have suited all three of them because it had lasted until well after both men had retired. The question of offspring was never mentioned so we assumed there weren't any.

The lady we had met was Mrs Carter and the reason they were putting the house on the market was that Mr Carter had recently suffered a stroke. This dramatic change to the status quo had triggered a new plan: Mr and Mrs Carter would seek specialized care in an old people's home and Col Young would take up permanent residence at Whites. How long this would take was uncertain but they were pleased to know that we were happy with their asking price and that the sale of 'Smuggler's Ridge' was assured. We confirmed that we were in no hurry and that they should take whatever time was necessary. However, to give us some certainty, I would write him a letter confirming our agreement to which he would formally respond. He was perfectly happy with this and I asked him if he would object to our surveyor inspecting the property? Again, he was content that we should proceed along these lines.

As it happened, some very close friends of ours had just celebrated their daughter's marriage and they had visited us some weeks earlier. The new son-in-law, who worked in the mortgage industry, had fallen in love with our house and said that if ever we were contemplating a sale, would I let him know. I was surprised he could afford it, but now that we had 'Smuggler's Ridge' in our sights, it seemed the right time to revisit the subject. Within a few days he had been back to see us again and made an offer we couldn't refuse. So, now we had two 'unofficial' deals on the table, neither involving agents or, at this stage, lawyers. I was nevertheless optimistic that with some goodwill on all sides, the timing could be made to work.

The, suddenly everything changed. Col Young called to say

that Mr Carter had sadly died and, therefore, he would have to put everything on hold for the time being. This was bad although not calamitous news for us as it appeared that, if anything, this would hasten the process of the remaining two parties leaving the house rather than delay it. How wrong we were.

What happened, of course, was that their share of the house now became part of Mr Carter's estate. The next generation of Carters became involved and the disposal of Smuggler's Ridge became tied up with probate and the executors. Col Young beat a hasty retreat to his club telling us over the 'phone that matters were now out of his hands and, anyway, it wouldn't be 'respectable' for him to remain in the house with Mrs Carter - and that from a near eighty-year-old who had been living in the same house as the lady in question for forty years!

And, that was that. I had a single communication from Mrs Carter's son-in-law saying that it would take several months to unwind matters and, when they were ready, the property would go on the market. I mentioned that we had spent two hundred and fifty pounds on a survey but that didn't seem to impress him.

That's when we started looking elsewhere.

David Jason

DAVID Jason and I first met in Leeds at the offices of Yorkshire Television. At the time he had made a couple of highly successful comedy series including, of course, 'Open All Hours' and 'Only Fools and Horses' and ITV were keen to poach him from the BBC. They had persuaded him to star in a series called 'A Bit of a Do' which, unusually, had been shot as comedy drama rather than a sitcom, meaning, amongst other differences, there was no studio audience. This was a significant move for David who, until then, had been considered a comedy rather than dramatic actor.

When we had first thought about casting the role of Pop Larkin, David had not readily come to mind. Bob Hoskins was our first choice followed closely by Phil Collins. However, both appeared beyond our reach. Mr Hoskins was enjoying the time of his life starring in major Hollywood movies and Phil, although having proved his worth as an actor in 'The Great Train Robbery', was earning a fortune as a musician. Anxious to find a new role for David, it was YTV who suggested him for 'The Darling Buds of May'.

We had all seen enough of David's work to know that he was

more than up to the job and he, in turn, was keen to take it on. This proved to be the start of a relationship that would last for the next nineteen years.

My first sight of David at work was at the read-through of episode one. With the cast assembled around a large table, I have to say that David's first effort to create the role of Pop was discouraging. It was painfully obvious that he was not a good reader and surprisingly lacking in confidence in this situation. Moreover, the slick professionalism of those around him accentuated his stumbling delivery. I was surprised that he didn't appear troubled by any of this. "Good script," he said, "don't worry about me, I am hopeless at reading, not like the others with their bags of tricks. But I don't mind that." He tapped the side of his nose. "Don't worry, I'll get there and when you're ready to shoot, I'll be ready to give you my performance. The others, well, they'll give you the same as you got today."

Which is precisely what happened – and it occurred to me that for a man who had started out as an electrician with no formal drama training, this was the way he had made his career work. Lacking in studied technique, the only route available to him was to 'think' his way into a role, much in the way that American actors are trained, although without the pretentiousness of the full-blown 'method' school. This enabled him to work well within himself most of the time – a bit like cruising at 60mph in a Ferrari.

It was also the reason why he was reluctant to alter his appearance or put on a funny voice. Unlike character actors who love to play with wigs, make-up, dialects and costume, disguising themselves as much as possible in the process, David instinctively knew how to act from the inside out, dredging the character from within. All the great leading actors have done this. Just because Cary Grant was always Cary Grant did not make his performances any less convincing. The same could be said of Spencer Tracey, Errol Flynn and John Wayne, and for the great leading ladies like Marilyn Monroe. But, it's a hard trick to pull and, when you see it, you know that something special is going on. Few manage it convincingly and consistently and when they do we call them stars.

Soon after the series was announced, David was asked to record some audio cassettes of the original books. As someone who readily confessed to disliking reading, David relished the task by giving every character their own voice – even Ma and Mariette - and he portrayed Pop as a kind of cockney country yokel. However, when it came to playing the part for real, there he was looking and talking very much like himself, the only obvious difference being the length of his sideburns. The rest is acting.

'Darling Buds' was very much an ensemble piece with the four leading characters, Pop and Ma and Charlie and Mariette more or less dominating the action. Needless to say, Catherine Zeta-Jones as Mariette received the lion's share of media attention, not least because of her fresh, youthful beauty. It was as if the whole country had fallen in love with her, men and women, young an old alike. In fact, Kelvin Mackenzie, at that time editor of the Sun newspaper, called me one day pleading for some item of 'Darling Buds' merchandise that he could sell to his readers. "Anything with that girl on", he said, "T-shirt, tie, pair of knickers – I don't care so long as she's on it!" Without even bothering to check I told him that our young leading lady would never agree to anything of the sort and offered him a specially written whole page cartoon-style Larkin's Christmas story instead. "Anything," he said, "but make sure that girl's in it!" The whole page duly appeared.

Pam Ferris had little difficulty bringing H.E.Bates' lovable Ma to life and the classically trained Philip Franks portrayed taxman Charlie's diffidence and newly discovered romanticism to perfection. But, without doubt, it was David who held the series together, his solid, subtly crafted performance providing the springboard from which the others launched their performances.

The first episode of 'Darling Buds' delivered an audience of more than eighteen million viewers, a record for the first episode of any series before or since. What's more, it held that audience throughout series one. ITV had a huge hit on its hands and there was no hesitation in commissioning series two. By now we had used up all the material in the first book and most of the second. Mariette and Charlie were happily married and so the series had lost much of its romantic edge. Still, we went ahead with some new stories mixed in with the originals. Ironically, H.E.Bates must have found himself in a similar quandary as, following the huge success of the original book (the one called 'The Darling Buds of May') he, too, went on to write four more. TV eats up material and we were only too aware that, if ITV wished to continue into a third and even a fourth series, we would need a further supply of new stories and characters interspersed with H.E.'s original material.

Still, thanks to some good new story ideas and excellent scripts, series two went well enough and a third series was soon commissioned - and this was when the problems started. For obvious reasons, we were working hard to keep the Mariette character to the forefront. Catherine was still riding on the crest of a wave in terms of popularity and with Mariette now happily settled with her own family, there was the obvious danger of her character stagnating. So, we briefed our writers to introduce some tension into her marriage, thus opening the door to fresh romantic prospects. At the same time we had Charlie (now devoid of his previous employment with the Inland Revenue) getting involved in a series of failed business initiatives. Whilst this succeeded in preserving a central role for Mariette, it didn't go down too well with rest of our 'ensemble' cast. Soon we received murmurings that both Pam and, to a lesser extent, Philip were unhappy with the way their characters were developing, or, as they saw it, not developing. Only David kept his own counsel for which we were grateful.

The situation culminated with lunch for two at the Royal Garden hotel in Kensington when I attempted to persuade Pam to sign up for a fourth series. After some perfectly pleasant preliminaries, she lost no time in telling me that Ma had become a mere appendage to Pop and that she should really have a life of her own – in short, Pam wanted Ma to become a liberated, independent woman, strong, self-opinionated and free to do what she wanted with storylines of her own. I tried to explain that not only was the series set in the 1950's, but Ma was all of those things already. She and Pop were a team, they did everything together through choice – two strong characters who were still very much in love. Sadly, this failed to mollify Pam who made it quite clear that unless there were some serious changes, she had no wish to carry on.

Elsewhere, we were having conversations with Catherine and her agent. Whilst she was grateful for the opportunity that 'Darling Buds' had provided, she didn't want to be typecast in the role of 'the girl next door' and had aspirations to sing and dance as well as act. Amusingly, she had turned up on the set at the beginning of series three made up to look ten years older, more sophisticated and decidedly more sexy. The director told her to go back to her caravan and take it all off!

When this was conveyed to the rest of the senior production team, it was agreed unanimously to call it a day. We had reached a point where the tail was wagging the dog and to attempt to carry on would result in the whole spirit of the series, not to mention the original books, being compromised. I sometimes wonder how many producers would take the same decision today. So many long-running programmes seem to go on chasing ratings well past their sell-by date.

Again, the pattern of the television series mirrored the books. We were left with H.E.s' final book, 'A Little of What You Fancy', still unmade. In this Pop has a heart attack, a bored Ma does indeed have a dalliance with a handsome barrister, and Pop's 'perfick' paradise is threatened by the construction of the Channel Tunnel. It was as if even H.E. could find nowhere else to go with his idyll of Kentish life. We had this story scripted but never did get round to making it for television although, some years later, it was recorded for radio with

David again playing Pop.

But, in the meantime, we had a serious problem – having created one of the most phenomenally successful TV series of all time, we were now out of work. We needed a good idea.

David had been loyal throughout all this – to such an extent that he always said that, providing we were able to re-assemble the original cast, he would be happy to make more episodes. Still, there seemed little chance of that. We were sure Pam wouldn't change her mind and Catherine was soon committed to other projects, eventually leading her to Hollywood.

It was time to sit back and think. What were we trying to achieve?

One of the few advantages of being in an erratic and unpredictable business is that when you're between jobs there is plenty of time to think. We had started Excelsior with the express intention of making long-form drama for television; in other words series that had 'legs' and would go on for years. 'Darling Buds' had given us a terrific start. We had made forty hours over three years and most producers would have been more than happy with that. But this being England and not America, the limos were not queuing outside our offices with broadcasters clamouring for us to do the same thing for them - in fact, quite the reverse. The general view in the industry was that we had been lucky. The timing of the first series coinciding with the war in the middle east, the recession, an unexpected resurgence of interest in the 1950's, the Catherine sensation – all of this was responsible for the success of the series. Well, so be it, and I am not saying for a moment that these weren't contributing factors, but the series still had to be conceived, scripted, cast and directed. It had to be edited, music composed, publicised and marketed – and paid for – the things that producers do - and it all had to be done well. Yes, there were elements of luck. We were fortunate, for example, that Greg Dyke at LWT had chosen to transmit it on Sunday evenings, the perfect time for the public to welcome the Larkins into their living rooms. We were lucky, too, that Yorkshire Television saw its potential from the start. But, in the end, its longevity was curbed by a fatal flaw. We started off with one star and three supporting actors and ended up with four stars. As H.E.Bates may well have discovered half a century earlier, it was the Larkin 'family' that inevitably sowed the seeds of its own destruction. Nobody can go on being that happy forever! Still, we certainly weren't complaining - we had much to be grateful for and now it was time to move on.

During this period of introspection we decided that one thing we wouldn't do was devise another series with an ensemble cast. We were also clear that, despite everything, David was and always had been our star. It was time to go to him to talk about what might happen next.

As David accurately describes in his autobiography, this particular piece of the future was sparked over lunch at the Intercontinental Hotel in Park Lane. Richard and I had planned to ask him what he would like to do next, whether there was a character that he had always wanted to play? The question came up over coffee and, as David himself admits, it took him completely by surprise - clearly, no-one had ever asked him that before. Like most actors, he had always been cast in parts that others thought he was suited to. For the first time he was being treated like a star.

The answer came quickly. "Now that you ask, I've always wanted to play a cop, a sort of Columbo character, dishevelled, chaotic, but passionate about what he does. A good cop, though." We said we would see what we could come up with and get back to him.

It often surprises people how many good ideas for film and television begin in public libraries. The reason is simple. Whatever you might have in mind has almost certainly been thought of before. If you are really lucky, the novelist will have already researched the subject matter, created and developed characters and storylines and even written further books creating a ready made 'series' in the process. The drawback, of course, is that the film and TV rights may have already been sold elsewhere, even if nothing came of them subsequently. But the process of locating suitable books, reading them and researching the underlying rights can be time-consuming, and we were keen to make progress quickly before David got caught up in other projects. We decided to employ a researcher with a very specific brief – to find a contemporary novel, preferably a series, featuring a lonely, eccentric detective with the potential for some humour. Although we saw this new series very much rooted in serious crime drama, we were keen to maximise on David's considerable aptitude to deliver the odd comic moment.

Whilst this was going on we took a close look at what else was on television in the same or similar genre. The three prominent British series at the time were 'Morse', 'Taggart' and 'Poirot' – with seemingly endless episodes of 'Columbo' still streaming in from the States. We knew how important it was not to replicate any of these and, at the same time, to try to move the genre of the UK television detective forwards. We wanted the series to be family friendly, which ruled out some of the gorier stuff that 'Taggart' indulged in. 'Morse' and 'Poirot' seemed too formulaic, rooted as they were in the 'who-done-it' school of murder mystery. Somewhere in all of this we felt there was an opportunity for something familiar yet different. But what it was we didn't quite know.

It wasn't long before our researcher came up with some news. She had identified three novels that might interest us, amongst them a book called 'A Touch of Frost' written by a little known writer, Rodney Wingfield. The rights to all three books were available.

I quickly set about reading them. The researcher had done a good job and, with some careful adaptation, all three of them could have worked. I discarded one, simply through lack of originality, leaving us with 'Frost' (which presented its own problems) and the other, a story about a taxi-driving private gumshoe who played jazz trumpet in Soho clubs. Somehow this character didn't seem right for David. We could see him playing Frost, but the problem with Mr Wingfield's book was that everything was so dark - not only the storylines involving macabre and often violent murders, but also the Frost character himself, a chain-smoking obsessive, incapable of forming any kind of relationship, least of all with his long suffering wife who was dying of cancer. Even his George Cross, awarded for exceptional bravery in the course of duty, turned out to be a sham since he was drunk at the time. And yet…

By the time we were ready to approach him with these ideas, David was in the Seychelles on a scuba-diving holiday. We duly despatched all three books to him with our thoughts and awaited his response. A week or so later I returned to the office to find a message on the answer phone machine – several, in fact, because David had so much to say that the machine kept cutting him off. He loved Frost and was confident that, with the amendments we had suggested, it could easily become the series we were looking for. With this enthusiastic reaction from our star, we set about obtaining the rights. Fortunately, we already knew the author's agent and it didn't take long to agree terms. Then, with David back from holiday, we met up to agree our tactics for persuading a broadcaster to come on board. Following our joint success with 'Darling Buds' there appeared to be no good reason why we shouldn't start with Yorkshire Television. We put together a pitch document and sent it up to their Head of Light Entertainment, Vernon Lawrence, who had guided 'Darling Buds' so successfully through the complex and intricate alleyways of the ITV network. We had always felt that YTV's Light Entertainment Department was the right home for 'Darling Buds' rather than their Drama Department. Comedy drama is a peculiar hybrid in television terms: it is not as plot heavy as traditional drama, nor does it take itself so seriously. On the other hand, it is not situation comedy with its laugh-every-ten-seconds scripting and long scenes shot multi-camera in front of a studio audience. For 'Darling Buds' we'd felt that working with YTV's light entertainment people would be more likely to retain the light touch we wanted. This proved to be the case. 'Frost', by contrast, was indisputably drama and Vernon was not so sure that he could legitimately route it through his department. So, that was another battle that lay ahead. We really did not want to find ourselves working with a completely different team of people.

Looking back I think YTV were scared of the project – not least because, despite David's great success in 'Buds', he was still an unknown quantity as a 'serious' actor. There were risks involved and they just weren't sure. This nervousness and uncertainty resulted in Vernon coming back to us with an offer to commission a pilot episode. We said 'no'. From our point-of-view setting up a single episode would be almost as much work as setting up a series, besides which it would convey the wrong impression and a lack of confidence to the network. We thanked Vernon but said that we would move on and offer the series to the BBC who, we believed, would be keen to get David back. The gamble paid off.

Vernon had already suggested an end-of-series dinner party for the four principal actors in 'Darling Buds', to be hosted by the top brass at YTV and ourselves. This was to be held in the executive dining room at their studios in Leeds and Vernon wanted us to stay behind with David after the rest of the 'Buds' cast had left to pitch 'Frost'. The dinner went well with Clive Leach, YTV's chief executive, John Fairley, their controller of programmes, Vernon, Richard, David and myself staying behind - in good enough spirits after a few bottles of wine.

It fell to Richard and I to introduce the background of the project before handing over to David to put some flesh on the bones. To say that he was brilliant would be an understatement. By the time he had finished the YTV senior management were left in no doubt that they had just been offered the deal of the century and, the following day, officially confirmed their commitment. 'Frost' was up and running.

It was time to meet the author. It had transpired that Rodney Wingfield was an ex-radio writer who had originally created Frost for a Radio Four play. His agent told us he lived in Basildon with his invalided wife and that he did his writing in an attic from where he could observe life going by on the streets below. With the television rights agreed and sorted, we asked to meet Mr Wingfield in person and introduce him to our chosen adaptor, the highly respected film and TV writer, Richard Harris. Richard 'Dickie' Harris (the author of 'Stepping Out' and 'Outside Edge') had written some episodes of 'Buds' for us and was intrigued by the task of adapting Mr Wingfield's work for television and bringing his Detective Inspector Jack Frost to life. Also at the meeting was veteran director, Don Leaver, fresh from the hugely successful 'Prime Suspect', who we had asked to line produce the series and direct our first episode. We had assembled quite a team.

Not that you would have thought so from Mr Wingfield's reaction. Few authors take readily to the idea of having their work adapted to the screen, understandably so. When you have 'owned' something and lived with it for a long time it is hard to give your baby away. Nevertheless the commercial benefits are tempting. A successful television series or film based on a book will not only net the novelist considerable additional income, but multiply his book sales tenfold. Like many others before him, our author was caught betwixt and between. Yes, he liked the idea of Jack Frost achieving TV status, but wanted it done his way. It became immediately apparent that he and Dickie were not going to get on. Dickie had his own thoughts as to how the stories would best translate to the small screen and, as a highly experienced TV writer, fully took on board our concerns about the nature of the central character. For example, we had promised David and YTV that, whatever other idiosyncrasies he might have, we couldn't have our hero chain smoking or repeatedly swearing – after all, this was a series intended for Sunday night family viewing, pretty much the same audience as 'Darling Buds'. Secondly, the explicitly sexual nature of some of Mr Wingfield's stories would be unsuitable as would much of the violence he liked to describe in such graphic detail. These factors were all conditions upon the series being commissioned and were non-negotiable. Needless to say, our agreement with the author enabled us to make such changes and, once he realised this, Rodney Wingfield withdrew from the meeting, protesting that he would prefer to let us get on with it and not get involved. We never met him again and all our further dealings were conducted amicably enough through the agent.

Another important decision taken at that meeting concerned the acceptance by the audience of David Jason in a serious dramatic role. We wanted to establish this quickly, so that viewers knew immediately what they were in for. I referred to the fact that in the first book Frost's wife is ill with cancer. We decided to open the series with her dying in hospital. In this way, whilst we didn't need to get to know her character (she was comatose in a hospital bed), we had the opportunity to see Frost's conflicting and complex feelings and to learn pretty much everything we needed to know about him before we even started to tell police stories. It also gave David the chance to act without having to be funny!

When the first episode was transmitted, it pulled in audience of over seventeen million virtually wiping out the BBC and the other channels on the night. Whereas we had made 'Darling Buds' by dividing each story into two one-hour episodes, this time we had managed to persuade ITV to let us script each episode as two hours, so, to all intents and purposes, each series comprised a series of feature films made for television. This 'extended' format also enabled us to run more than one storyline in an episode – thus providing a more accurate insight into police life - as well as delving into Frost's personal and domestic situation. Combined with the fact that our stories were just as often 'why-dunnits' as 'who-dunnits', this is what made 'Frost' different to its predecessors. Still, a good television format should be like the clothes of a well-dressed man, unnoticeable. All this was established at the outset and, other than an occasional reminder to a new writer, seldom referred to again.

Frost was a great personal triumph for David and, as the series progressed, it attracted the best writers and directors in the country. It also launched the careers of many aspiring young actors in supporting roles, amongst them Damian Lewis.

'A Touch of Frost' ran from 1992 to 2010 and could easily have continued for a further season or two. In the end, David became embarrassed that he was too old for the part, announcing at a press conference as early as 2008 that "he didn't want to become the oldest detective in television history", pointing out that in real life he would have already retired six years ago!

Compared with some other actors it never struck me that David had a huge ego – in fact, he valued his privacy almost to a fault, seemingly unimpressed with awards ceremonies and extra curricular public appearances. Still, following his great success and popularity over such a long period of time, it would have been surprising if he hadn't gained great confidence as a performer and I am certain that when he 'retired' from 'Frost' he fully expected to be offered another starring role in a new series. Sadly for him, this never happened. When all is said and done, television executives are unlikely to go out of their way to find a new series for a seventy year old actor, however accomplished and popular. His attempt at a new situation comedy for the BBC, 'The Royal Bodyguard', flopped badly in 2011 and, since then, he has only appeared in brief reprisals of 'Open all Hours' (which later evolved into 'Still Open All Hours') and an 'Only Fools and Horses' sketch for Comic Relief.

On the domestic front, however, his life went from strength to strength. Having lost his long-term partner, Welsh actress Mfanwy Talog from cancer, tragically, at the same time as his screen wife in 'Frost' was suffering the same fate, he had met and eventually married Gill Hinchcliffe, when she was a researcher at YTV. Gill gave birth to a baby girl in 2001 and David became a father for the first time at the age of sixty-one.

When he received his knighthood in 2009, it was generally felt to be largely due to his success in 'Only Fools and Horses' which, of course, pre-dated both 'Darling Buds' and 'A Touch of Frost' and has been shamelessy repeated by the BBC ever since – something that

David claimed to hate on the basis that he was not only being over-exposed, but that it was a constant reminder to viewers as to how he looked fifteen years earlier!

There is no doubt that David has made a unique contribution to British television over the last forty years. He has always acknowledged that his old compatriot and mentor Ronnie Barker was the 'governor'. The difference being, of course, that Ronnie Barker was not only a fine performer but also a brilliant writer. Arguably though, thanks to 'Frost', David went on to achieve the status of being the greater actor. Not much to choose between them you might say, but it was Sir David who got the knighthood.

A postscript. They say that certain parts are made for certain actors. Well, when Rodney Wingfield describes Frost in his first book he refers to him having a pronounced scar above his left eye that he has a habit of 'worrying' when he is tense or troubled. In real life David has exactly that scar in the same place, a remarkable coincidence which, of course, was lost to all but the most observant and keenest Frost afficianados: a tiny fraction of the television audience, needless to say.

Rodney Wingfiled was never in favour of casting David as Frost so it certainly wasn't his idea!

Catherine Zeta-Jones

CATHERINE was nineteen when Christine and I first saw her in '42nd Street' in the West End. She had started in the show as a dancer, progressed to understudying one of the leads and, finally, to playing the part herself. I cannot recall what stage of this process she had reached when we saw her, but I have to confess she made no great impression on me that night. I promptly forgot her again. But it was round about the same time that we were casting 'Darling Buds'.

Mariette was by far the hardest part to cast in 'The Darling Buds of May'. There were a number of reasons for this. Firstly we had the character as described by H.E.Bates in the book. For the story to work Mariette had to be beautiful, sexy and voluptuous whilst, at the same, possessing a fresh, youthful innocence which made her lovable and non-threatening to both men and women alike. H.E. leaves us in no doubt that she is sexually experienced, in fact she confesses to Ma that she might be pregnant in the first book. Not that we hear any more about it. "It seems unkind to say 'no'", she says in the book, "when a young man asks nicely, well why not?" But H.E. also makes it clear that she is not a tart. A tall order you might think and much easier for a novelist to create on the page than to portray successfully on the screen. But we had another problem.

We had auditioned dozens of highly skilled young actresses in their late teens and early twenties but, at that time, the drama schools were turning out interesting, attractive-looking young actresses rather than encouraging them to be glamorously gorgeous. Which was what we needed. When Charley the tax man first casts his eyes on Mariette his jaw had to drop at least six inches and every man, woman and child watching had to understand why. All in all, it was quite a package and, frankly, we hadn't got anywhere close.

Time was marching on when an extraordinary thing happened. We were due to meet the last few candidates at a final meeting at YTV's London offices in Burlington Square, expecting to have to settle for the best of what we had seen. As Richard and I announced ourselves to the receptionist, we noticed two of the young returning actresses patiently waiting, plus a third, stunningly beautiful dark-haired girl who we didn't recognise. She flashed us a dazzling smile at which point we were ushered upstairs to join our fellow executive producer, Vernon Lawrence and the director for episode one, Rodney Bennett. The girls were sent up and we found ourselves politely dismissing the first two. Rodney then turned to us saying: "Well that's it, gentlemen, it's decision time." Richard and I looked at each other and asked what had happened to the third girl who we'd seen in reception. Rodney consulted his list and replied that there was no third girl. That was it.

Protesting, we rang down to reception to ask what had happened to girl number three – only to be told that she was indeed in the building but was auditioning for a dancing role in a forthcoming light entertainment show. I asked the receptionist to make sure that she wasn't allowed to leave the building until we'd had the chance to talk to her. We sat chatting for another ten minutes or so when the 'phone rang to say that a Miss Zeta-Jones was on her way up. As she came into the room to face four middle-aged men, she tossed back her hair and delivered another devastating smile. In unison, our jaws duly dropped and we proceeded to stumble through a few rather inept questions about her previous experience. I am sure she answered them very well - although, ten minutes later when she got up to go, I am not so sure we remembered much of what she had said.

"Well," said Vernon, "I think we've found our Mariette." Rodney replied, "Yes, but can she act?" For the second time that afternoon we reacted in unison. "It doesn't matter!"

And that is how we got our Mariette and how Catherine took her first step towards stardom and, ultimately, the road to Hollywood, the Oscars - and Michael Douglas.

Truthfully, at that stage of her career she wasn't a very good actress but transpired to be a fast learner. She was in the experienced hands of some excellent directors and surrounded by a cast of fine actors all keen to help her. She was also cursed with a Welsh accent. I say 'cursed' because of all the British dialects, Welsh has proved itself the least able to travel, especially to the States. You only have to think of the great Welsh actors like Richard Burton and Anthony Hopkins to see how quickly they ditched their dialects and adopted the Olivier-style delivery! In fact, Catherine had to wait until 'Mask of Zorro' when she spoke with a Spanish accent, before she found universal success. All her major roles subsequently were played as an American.

She also had another great quality. Not only was she lovely to look at, she had a wonderful sunny nature. She really was a delight.

When we making the last episodes of Darling Buds, I invited her to dinner to discuss the possibility of devising a series especially for her. We arranged to meet at the Inn on the Park in Park Lane. The largish restaurant was upstairs and relatively dimly lit. I had chosen a corner table so that she could either sit with her back to the room affording her some privacy or look out - whichever she preferred. This was a practice I had developed especially for these situations. Simply put, you never knew what mood a famous and easily recognisable person would be in. Sometimes they liked to be on display, other times they didn't.

I arrived a few minutes early and took the corner seat looking out. Rightly, Catherine arrived a few minutes later. As she stood silhouetted in the doorway, a hush descended in the room and I was aware of the rattling of knives and forks upon plates as my fellow diners stopped eating to gaze upon the apparition before them. Whether they recognised her or not I don't know - nor was I particularly interested for, like them, I was focussed on the vision of this beautiful girl in a demure black knee length dress with long dark glossy hair tumbling about her shoulders. As she stood looking around her for what could only have been a few seconds, I realised that this was that legendary star quality, so elusive it can barely be defined.

The Maitre 'D was obviously caught off guard too, for, by the time he had summoned up the presence of mind to attend to his lovely young client, she had already spotted me and was sashaying her way over. I was only too aware that every eye in the room was waiting to see who her dining companion would turn out to be and, feeling an adolescent sense of pride, I stood up to greet her. I am sure I beamed as she gave me a light peck on each cheek before sitting down quite happily with her back to her unintended audience.

The idea that Richard and I had come up with for her was simple. Catherine was to play the part of a young woman who wants to be a singer. We first meet her as she is performing in an out-of-town club in front of an audience decidedly more interested in her figure than her voice. Nevertheless, it is clear that she has more talent than this crowd deserves. Watching her are her manager, a well-meaning but ineffectual young man, and two grey-suited strangers who he wrongly takes to be talent spotters. When she has finished her act he shows them backstage to meet her. They reveal themselves to be from a firm of solicitors and want her to accompany them to

London. As the story unfolds it transpires that, unbeknown to her, she is related to an elderly man living in Switzerland. All they tell her is that he is a wealthy entrepreneur who has built an international group of companies ranging from fashion to boat building. And that he is dying. At the lawyers' insistence she agrees to fly to Geneva, all expenses paid, to meet him.

She joins him in the grounds of his mansion overlooking Lake Geneva. Sitting in a wheelchair, he explains that she is his only living relative resulting from a brief but passionate relationship he had had twenty or more years ago in Paris. Although this is news to her, she can just about piece it together based on her scant knowledge of her early upbringing. It begins to make sense as she comes to feel more at home with the old man and finds herself enjoying his company as he shares his memories. In fact, on her return to London, she is surprised to discover how upset she feels at the prospect of not seeing him again.

A week or so later the news arrives that the old man has died and that she has inherited his entire business empire. She is projected into a new and unfamiliar world - a world of bankers, high finance and political in-fighting. There is no shortage of advice, mostly from those whose self-interest would be best served by her selling out. But the young woman has other ideas. The courage and fortitude that the old man recognised during their conversation on the banks of the lake comes to the fore and soon we see our star travelling the world, visiting her bizarre empire of businesses, each one providing her with new friends and enemies, new experiences, opportunities and problems that need solving.

Almost word for word, that is how I described the project to Catherine that evening. She was entranced - by the idea, by her character and by the breadth of the subject matter. There was nothing remotely like it on television and she loved it. "And I have title for you," she said. I wasn't expecting this, although it was true we hadn't come up with a name for the series. "Klay's Kingdom", she went on. "Klay was my nickname when I was younger." A very good title, too, I thought.

But for the vagaries of the television industry, history might have taken a quite different turn. You now know the concept for the series exactly as I then presented it to ITV. Talk about having all the ducks in a row! Vernon Lawrence, the man who had worked with us on "Darling Buds" at Yorkshire Television had been promoted to Network Controller of Drama for ITV, responsible for all ITV commissioning, Catherine was the biggest TV phenomenon of the last ten years and my company, Excelsior, had just been responsible for two of the biggest, most successful series on ITV for more than a decade. You would have thought that a commission for "Klay's Kingdom" would have been a formality.

Not a bit of it. Vernon turned it down on the basis that Catherine couldn't act. The BBC turned it down because the storyline was implausible. And that was that. So, "Klay's Kingdom" never got made and the rest *is* history. Dispirited, Catherine went to America, became a big star winning both an Academy Award and a Tony (despite her 'lack' of acting ability!) and then famously went on to marry into a Hollywood dynasty. She was awarded the CBE in 2010.

Bearing in mind her later international stardom, imagine for a moment how successful "Klay's Kingdom" would have been as an ongoing television series, not only here but in the States and all over the world.

Some years later when I was Chief Barker I proposed Catherine as a category winner at the Variety Club Showbusiness Awards. She accepted and, although she was unable to fly over for the ceremony, she sent us a charming acceptance speech on video. She wore a knee-length black dress, which, I like to think, was the same one she had worn that night at the Inn on the Park.

But it probably wasn't.

Oliver Reed

FOLLOWING the huge success of 'Darling Buds' - and having engendered some awareness of H.E.Bates amongst the television audience - we naturally looked at his other works to see if there was anything else that might translate well to the small screen. One character stood out, Uncle Silas, the heavy-drinking, flirtatious old countryman featured in a collection of H.E.'s short stories.

We knew that for the series to work, firstly we had to find a way of adapting these fragile little tales and, secondly, find an actor who could convincingly convey the dangerous magnetism of this irascible old reprobate.

The answer to the first question came more readily than the second. We would make them as half-hour episodes, using the very best writers we could find, but in such a way that, if the broadcaster wanted, they could be transmitted consecutively as one-hour shows. Finding the right actor was harder.

The idea of casting Oliver Reed was a flash of inspiration. He was exactly right for the part - the right age, dangerous and still with that raw sexuality that had enabled him to become an international star of more than sixty films. He was also a drunk (like Silas) and, following a disastrous appearance on a Channel 4 chat show, had made pretty certain that he was unemployable.

Oliver was represented by one of the last of the old-time agents, the formidable Denis Selinger, who, luckily, we knew. I rang Denis to ask whether he believed the proposition was remotely practical. He said two things: firstly that Oliver had never done television and, secondly, if he agreed to take the part, then he, Denis, would guarantee that he would be reliable and behave on set. Quite an undertaking, I thought.

There was also a further complication. Oliver, aged sixty, had just got married to a twenty year-old girl called Josephine who he had first met when she was still at school. The couple had set up home in Guernsey. Not surprisingly, this relationship had caused some furore in the media, and they had rather gone to ground. Anyway, Denis promised to speak to Oliver to see how the land lay.

It wasn't long before we heard back. Not only had Oliver read the books but he was keen to meet up to discuss the project. I said we would be happy to fly to Guernsey to see him and talk things over.

Armed with this expression of interest, I called David Reynolds (Vernon Lawrence's successor at Yorkshire TV) and told him about our idea. David was understandably nervous about Oliver but, like us, saw the potential. I told him what Denis had said but David wanted to be on the safe side. After all, the series hadn't been commissioned yet and it would be his job to sell the package to the powers that be. He had never met our proposed star and asked us to arrange for Oliver to come to London and we would have lunch together at the Hilton, Park Lane.

But first we had to meet him ourselves. The trip was duly arranged and before long Richard and I found ourselves in a taxi en route from Guernsey airport to Oliver's new home, a relatively modest but perfectly pleasant bungalow just outside St Peterport. We were greeted warmly; Oliver in white flannels and an MCC blazer complete with cravat was the picture of an English gentleman,

Jo, his lovely young wife, scuttling around serving us tea and coffee and discreetly absenting herself when we were discussing business. I suppose we had arrived at about 11am, and it wasn't long before our host was telling us that he had booked a table at his local restaurant, the Coq du Nord, for lunch. He had already ordered a taxi and it was due any minute.

The restaurant was not far from his house and empty apart from us. Not surprisingly, we had the best table, set in a bay window with a view across the road to the sea beyond.

Well, I have to say that during lunch Oliver was a model of sobriety, drinking bottled water throughout and, amongst many other topics of conversation, discussing openly his realisation that he needed to move away from drink-related characters and themes. In fact, his only reservation about playing Silas was that drink featured heavily in the stories. We explained that there was much more to H.E.'s complex character than that and, anyway, Silas was more likely to binge on local cider or strong beer than spirits. That seemed to satisfy him and we went on to discuss David Reynolds' request to meet him over lunch in town.

"That's fine," Oliver said. "He wants to see me on my best behaviour. No problem, I'm happy to fly over, just let me know when."

The formal part of our mission successfully accomplished, we moved on to quiz him about some of the highlights of his movie career. All actors like to talk about themselves and Mr Reed was no exception and for three quarters of an hour or so he regaled us with libellous tales about Michael Winner for whom he had starred in several of his films, the time on location when he had purchased a Chinese junk on the spur of the moment, as well as his well-reported spending sprees which frequently left him on his uppers.

"Never worried me," he explained, "I always knew I could make another film, earn a million and get back to where I was."

The time soon came for us to make our way back to the airport and head off home to Gatwick. A taxi was summoned and we shook hands and bid farewells. It had been a thoroughly enjoyable and entertaining lunch. As we left the restaurant, he stopped in his tracks.

"Sorry, I've just remembered I've got to talk to the owner about a party I'm having here in a week or so. I'll say goodbye and see you soon, then. Have a good flight back and let me know when you want me in London."

Again, we bade him farewell as he re-entered the restaurant and we walked to the car park where our taxi was waiting. As we got to the car, a thought occurred to me and I asked the driver to give us a minute. I turned around, went back to the road and took a look through the bay window where we had been sitting. Oliver was back at the table talking to the owner whilst pouring himself a large glass of red wine. I suspected that poor Jo wouldn't be seeing him for the rest of the afternoon.

Nevertheless, it seemed to us that he had proved a point namely that when necessary he was perfectly capable of staying sober, which was what we needed to know.

A week later I collected him from Gatwick and drove him up to town. Driving towards the A3 we passed through Cheam.

"That's where I went to school," he said pointing out a place that I had driven passed many times.

"I didn't know you were local," I said.

"Oh yes," came the reply, "I was born in Wimbledon and lived in Coldharbour just outside Dorking for years."

I subsequently discovered that he had purchased the nine-bedroom mansion, Broome Hall, where he had revelled and partied in the sixties and early seventies.

"Where you live is so important, don't you think?" he went on. "I need to be somewhere I can be a character. Very difficult in Guernsey. I must say Ireland appeals".

I took that to mean, roughly translated, that he would be happier in some mythical place where he could go out and get drunk, behave badly, get taken home by his mates and not get banned by the local pubs. Not to mention appearing before the magistrates the following week. Which is pretty much what had happened more than once in Surrey. Still, during our two-hour drive he was good company and clearly totally sober.

This continued through lunch at the Windows Restaurant on top of the Hilton and I could tell that David Reynolds was both intrigued to be lunching with this famous star and happy to get behind the project.

This proved more time-consuming than any of us had imagined, however, and it was several months before we were able to go back to Denis Selinger and offer Oliver a contract. By that time Oliver had been offered a major part by Ridley Scott in a forthcoming film called 'Gladiator' starring Russell Crowe. Whereas a few months earlier we could have dictated the schedule to Oliver, now we had to wait for him to finish filming in Malta.

Still, up against a major multi-million dollar feature film, beggars can't be choosers and so we patiently re-scheduled to start shooting in May, giving Oliver a two-week break between the two projects. We sat back and waited.

Three weeks before we were due to start filming the news came through that Oliver had died in Malta without completing his scenes. Apparently (and perhaps appropriately) he had suffered a massive heart attack whilst drinking in a Maltese bar one evening after the day's shoot. He was in the company of his wife Jo and members of the crew.

It was a tribute to Oliver's performance when Ridley Scott completed his scenes using a body double and superimposing Oliver's face from previously shot material. Technically very difficult and expensive at a time when computer imaging was not as advanced as it is today. It would have been cheaper to re-shoot the whole part with another actor.

Still, more to the point, where did that leave us?

Well, by some miracle, when we read and re-read our commissioning contract from ITV, we discovered there was no mention of the production being dependent on the participation of Oliver Reed or, for that matter, anyone else. So, if we were to save the series, the immediate job in hand was to re-cast the leading role with a real marquee name. We held a number of meetings with potential artists and their agents but the one who rose head and shoulders above the others was that fine British actor, Albert Finney. Terms were quickly agreed, Albert was available and with the minimum of re-scheduling we were in business again.

Of course, with Albert in the lead, we had our choice of supporting actors, male and female, not to mention directors, all keen to work with the great man. Our cast list looked like a 'who's who' of the British film industry with Sue Johnstone, Lynda Bellingham, Charlotte Rampling, Julian Holloway and Harriet Walter all making appearance alongside Albert.

But, amidst the furore something changed, subtly and, somehow, outside of our control. The series transmogrified into an 'art' piece, losing in the process its earthiness and popular appeal. The truth was, fine actor that he is, Albert was not Oliver and lacked that threatening darkness which Oliver could conjure up so easily.

At the end of the day, the two series were well enough received but never managed to gel with the wider audience in the way that 'Darling Buds' had done.

They say that actors dredge up their performances from the bottom of their souls. Clever as Albert was, he was only ever going to act the part of Silas. Oliver would have lived it. He'd been there and got the t-shirt.

Sir Henry Cooper

I was privileged to know Sir Henry Cooper, mainly through golf - I played with him many times - but also as a friend in his later years. One of many hundreds, I should add. He was a wonderful and quite remarkable man, kind, generous, exceedingly polite and always self-effacing.

He was born in Lambeth to Henry and Lily Cooper in 1934. With his identical twin brother, George, and elder brother Bern, he grew up in a council house on the Bellingham Estate on Farmstead Road, South East London. During the Second World War the family was evacuated to Lancing on the Sussex coast. Around 1942, Henry senior, was called up to serve in the war and the rest of the family did not see him again for almost three years.

The twins attended school in Lewisham. They were particularly close growing up and in his biography Henry talks of how they came to each other's aid when things turned nasty in the school playground. One particular incident landed the young Henry his first knockout in the playground. At school, the only subject that seemed to interest Henry was history, where he enjoyed acting out scenarios. Life was tough in the latter years of the war, and London life especially brought frequent dangers during the blackouts. Henry did many jobs, including a paper round before school and made money out of recycling golf balls to the clubhouse on the Beckenham course. All three brothers excelled in sport, with George and Henry exercising their talents particularly in football and also cricket.

He entered public consciousness in the fifties and sixties as a professional boxer, attaining worldwide fame and respect through his achievements. It was on 18th June 1963 that his left hand (known fondly in boxing circles as 'Enry's 'Ammer) sent a young up-and-coming boxer called Casius Clay, later known as Muhammed Ali, flat on his back in front of a packed Wembley Stadium. They subsequently became firm friends and remained so.

Henry was the only British boxer to win three Lonsdale Belts outright and was regarded as the most popular of all English boxers becoming known affectionately by the British public as 'Our 'Enry'.

Following his retirement from boxing in 1971, Henry maintained a high public profile with appearances on the BBC quiz show 'A Question of Sport' and various advertisements, most famously for Brut aftershave which have been credited with removing a lingering suspicion that men who wore cologne were effeminate.

Although generally a traditionalist, he was officially the co-founder of the Anti-Nazi League, a largely left-wing campaign focused on far-right groups which opposed immigration. He was also a frequent and popular guest at charity fund-raising events. He appeared as boxer John Gully in the 1975 film 'Royal Flash' and in his latter years featured in a series of UK public service announcements urging vulnerable groups to go to their doctor for vaccination against influenza called 'Get your Jab in First!'

He was the first celebrity to win the BBC's Sports Personality of the Year award twice in 1967 and 1970 and one of only three two-time winners in the award's history. Henry maintained this respect and fame throughout world of sport and the wider community after that and was knighted in 2000 in recognition of his work for charity.

He had invested much of his fortune as a 'name' at Lloyd's of London, a supposedly 'blue chip' investment, but in the 1990s he was reportedly one of those who suffered enormous personal losses because of the unlimited liability which a 'name' was then responsible for, and he was forced to sell his hard won Lonsdale belts. Subsequently, Cooper's enduring popularity as an after dinner speaker provided a source of income, and he was in most respects a picture of contentment.

Considering his long career, he had suffered relatively little boxing-related damage to his health, apart from "a bit of arthritis", remaining an imposing figure into his seventies; in the words of one journalist, "the living manifestation of an age of tuxedos in ringside seats, Harry Carpenter commentaries, sponge buckets and 'seconds out'". He lived in Hildenborough, Kent and was the president of Nizels Golf Club. He was also a past-Captain and, for many years, Chairman of the Variety Club Golf Society.

He had been married to Albina, the love of his life since 1960. They were clearly devoted to each other and he had converted to her faith. In an interview he once described Albina, who "hated" his sport, as "an ideal wife for a boxer", never grumbling about his long absences before big fights and inviting journalists to wait downstairs with a cup of tea on the morning after a fight while he roused himself from his slumbers.

I remember playing with him at a charity golfing event which I was sponsoring in 2008 at the beautiful Burgh Hill Golf Club, not far from Walton-on-Thames. Unusually, he turned up on the first tee looking less than sprightly and was clearly subdued during the first two or three holes. Knowing that he had been suffering from worsening arthritis, I asked him if he was okay. As we walked along the fairway he told me that he had just received the results of some tests which had revealed a mild heart condition. Somewhat alarmed, I queried the precise nature of the condition. Now this was not Henry's strong point. Detailed answers to detailed questions had always thrown him.

"Not sure," he replied. "Its some kind of virus – in the heart. They say they can help control it, but they can't cure it." I asked him whether he had told Albina. "No, no," he said, "it would only worry her and I don't want that."

"How is she?" I asked. His face lit up. "She's fine," he said, "just fine. Fit as the proverbial fiddle."

As we carried on playing, I couldn't help thinking that Henry had been prescribed a death sentence – how long it would be, no-one knew, but I was sure he would accept the hand that he had been dealt and embrace it with courage and dignity.

Two weeks later, without warning, Albina had a heart attack and died. Henry was never the same after that. I don't think he could come to terms with the cruel irony of the situation, let alone the loss of his beloved Albina. He was the one who was supposed to go first. Of course, he soldiered on supported by his two sons, and I was pleased to have been instrumental in setting up a dinner in his honour at the Guildhall during this time. But by then he was looking frail and within another eighteen months, he too died on May 1st, 2011 at his son's house in Oxted, Surrey, two days before his 77th birthday.

Leading the tributes from all over the world, Muhammed Ali said he was at a loss for words.

"I was not aware he was ill. I visited him two summers ago during a brief visit to Windsor as part of the Equestrian Games being held there. He was in good humour and looked quite fit. Henry always had a smile for me; a warm and embracing smile. It was always a great pleasure being in Henry's company. I will miss my 'ole friend. He was a great fighter and a gentleman."

But we all knew that the fight had deserted Our 'Enry when he lost his Albina.

The year after his death we re-named the annual golf event that we had played at Burgh Hill the 'Henry Cooper Memorial Classic' and for the last several years it has been played at Kingswood Golf Club. The winner's trophy is an exact replica of the Lonsdale belt Henry had to sell due to the Lloyds debacle and made by the same firm who crafted the original.

Sometimes a strange thing happens when someone of Henry's stature departs this world. It is as if everything that can be said has been said and there follows a vacuum when the person becomes not exactly forgotten but taken for granted. Many who knew and loved him didn't want this to happen in Henry's case and so this tournament is designed to remind us once a year how he touched us all.

Of course, it is not the only thing to have been set up in his memory. As I write this there are a number of other initiatives in progress, including a life-size statue of him which is to be erected near his birthplace in Hackney.

He deserved no less. He was an example to us all as to how you can achieve great things in life through talent, perseverance and hard work without success going to your head. Not only did he sustain a wonderful career until the end of his life, he remained the same modest, unaffected human being as when he started out.

Freddie Laker

DO you remember Skytrain? It was going to be the first 'step-on-step-off' scheduled air service across the Atlantic - from a charter operator with absolutely no experience of running a scheduled airline at all.

Still it seemed like a good idea at the time and received a lot of positive media attention. The public was tired of the monopoly of a few national airlines dominating the trans-Atlantic route. Prices were high, service indifferent and 747's were flying across the Atlantic half empty. Passengers were pleased to see a gutsy, 'up-yours' challenge from the private sector. And from a man who had an almost unprecedented appetite for self-promotion.

So, at the time, Freddie Laker was a bit of a folk hero. Well, he was no hero of mine for reasons I'll explain in a moment.

But first a little history. Freddie Laker got his first job at the age of sixteen sweeping floors and making tea. He flew cargo planes during the war and afterwards bought some old bombers, which he used during the Berlin airlift to fly people and cargo in and out of Berlin making his first fortune. He then went into the charter business assembling a large fleet of jets flying mainly to European holiday destinations. Once he had dreamt up the idea of offering the public cheap transatlantic fares he frequently flouted the law whilst awaiting a government license to operate Laker Airways as a scheduled airline - simply by assembling groups from individuals who had turned up at Gatwick hoping for cheap fares.

Nevertheless, he was a pioneer and gave the complacent international carriers (who the public believed to be operating a cartel anyway) much to think about. In the end they matched his prices and his business fell away, finally going into liquidation in 1982. Although he was awarded damages in court against his competitors, he lost much of his personal wealth and retired to Florida and subsequently to the Bahamas, with his fourth wife.

Despite the enduring success of Richard Branson and a couple of others who followed in his footsteps, Laker professed no bitterness saying that he was proud to have given the 'big boys' a run for their money.

At the time I was running the magazine business and we had picked up the contract to publish an in-flight magazine for Caribbean Airways, which was, notionally, the national airline of Barbados, but in reality was operated by Laker Airways. As a magazine it had proved quite profitable, with the added benefit that every year I would send a couple of sales people to Barbados to sell advertising and occasionally go myself. These days, as you will have observed, such magazines are packed full of advertisements from the airline's duty free suppliers but, in the case of 'Caribjet' – the name of the publication – these companies were all suppliers of Laker and so we were precluded from approaching them. Still, we did very well from local advertising.

By the time Freddie announced the launch of Skytrain, we had picked up a couple more in-flight magazines, one for Air Europe and another for Orion, the charter airline set up by Horizon Holidays. So, by now we had some real experience in this field. I was just as excited as everyone else about the launch of Skytrain and, full of admiration for the idea and Freddie's courage as an entrepreneur. I got in touch with his marketing people to propose a Skytrain in-flight magazine that we would publish and supply to Laker Airways for nothing in exchange for keeping the advertising revenue. I was immediately summoned to Gatwick for a meeting, not with Freddie on that occasion but with his commercial manager, who happened to be his son-in-law. Anyway, I went through the bones of how things would work and left him with a draft contract, which effectively gave us exclusive rights to produce a magazine in the quantities required in exchange for standing the risk if revenue failed to match production costs - and retaining any additional income. In other words, regardless of whether it made a profit or loss, Laker would get 300,000 copies of a 48-page magazine promoting the airline and their onboard sales for nothing - one less problem for them to worry about and a prestigious addition to their new brand. The contract came back duly signed. Needless to say, with the benefit of our experience with the other three magazines, I had carefully assessed the potential and believed that we would come out on the right side.

We quickly got started on putting the magazine together. I put two sales people onto securing the advertising revenue and had the editorial department come up with some draft content. Laker had understandably asked for rights of approval; in particular the front cover. I wanted to do something special and came up with the idea of photographing a plasticine model of Freddie posing in front of a fully liveried Skytrain DC-10. This seemed the right kind of thing from several angles – it was amusing, acknowledged Freddie's personal dominance in an appealing and self-deprecating way and established the identity of the Laker Syktrain aircraft. Most importantly, it would make the passengers smile.

Such caricatures were quite the thing at the time (think 'Spitting Image') and it didn't take long for the art department to come up with a sculptor prepared to take on the task. Within a week I had a gloriously amusing ten-inch tall model of Freddie on my desk, complete with a roll of blueprints under his arm. It was charming, funny and, in my view, wholly inoffensive. It was simple to get hold of a model of a Skytrain DC-10 and soon I had my front cover picture.

I had it mocked up as a front cover and took it down to the Laker offices at Gatwick for approval. It looked great and I was pleased with our effort. The commercial manager took one look, excused himself and left me sitting in his office. Ten minutes later he returned with Freddie himself.

"Very interesting," said Freddie. "Listen, I don't mind you making fun of me but not my aircraft. That is obviously a model. So, I suggest you drop the picture of me and simply use a proper photograph of the DC-10 in flight. John has got lots of good pictures, haven't you, John?"

And with that he turned on his heel and we ended up with the most boring front cover you could imagine. I'll come back to the little sculpture of Fred in a moment.

Meanwhile the ad sales were going apace. Not only were a lot of local and national advertisers keen to be associated with the new airline but all the duty free suppliers were anxious to take space as well. It was clear that the magazine was going to be a huge success. As the sales built up I added more editorial pages and more colour to make sure that not only would it exceed the client's expectations but that, as publishers, we would be seen as not being greedy but ploughing back potential profit into the publication.

The time had come to proof up the whole thing and present it to Laker so that we could make any last minute revisions and go to print.

For the first time I was summoned directly into Freddie Laker's office.

"So, I gather we have a success on our hands," he said. I hadn't even got the dummy out of my briefcase. "John tells me you've sold much more advertising than you expected."

"Well, we didn't know what to expect," I replied, "but, yes, I think you'll be pleased. We've been able to make the magazine much bigger and more colourful as a result." I put the dummy in front of him. He made a dismissive gesture.

"So this is what we'll do," he went on. "You can have what you were expecting to make out of it and we'll take the rest. After all, it is our magazine, isn't it?" I was dumbfounded and wondered how to deal with this. I didn't want to refer to the contract, which was quite specific. We kept the profits.

"It isn't quite as simple as that," I replied. The minimum specification was for a forty-eight page magazine." I pushed the dummy towards him; he hadn't even opened it. "As you'll see we've already increased it to seventy-two. This has significantly increased the costs."

"Okay, I'll tell you what we'll do. We'll split the profits fifty/fifty. What do you say?"

I took a deep breath. "Mr Laker, you're in the business of flying planes, my business is magazines. I had these discussions with John two months ago. He agreed the principle and you signed a contract. Now that we've done well – to our mutual benefit – you're telling me you want to change the rules of the game."

"Don't say that," he protested, getting up and strutting around, "The game's changed. Come on, you never thought you were going to sell this much advertising!"

I realised that he had to have his victory. This is what he was known for. The great Freddie Laker, the hard man, the guy who always got the deal. I was reminded of a story I had heard from John, the commercial manager, earlier. When Macdonald Douglas the aircraft manufacturers had sent a negotiating team over to talk about supplying Laker's new fleet of DC-10's, eventually a price had been agreed; at which point Freddie had asked everyone to leave the room, his own team included, leaving him and the CEO of Macdonalds alone. Afterwards, Freddie told his colleagues that he had successfully achieved a further reduction by asking the CEO what was in it for him personally. Faced with an embarrassing situation, the American had agreed to a further discount to Fred's personal advantage only to be told: "If you can afford to give it to me, you can afford to give it to my company." Cheers all round. Except, of course, no-one actually knew what had happened behind those closed doors. They only had Fred's version.

I felt I was in a similar position. If I had stuck to my guns and despite the contract, I wouldn't have put it past him to refuse to put the magazines on the aircraft. Plus, we had a three-year contract and I didn't want to start out on the wrong foot. Pragmatism prevailed.

"Okay," I said. "You win. I'll agree to fifty/fifty."

"Good," he said. I imagined how he'd brag about his little victory later. He hadn't even looked at the dummy or shown the slightest interest in the content of the magazine.

The magazine went ahead and was duly delivered to Gatwick in time for the inaugural flight. Apart from the bland front cover, it looked excellent and everyone seemed delighted. No word, of course, from the great man himself. Despite the new arrangement we had still made a tidy, albeit reduced, profit and, overall, I was pleased with the outcome.

Pretty soon it was time to get on with the second issue and, once again, I found myself down at Gatwick talking to John, Freddie's sidekick.

"I'm sorry," he said, "but we've had a better offer. We're going to change publishers." I realised there was no point in debating the issue. "We have three-year contract, you know I could enforce that." But I knew it was futile.

"Yes, we've thought of that. We'll take our chances. We can't see you litigating against us somehow. The publicity wouldn't do you much good, would it?"

"Well, thanks for dragging me down here to tell me," I said. "And good luck." And that was that.

I subsequently discovered that Laker had given the magazine contract to a firm who printed record sleeves. Apparently the chairman was a personal friend.

I went back to London feeling wretched. We had put our heart and souls into a project which was my idea, done it as well as we possibly could and been chucked out with the dishwater. Horrible. What's more I knew that the new publishers would not make anything like such a good job. What they had offered Laker one can only speculate.

Back in my office I unloaded all this on to Heather my secretary. She had lived through the whole project with me and was outraged.

Since the original front cover idea had been jettisoned, that little model of Freddie Laker had been standing on her window ledge. By the next morning it had pins sticking out of it.

Shortly before the next issue of the magazine was due to be delivered, Laker Airways went bust leaving our successors with 300,000 copies of the Skytrain magazine with no aircraft to put them on.

They say the gods smile on the righteous.

John Sullivan

IT was quite a co-incidence that two of the people who had much to do with David Jason's great success lived only a few hundred yards apart. My company, Excelsior, had produced 'The Darling Buds of May' and 'A Touch of Frost' and the great John Sullivan had written and produced that wonderful situation comedy 'Only Fools and Horses'. Between us we had supplied David Jason with his most of material for more than twenty-five years.

John's life was an extraordinary testament to talent and perseverance. He was from a poor working-class background and grew up in Balham. His Irish father, John Senior, was a plumber and his mother, Hilda, worked as a charlady. It was in Balham where he observed the sort of market trader who would later appear in 'Only Fools and Horses'. He failed his eleven-plus and attended Telferscot Secondary Modern School, where an English teacher sparked an interest in reading the novels of Charles Dickens and discovered young John's talent for writing stories.

He left school at fifteen with no qualifications although he did go on to attend evening classes in German and English and read 'Teach

Yourself' books after leaving school. His first paid employment was as a messenger boy for Reuters, and he continued to work in a number of low-paid jobs in South London for a further fifteen years.

During this time, he started to submit scripts to the BBC (unsuccessfully) before getting a job in the BBC props department. In 1976 he approached television producer Dennis Main Wilson with a script about a young Marxist which led to a pilot for the BBC 'Comedy Special' series. Following a positive reaction, it was commissioned for a full series and John had broken through. 'Citizen Smith' ran for four series, after which he was asked to submit something else. An initial idea for a comedy set in the world of football was rejected, so he proposed an alternative idea for a sit-com about a cockney market trader in working-class, modern-day London. He called it 'Readies'.

Through Ray Butt, a BBC producer and director whom Sullivan had met and befriended when they were working on 'Citizen Smith', a draft script was presented to the Corporation's Head of Comedy, John Howard Davies who commissioned Sullivan to write a full series under an alternative title 'Only Fools and Horses', which had also been the name of a 'Citizen Smith' episode. Sullivan believed the key factor in getting it accepted was the success of ITV's new drama 'Minder' starring George Cole and Denis Waterman, a series with a similar premise and also set in modern-day London. Interestingly, David Jason was not the first choice to play Del Boy, this should have gone to a Scottish actor called Enn Reitel who, incidentally, looked very much more like Rodney (played by Nicholas Lyndhurst), than David. However, when it came to shooting the first episodes, En had just picked up a season at Butlins and turned down the opportunity. Since then he has made a good living as a TV actor and voice over specialist, most recently in the 'X-Factor'. He is also well-known for impersonating David Jason!

Much of the material for 'Only Fools and Horses' came from John's real-life experiences: falling through a raised bar flap, the chandelier crashing, his father's poker sessions, his niece working in the police force, and his grandfather falling down holes to claim money - all made their appearances. It is arguable that the economic insecurity experienced by the Trotter family, and their eventual rise to wealth, is based on Sullivan's own personal background, who grew up in a poor household and noted in an interview that he and his friends seemingly had no other opportunities after leaving school apart from becoming, as Sullivan put it, "factory fodder." The success of 'Only Fools and Horses', however, put paid to that.

With the success of 'Only Fools and Horses', at the suggestion of his wife, Sharon, he decided to write a romantic comedy series featuring a strong female lead character. 'Just Good Friends', Starring Jan Francis and Paul Nicholas in his first television role, ran for three series plus a feature-length special between 1983 and 1986. Other sitcoms included 'Dear John', starring Ralph Bates and Belinda Lang, which had been inspired by a letter in a magazine, written by a woman who had been jilted by her fiancé on their wedding day

We had met the Sullivans soon after we moved to Kingswood in 1980. By chance they lived next door to my accountant and, although John and his wife Sharon were very private people, it wasn't long before we were invited round to dinner.

Of course, we talked about David Jason and our mutual interest in him. At the time John was quite happy to see David's career moving on and seemed reconciled to the fact that 'Only Fools and Horses' had run its course, save for the odd future Christmas special for which he already had some ideas. Perhaps surprisingly, there was no rivalry between us: I was pleased to express my admiration for him and his great contribution to the world of TV comedy. In turn, he was complimentary about 'Darling Buds' and 'Frost'.

As we got to know each better through an occasional chat over a beer at the Chequers, he confided in me that he was getting increasingly frustrated with the way he was being treated at the BBC. Like nearly all acclaimed, successful people, John wanted to carry on writing; money was no longer the object. He was by no means a conceited man but rightly perceived himself as the leading comedy writer of his era, ranking amongst the best ever. Following 'Fools' he had proposed a number of new series ideas to the BBC, none of which had come to fruition. He told me that he was thoroughly fed up with talking to script editors and development executives who were half his age and had never written anything, let alone got close to his track record - endlessly being told that maybe if he changed this or that, produce another draft, etc, etc…

Of course, what John was experiencing was nothing new. A long line of other leading writers, too many to mention, had suffered the same fate, struggling to stay in business once their biggest hits had come and gone. Why this happened so regularly and consistently is hard to explain. It is as if the successful artist could not possibly eclipse his own achievements, even though a lesser effort from him would probably still be vastly superior to the work of an up-and-coming youngster learning the tricks of the trade for the first time! But maybe this syndrome pervades all British life: intrigued as we are with the fresh energy of youth rather than the experience and skills that come through age. In any event, this is how John felt he was being treated and it was making this otherwise mild-mannered man angry and a touch bitter.

John had an agent called Roger Hancock who I knew fairly well. The brother of Tony Hancock, Roger had all of Tony's charm and humour without the addictive personality that finally destroyed that great comic actor. I had met Roger a number of times and, although we had never done any business, we got on rather well. On one such occasion - in fact, on his hired yacht at the Cannes Television Festival - I had floated the idea that John might like to work with us on a new project to take to ITV. Roger had dismissed the idea out of hand. "Why would John want to do that?" he laughed, "he's making a fortune at the BBC!"

I didn't pursue the idea for two reasons. Firstly, I wasn't sure that John wanted to work with us anyway. Why should he? After all, he would reason (although he was far too nice to say so) that he had been far more successful than us – and, frankly, what would we bring to the table that he didn't already know? Secondly, I got the distinct impression that Roger wasn't in the slightest bit aware of John's dissatisfaction with the BBC and, if that was so, it certainly wasn't my job to enlighten him. Subsequently, I did chat to John directly about a number of ideas we were working on but John, very politely, turned them all down. He wasn't going to be a hack for hire and I didn't blame him.

Ironically, he did end up doing something for ITV. By now, of course, David Jason had his own contacts at ITV having already 'defected' from the BBC and he, too, must have known of John's frustrations. He knew that John was a great Charles Dickens fan and encouraged him to write a TV series based around the adventures of Mr Micawber with, predictably, David playing the lead. The Sullivan/Jason combination was too much for ITV to resist and the series went ahead in 2001. It was a gentle piece, neither sitcom nor comedy drama, and although it received mild critical acclaim, disappeared without trace.

He went on to writing series for the BBC which were, effectively, 'spin-offs' of 'Only Fools and Horses', including the famous Christmas special where Del and Rodney appear as Batman and Robin. In the end, John made Del and Rodney very rich; fiction mirroring fact, as had been the case in his own life.

He died, unexpectedly and tragically, from viral pneumonia. We had heard through Sharon that he had been ill in hospital, but all seemed to be progressing okay and the family were expecting him home for a birthday party the following weekend. He never made it. He was only sixty-four.

John made a fortune – not through running a business, doing deals, buying and selling houses, gambling or investing in the stock market. He made it through pure talent, sticking to his last and a rare ability to judge the mood of the public.

Not to mention his genius for giving millions of people huge delight, lifting their spirits and yes, making them laugh.

PS – I referred to John's agent, Roger Hancock, who had managed his affairs until the end of both their lives. By an uncanny coincidence both men died on the same day, April 23rd, 2011.

Robert Powell

MY first meeting with Robert Powell was on the set of 'Hannay' at the Thames Television Studios by the river in Twickenham in 1989. The series, devised and produced by my colleague, Richard Bates, was based around the stories of John Buchan whose book 'The Thirty Nine Steps' had been filmed with Robert in the starring role ten years earlier. I was struck not only by Robert's famed good looks, with his mass of tightly curled black air, but also by his obvious intelligence and easy manner. He struck me as being confident, knowledgeable, good at his job and, above all, totally clear about what he was doing and why. He was one of that rare breed; an actor with his feet firmly on the ground.

As I got to know him better I discovered why. Unlike many of his colleagues Robert had been blessed with an excellent education and had not always wanted to be an actor.

He was born in Salford, educated at Manchester Grammar School and later went to the University of Salford. He took up acting whilst an undergraduate. He had wanted to become a lawyer and in the early sixties attended an external London University LLB degree Course at the Manchester College of Commerce, at the same time quietly taking acting roles under the direction of Trevor Nunn. After this he got a job at a repertory theatre in Stoke-on-Trent. He had a small role in the original film version of 'The Italian Job' playing one of the gang, but had to wait a few years for his first notable success as scientist Toby Wren in the BBC's science fiction series, 'Doomwatch' in 1970.

Having been killed off at his own request in the last episode, he became a household name and, during the seventies, was a television regular, with occasional forays into film, particularly with Ken Russell, including Gustav Mahler in the biopic 'Mahler' and Captain in the film 'Tommy'. But he had to wait until 1977 to land his most famous role, Jesus Christ in 'Jesus of Nazareth' following a successful second audition with Franco Zeffirelli. For this he was nominated for a BAFTA and collected the TV Times Best Actor award. Shortly before shooting started he married Pan's People dancer, Babs Lord.

In 1978, he played the leading role of Richard Hannay in the third film version of 'The Thirty Nine Steps'. It was ten years later that the television series entitled 'Hannay', devised and produced for ITV by Richard, appeared with Powell back in the role. It ran for two seasons.

During the eighties he appeared in the film 'Harlequin' for which he won the Best Actor Award at the Paris Film Festival. He later won Best Actor at the Venice Film Festival for his role in 'Imperativ'. He then agreed to a request from his old friend and golf partner, comedian Jasper Carrott, playing the part of an incompetent detective in a succession of sketches that formed part of Carrott's television series. 'The Detectives' was so popular that it was rolled out as a sitcom, Robert's first and only venture into this genre.

At about that time we were exploring the possibility of making a TV series based on a train journey, rather like 'Murder on the Orient Express'. Trains provide a wonderful backdrop for thrillers and crime stories with a multitude of characters 'locked' in a closed environment. We had been turning this idea over in our minds for some while and had even approached the current owners of The Orient Express to discuss its feasibility. However, the project only really took off when we discovered an old 1930's train that had been lovingly restored by a South African businessman and was running a weekly service from Capetown to Pretoria. The train was called 'Pride of Africa'.

At the time South Africa was attracting a lot of attention from film makers - not only because of the sheer beauty of its locations and its reliable sunny climate, but because, largely due to the diminished value of the Rand, you could film there for a fraction of what it would cost elsewhere. The combination of the old train and its whereabouts made a pretty attractive package. We started work on the script, based around a central character called Webb, an ex-priest who had lost his wife and his faith and taken to a life of adventuring. When we meet first him we see him being fired from his job leading big game expeditions and about to start work as a security man on the train.

Rather than going via a broadcaster in the usual way and losing many of the rights in the process, we had decided to finance the venture ourselves using a specially created fund to which private investors would be invited to subscribe. The combination of the exotic story, our track record and Robert's name and reputation - coupled with a ridiculously low budget - meant that the finance was relatively simple to procure. We believed that once we had made a good pilot episode we were in with an excellent chance of landing a commission for a full series from ITV or BBC, whilst selling it all over the world. How wrong that assumption was to prove. Still, the die was cast and away we went.

When it came to casting, the only part that really mattered was Webb himself, all the other characters could be cast locally. Robert was ideal for the part. He looked great, he was the right age and had

plenty of experience of working abroad. We sent him the script and asked if he would be happy to spend six weeks in and around Pretoria where 'The Pride of Africa' was based. The answer came back a resounding 'yes'.

I immediately got on a plane and went off to recce the project. The first stop was to see the owner of the train, a Mr Rohan Voss. Then, with his co-operation secured, we could look for a local production company to set up the shoot, lay on the facilities and crew and, most importantly, assist us with the local casting. Also, I was keen to establish contact with the South African broadcasters to see if we could raise any pre-production finance from then.

All of this went well. Rohan Voss was a tough Aficaaner in his early fifties who had made his fortune from motor-cars but loved trains. His entrepreneurial nature pre-disposed him to our project and he was quick to see the publicity potential that a widely distributed TV series could provide. Having said that, he still charged us for the use of his train and drivers! I also concluded a deal with a production company run by Herman Binge (a well-known television director in South Africa) and his colleague, Lindsay Reid-Ross. They were full of enthusiasm and showed every sign of earning their associate producer credits. I also concluded a pre-sale to M-Net, South Africa's leading cable broadcaster, which meant that we had money to spare in the bank. All in all, a successful trip. Filming was scheduled to start in early May when I was assured by the locals the weather would be good. I returned home, pleased with the outcome. It looked as though the only people going out from the UK would be myself, Robert and the director, whom we still had to confirm.

Back in the UK there was the usual rush to arrange visas and flights as well as finalising the financing which was nearly complete. We appointed a director, Graham Theakston, who we had worked with before and who had directed a very good episode of 'Frost'. He had an excellent CV and had recently won a BAFTA award for best director for the TV series 'A Politician's Wife'. He was excited by the idea of filming in South Africa and with his contract successfully negotiated, the UK contingent was complete.

Our production schedule coincided with the Cannes Television Festival where all the major international broadcasters and distributors would be gathering to do their deals for the forthcoming year. Richard and I agreed that he would go to Cannes whilst I went to SA to start filming. As soon as I had enough footage in the can, I would assemble a trailer and send it to him in Cannes to drum up some international sales.

So, with pre-production complete, it was time to head back to Jo'burg, then on to Pretoria.

We had allowed a day or two to finish the casting. Our local producers had short-listed a number of local actors for us to see and, although we weren't exactly spoilt for choice, it was apparent that we could assemble a better than average cast from those available. As director, Graham had the final say, but there was little disagreement between us. They had also set up a production office in an old railway building near the station yard just outside Pretoria where some 'Pride of Africa' carriages would be shunted into a shed for our exclusive use during the shoot. The engines were a different matter. Whilst Mr Rovos could spare a couple of coaches on loan for six weeks, we had to be quite specific about the days we wanted an engine. These were the old restored 1930's working steam locomotives required for the day-to-day running of the Vos Rail trips.

The few days gave Graham the opportunity to get to know his cast and crew, indeed, he busied himself with wardrobe and sets, confirming locations and generally fraternising with his colleagues; with one notable exception, his leading man. Despite a number of heady, talkative evenings in local hostelries, Graham appeared to studiously avoid any real discussion with Robert about the way he intended to direct the film or how the Webb character should be portrayed. This was not what I had expected and it didn't take long for Robert to become acutely aware of the fact that he was being left out of things. Rightly, he believed that his experience of film making, especially in foreign environments, exceeded everyone else's and that he had much to contribute on a day-to-day basis apart from acting out the starring role. I had no choice but to bring the matter up with Graham.

His response was curious: simply to point out that he wasn't worried about Robert, whom he knew perfectly well would deliver a thoroughly professional performance. Besides which he had far more pressing problems to deal with. Until that point I had no idea there *were* any problems but he went on to say that virtually every head of department - design, wardrobe, props, in particular - was useless. Not only that, but he had no faith in his two assistant directors. In fact, the entire team was not up to his expected standards. I disagreed. Whilst acknowledging the team was smaller and less experienced than its UK equivalent, nevertheless, all the department heads had worked on international films and had plenty of combined experience between them. We had hand picked the best talent available. He then said an extraordinary thing - that he would 'give it go' but wasn't optimistic about the outcome. Disturbed by this, I decided to keep his remarks to myself, at least until we saw the rushes of his early scenes.

Graham had chosen his scenes for the first day's shoot. The weather was fine and we were on location not far from the production office. Robert was not required for these scenes, however, rather than clicking his heels, he decided to come and watch the shoot. We arrived together to see our director preparing to film a young actor driving up to small row of shanty shops in a horse and cart. Not a difficult scene, but Graham was anxious to get it right. It took a little longer than anticipated but looked well enough. We were about to go inside the shop to shoot the second scene of the sequence but Graham decided it was time for an early lunch. Afterwards he completed the interior shots before asking the crew to set up the final scene of the sequence when a father shows his young son the last resting place of his two old war buddies.

The art department had created the graveyard in a nearby field so that there was no need to move the unit too far. The scene never got shot. Graham was not happy with the quality of the mock graves, even though they only appeared in frame briefly, insisting they were re-made. With this he stormed off the set causing puzzlement all round. Anyway, the upshot was we were already half a day behind schedule, and we had only started filming that morning!

Back at the office I took Graham to one side and challenged him about his decision to re-schedule the scene. He responded that it was hopeless, we were never going to make a decent film and he was going home. However, he was prepared to stay on for a day or two to help me wrap things up. Dumbfounded, I thanked him for his generous offer, but suggested that he flew back immediately. I had investors to consider and I was going to complete the film. I was cancelling his accommodation forthwith and, if that was his frame of mind, I didn't want him anywhere near the project.

Dejected, I returned to our little bed and breakfast, had a shower and prepared myself to break the news to Robert. "Thank God," he said to my great relief, "you did the right thing, there's something wrong with that guy."

With very little time to audition new directors - and little hope of getting one from the UK at such short notice - I contemplated the first of a series of risky decisions, namely, whether to ask Herman Binge to take over and direct. The advantages were obvious. Herman already knew the material inside out; plus, he was there, ready to go and already on the payroll! The drawback was that he had only ever worked in South Africa and I had no idea how good he was.

But - and this was important - I liked him and so did the crew and the local actors.

Before I went ahead, however, I did two things: firstly, I telephoned Richard in the UK; he was just off to Cannes and was distressed and angry to hear than Graham had let us down and said he would back whatever decision I made. Secondly, I decided to take Robert into my confidence. Robert, too, was happy to go with Herman saying that whatever his shortcomings might turn out to be, he would lend his support and advice. In fact, I think it was the first time Robert had felt fully engaged with the project.

Herman was a great, cuddly bear of a man, larger than life, but sensitive, emotional and, happily, diplomatic. When I asked him he said that he had been longing to offer his services but didn't believe he should. He had fully expected me to postpone the shoot until a new director could be flown over from the UK, but, yes, he was honoured to be asked and would devote himself to doing the very best job he could.

I then called the entire cast and crew together for a meeting at 7am the following morning. Most of them knew or had guessed what had happened and were anxious for their jobs. When I explained that we were going ahead as planned with Herman at the helm there was an audible sigh of relief in the room. The first AD, a man of great skill and experience himself, spoke up and expressed his total support for Herman and everyone else followed suit. He was greeted with a round of applause. It was an emotional meeting with a few tears shed, mostly by Herman. Still, we were up and running again with a good chance of getting back on schedule.

Then it started to rain.

I cannot describe how the local crew responded to the rain - not only were they not used to it, they were frightened of it! To them, filming was impossible. I explained that it was likely the rain would only last for a day or two and, in the meantime, we had plenty of cover and would simply re-schedule and shoot interiors. So, we repaired to the sheds and started to film the many scenes that took place in the carriages.

I was wrong and so were the weather forecasters. The heavy rain went on for days; one night it was so bad that Robert and I couldn't find our way back from the restaurant to our lodgings. Part of the attraction of the film was that much of it would show off the magnificent African terrain and its wild life. This was looking less and less likely every day that went by.

A good scheduler will always try to retain some weather cover in his schedule, in other words try to keep back a number of interior scenes so that should the weather turn against you, you don't waste time waiting for the sun to shine. In fact, to stay on budget, this is essential. In our case, with the unrelenting rain, pretty soon we would run out of interiors to shoot. Our scheduler was panicking, and so was I. We were faced with a choice: either to postpone filming and resume when the weather improved, or, carry on filming interiors with our fingers crossed, taking the risk that we would run out of weather cover and fail to complete the film on time. Either way we would come in considerably over budget with no guarantee that we would keep our cast and crew together. Night after soaking wet night I would go to bed worrying about what to do. It was my decision and nobody was going to make it for me.

As we approached the third week the rain was still torrential. We needed at least ten days of sunshine to complete the exteriors, which meant the rain had to stop in less than a fortnight. The local forecasters predicted that it would continue raining into the foreseeable future, so no comfort there. The meteorologists were describing the rainfall as 'freakish' and 'unprecedented' for the time of year. I decided to go for bust. We would go on filming interiors until either we ran out of scenes or the sun came out. Once set on this course there was nowhere to hide. Robert was a tower of strength during all of this; always supportive, always encouraging. It was a pleasure to have him around.

By now we had enough material in the can for me to go into a local studio to put together the promo for Richard in Cannes. I had brought some music I had written with me and sat down with the film editor to put the short film together. With some specially written narration voiced by one of the other actors in the cast, I thought it came together pretty well, so, off it went to Richard. Imagine how delighted I was a few days later to hear that on the strength of the promo one of the major German broadcasters, RTN, had bought the film. This was great news and meant that we would already be showing a return to our investors - providing we were able to complete it!

But the rain was trying its utmost to make this impossible. By now we had been reduced to shooting some of the more static exterior scenes under tarpaulins. The noise of the rain beating down on the canvas was horrific but I knew we had the technology back home to reduce it dramatically. We could also re-grade the pictures to make them look sunnier. But we were scraping the barrel.

Then, miracle of miracles, the rain went away as quickly and unexpectedly as it had arrived. We had our ten days and completed the remaining scenes, in glorious sunshine. We'd come out on budget and only half a day over schedule, the same half day I recalled ruefully that Graham had lost at the start. Meanwhile it was a wrap.

At the end of each day Lindsay, Robert and I would gather to watch the day's rushes whilst Herman returned to his room to plan the following day's shoot. With very few exceptions we were delighted with what we saw. Herman had done a brilliant job, the performances were good and we knew we had something special. Knowing that this was intended to be not only a two hour stand-alone film but as the first of a series, Robert had said to me: "We'll be back." He had been a first-class team leader, performed with total professionalism and been hugely supportive at a personal level. But, unfortunately, he was wrong. We didn't come back.

Despite its success in more than thirteen countries and dubbed into four languages, without a UK broadcaster onboard it could never sustain a full series. Also, without a UK broadcaster, we had little credibility in the international market place.

Why no UK broadcaster, you might ask? I wish I knew. Probably at the end of the day neither ITV nor the BBC really wanted to encourage small independents like us to go off on their own making serious drama. I remember taking the final film to Nick Elliot, then Controller of Drama at ITV. He watched the title sequence and then said: "Sorry, Philip, but we would never transmit something made in Africa. The audience wouldn't be interested." The following year Granada made a series called 'Wild at Heart', filmed entirely in South Africa, which was transmitted at peak hour and came back for a second and third series. Inexplicable and duplicitous, or so it seemed to me at the time.

A couple of years later I played golf with Robert and Denis Waterman at Foxhills near Chertsey. By now his career was in the doldrums. His comedy series with his friend Jasper Carrot, 'The Detectives', had not been re-commissioned and, to make things worse, he wasn't getting any voiceover work, the glue that had held his acting career together for some years and provided him with a regular income between 'proper' jobs. The reality was that voiceover actors had been charging too much for too long, encouraged by the actor's union Equity and greedy agents who perceived the advertising market as a bottomless pit to be plundered at will. In the end the ad agencies had got together and set their own rates, less than half what the voiceover artists had been getting. Many realised that they had enjoyed a good run and that the game was up. Some, however, and Robert was one of them, protested on principle and had gone on strike. Unfortunately, there were plenty more voice-over artists willing to accept the new rates and the strike simply left Robert and his few supporters out of work.

It seemed to me that Robert needed to take a more pragmatic view of things if he wanted to prolong his career successfully into middle age and beyond. Denis was earning good money in 'New

Tricks' and a number of other well-known performers had taken parts in soaps. I suggested that Robert might think about doing something similar.

He appeared to take great offence at this. To sum up his feelings on the matter: (a) he was a leading actor and couldn't be expected to work for next to nothing (b) the hours were unacceptable and the conditions not good enough and (c) he really didn't want to take a part in a soap - what would it do to his reputation?

I looked at Denis and Denis looked at me. "It's all work, though, isn't it?" Denis said sensibly, "and it keeps you in the public eye." Robert looked at us as if he couldn't believe what he had just heard. I nodded in agreement.

"Well then," he said, "maybe I should think about it."

In early 2005 he became a regular in the medical drama, 'Holby City'. I called and asked how it was going. "Wonderful," he replied. "These young actors are all so good, and the directors and writers, too. I'm loving it. I should have done it years ago."

I had seldom heard him sound happier. He remained with 'Holby' for six years before leaving to return to the theatre.

Nowadays Robert appears in person less often, but his distinctive voice is once again heard frequently on voice-overs, advertisements, and as a narrator of television programmes. In 2001, a state-of-the-art theatre was named after him at the University of Salford.

As for 'Pride of Africa', it still crops up and now and then and has stood the test of time very well. If you want to see it, you can get the DVD on Amazon. But make sure it's the UK specification.

Golfing Encounters

LIKE most of my generation I took up golf far too late. It's a time-consuming and infuriatingly difficult game to play requiring great concentration, perseverance and practice - which, in the end, could just be its downfall. The days are gone when younger men and women can justify a whole day apart from each other and their families at weekends or take a day off from work during the week and it is difficult to see how the game can be modified, in the same way that cricket has managed to change with the times, so that it can be enjoyed in a shorter form.

Still, if you are going to play golf, even to a moderate standard, it helps enormously if you had an early start. I took it up when I was in my forties and am constantly reminded when I play with others who learnt the rudiments of the golf swing when they were children, that I will always have to think about things that come naturally to them. Having said that I have managed to play a reasonable game off a handicap of around 15 or 16 for the last twenty years or so and, whilst I have never taken it too seriously, I have had a great deal of fun and met a lot of fascinating people in the process.

It is often said that golf, more than any other sport, reflects real life and that when you meet people on the golf course you see them as they really are. I think this may be true. There are many areas of life where you can bluff and bluster your way through. Socially, in business, politics, showbusiness, we have all met and know people who like to present a face to the world which, shall we say, enhances who they are or what they have actually achieved. Self aggrandisement, arrogance, pomposity - all too common in everyday life - count for nothing on the golf course. You can either play the game or you can't. Plus (and this may be the biggest difference of all) you are playing against yourself and the course. No-one is throwing a ball at you or hitting it back, your opponents are not leaving you in tricky places or making the game hard for you. There is literally no-one else to blame. Golf is a battle against the terrain and your own mind - and that cuts even the most expert 'bluffer' down to size. Like music, golf is a hard master. If an actor gets a word wrong, it may go unnoticed. If a pianist plays a wrong note, everybody knows! It's the same with golf, so, yes, there is a likelihood that people who pursue the game and achieve a degree of proficiency are the ones who do not rely on artifact or pretence to get by. Consequently, you meet few unpleasant or pretentious people on the golf course.

It is not surprising that many well-known sporting celebrities take up golf - not only when they retire from their own sport, but often while they are still playing it professionally. The worlds of cricket, snooker, tennis, boxing, racing (both horses and motors) - to mention just a few - have all produced excellent amateur golfers, highly competitive professional sportsmen who are attracted to what might be regarded as the ultimate game of the mind rather than the body. They also know that they can go on playing golf long after their principle sport becomes too strenuous. I have met and had the pleasure of playing with many of them.

You might not think it quite so likely that the game provides committed recreation for another kind of performer, too. Those from stage, film and TV have always been attracted to the game, maybe for the very reason that it offers a refreshing change from the falseness of their everyday worlds. It is an honest sport that helps keep your feet on the ground.

I have always been a great fan of the legendary Bing Crosby and I remember going to see him at what transpired to be his last concert at the Brighton Conference Centre in October, 1977. In front of a packed house, together with Rosemary Clooney, his wife Kathryn

and daughter, Mary, backed by a full orchestra, he performed brilliantly to a standing ovation. In fact, by chance, I found myself right next to him as we left the Centre (the way the stage had been set up there was no exit for the artists other than to come down from the side amongst the audience) and, other than looking a little tired, quite understandably, he seemed in good fettle.

The following day he flew to Spain for a game of golf at the La Moraleja golf course near Madrid. He finished 18 holes - carding a very respectable 85 - and, with his partner, the club president, took the money off Spanish golf pros, Manuel Pinero and Valentine Barrious. After his final putt Bing shook hands with his playing partners, bowed to acknowledge the applause of some fans and remarked: "That was a great game of golf, fellas." As he was walking to the clubhouse he collapsed from a massive heart attack. Unable to break his fall, he landed head-first on the red-brick pavement, producing a large bruise on the left side of his forehead. "We thought he had just slipped," said Pinero. "Bing had shown no sign of fatigue. He was happy and singing as he went around the course." He was seventy-four.

I tell this story because it emphasizes how important the game was to a world-famous entertainer in the declining years of his life and career. One might have thought that at the end of an exhausting concert tour Bing would have chosen to put his feet up somewhere, probably on a beach lying in the sun. Instead, he preferred the therapy of the golf course to bring him back down to earth as quickly as possible. What a way to go - a triumphant and (as it transpired) farewell concert followed by a win amongst friends playing the game he loved. I don't suppose many of us will better that for a perfect departure from this life, however tough it may be on those left behind.

The late Mike Read, the comedian and actor, whilst not being the easiest of men to get on with and who had suffered a tragic life in many respects, was another celebrity who loved his golf. Standing next to me on the tee of a tricky par three at the beautiful Santa Maria course near Marbella on a gloriously hot Mediterranean afternoon, he shanked his ball into the rough. Expecting the usual string of expletives, I was surprised when he turned to me, looked up at the sky and proclaimed: "What does one lousy shot matter when you are privileged to be here in the first place?" He, too, had found solace in the peace and tranquility of the golf course.

I have played many times with Jimmy Tarbuck who became a household name in the 60's as host of the TV series 'Sunday Night at the London Palladium' and has been a keen golfer all his life. A member of the Variety Club Golf Society for fifty years, Jim has been captain twice and at the time of writing is President. I have found Jim to be a kind and charitable man, not at all the rough-edged scouser that his image and reputation might suggest.

Refreshingly, he is not a manic-depressive like so many of his compatriots who have earned their living by making others laugh - and he cares passionately about the things he gets involved with. A long-standing member of Coombe Hill Golf Club, just around the corner from where he lives, at his best Jim has played off single figures and has enjoyed the company, on and off the course, of some of the most famous names in golf including Arnold Palmer and

Jack Nicklaus - oh and Bob Hope! He has some wonderful stories to tell which I wouldn't attempt to repeat here.

In 2013 Jim was arrested without charge on allegations of sexual improprieties with a young man in the 1970s. Jim made it immediately clear to his friends and acquaintances that there wasn't a scrap of truth in the allegations - in fact, his agent, the late legendary Peter Pritchard (who had also happened to be a Special Constable in his younger days), had kept records of all Jimmy's engagements at the time which proved that he wasn't even where the so-called victim had said the incidents took place. It still took the police a year to drop the charges. I spoke to him on the telephone several times during that time to wish him well and to assure him that not only were all his friends standing by him but so was the Variety Club. He conducted himself with great dignity during this distressing time, which not only played havoc with his professional life but, one can only imagine, caused misery at home, too. I have absolutely no doubt that his wife of forty years, Pauline, son James and daughter, Lisa, stood by him resolutely throughout, but it couldn't have been easy. Famous celebrities are easy meat for these witch-hunters and, as we know, only very few of these charges have led to prosecutions. In fact, it increasingly appears that the police are pursuing these cases now with almost manic relish simply to make up for not having done so thirty years ago! No doubt our politicians will eventually get round to enforcing the old principle of a man being innocent until he is proved guilty, but, in the meantime, mud sticks and the lives of innocent men are being ruined.

Jim is fussy about who he plays golf with and, I am pleased to say, I have been 'chosen' to accompany him on many occasions - probably because he knows he can beat me! One time we were playing at the beautiful Burgh Hill course in Surrey and Jim, who by now was playing off 12, confided in me that he was worried that his game was no longer up to his previously high standards. I tried to reassure him that this happens to us all as we get older, the body loses its flexibility and, although you believe you are swinging the club just as you always did, somehow the ball doesn't go so far (or so straight). Jim said that whilst he accepted that, he was conscious that the people he found himself playing with - often as the guest celebrity at corporate or charity events - would be disappointed. I have no doubt that he meant it and I was reminded again that being famous has its drawbacks and insecurities.

Robert Powell, another keen player, described what it was like to play in front crowds and cameras when your golf might not necessarily be up to the pressures of the moment. "The main thing, Pip", he said, "is to look good. I usually mimic the swing of a professional golfer - big backswing, accelerate at the point of impact and follow through, keeping your head down throughout. Even if you hit the ball fifteen yards along the ground, the cameras won't see that and it will at least look as if you know what you are doing!" Oh, to be that good an actor.

Another amusing companion on the fairways is the singer and actor Jess Conrad. Born Gerald James he was born in Brixton in 1936. He was popular in the late 1950s and early 1960s with a number of hits to his credit and he also appeared in a number of films, including most recently Mike Moran's 'Telstar - The Movie' in which he played the part of pop svengali Larry Parnes. He starred in many musicals throughout the 1970s and 1980s when his portrayal of 'Jesus' in 'Godspell' led to his landing the title role in 'Joseph and the Amazing Technicolour Dreamcoat' when it first ran in the West End. He went on to tour with the show for nine years and still appears regularly today in cabaret and concerts.

Jess is never short of a story, often talking about his experiences in an engagingly self-deprecating way. "My wife is often asked what it is like to be married to Jess Conrad," he is fond of saying. "She always replies that it really helps when you are both in love with the same man." He also has a habit of referring to himself in the third person. "Would Jess Conrad like living in that house," he once remarked on a TV reality show. "Yes, I think he would!" Although now over eighty, Jess looks startlingly young and, yes, good looking (see the relatively recent picture opposite). He first saw his wife, Renee, in a television commercial for Camay soap, rang his agent and said this was the girl he was going to marry. That marriage has lasted nearly fifty years. I have booked him several times for private parties and concerts: he always gives good value, is original, disarmingly modest and very funny.

Another very funny man is Bobby Davro, probably the best and quickest stand-up comic of his era. He really is an extraordinary chap. His father, Bill Nankerville, was a runner; a British national mile and 1500m champion, world record holder, and represented Great Britain in two Olympic Games. In 2003 Bobby was one of the contestants in the Channel 4 reality TV show, 'The Games' in which ten celebrities competed against each other in Olympic style events.

He got his first break in 'Live at Her Majesty's and went on to have his own Saturday night shows on ITV during the 80s. The 90s saw him switching channels to the BBC, appearing on television shows such as 'Public Enemy Number One' during an episode of which he suffered a broken nose when some stocks he was placed in toppled over and caused him to fall face-first onto the studio's concrete floor. The incident was not televised but was later used in a BBC health and safety video! Throughout a rich and varied career he has been constantly in demand, not only on television but also as a stage performer and after dinner speaker. Professionally, he has done very well.

Like all fine performers, Bobby takes his work very seriously, attends to every detail and hates to let people down. I asked him once if he would come along to entertain the 'troops' at an after-golf dinner held at my local pub - not exactly the sort of gig Bobby was used to! He turned up on time in his brand new Aston Martin looking dreadful and sweating profusely. "Sorry, I've got a bad dose of 'flu," he explained, "but don't worry, I'll be fine - just don't get too close." Well, he performed brilliantly when it would have been so easy to have cried off. On another occasion, I booked him to entertain us at Christine's 60th birthday party onboard *HMS Hispaniola* on the Thames. Again, it would have been easy for him to turn up and just tell a few gags but, instead, he brought an array of props, not least a life-size Pavarotti suit, which he used to great effect to impersonate the great Italian opera star. It was hilarious. He is a very talented man.

There are so many other celebrity golfers as to be too numerous to mention. The lovely Russ Abbott, who reduced his audience to tears at an after golf dinner in the splendid officers' dining room at Sandhurst with his mime of a drunk returning home after a hard night out, Denis Waterman, shy and retiring off screen, the surprisingly intellectual Jasper Carrott, the self-effacing actor Kevin Whately, the boxer John Conteh, the great and hugely talented Ronnie Corbett,

John Lodge of the Moody Blues, the singer Kenny Lynch - not to mention football stars like Pat Jennings, Geoff Hurst and Trevor Brooking. I have played with them all; to a man they are all great characters, genuine from head to toe and with little if anything left to prove. I have enjoyed their company immensely.

* * *

One of the most enjoyable fixtures I have played in over the years is an annual match against 'The Generals'. Originally intended by the Army Benevolent Fund to feature a team comprised entirely of Army Generals, mostly retired, the ABS now include a few Lt Generals as well, maybe even the odd Brigadier! Still, this broadening of the ranks in no way lessens the novelty of a fantastic day.

The event, which has been going on for many years, alternates between their home club, the North Hants near Fleet and my own club, Kingswood in Surrey. One of the pleasures of the North Hants fixture is that we all go on to dine in full evening dress in the magnificent officers' mess at Sandhurst Military College, just down the road. This is a great experience for many reasons. Firstly, the army does these things in great style - the laying of the table alone with its serried ranks of regimental silverware must take hours to set out; then there is the atmosphere of the historic room itself, walls festooned with portraits of battle scenes and military heroes - not to mention the fine food and wines and the live military music which accompanies the feast.

But, more interesting than the golf and the ceremony, is the experience of meeting and talking to the 'generals' themselves - men who have spent a lifetime serving their country and, it is easy to forget, risking their lives in the process. It can be both an inspiring and humbling experience. Remember, these are the highest ranking officers - soldiers who have risen to the top through merit, devotion to duty and loyal service to their country. Indeed, if you had any sense of cynicism about what being a professional soldier in today's world entails, these men will dispel it in an instant. Many of them, operating at the highest level, have spent years interfacing with politicians and bureaucrats, and will privately express their exasperation and despair at some of the decisions with which they are expected to comply - but, to a man, they will accept their orders and get on with the job in hand.

Again, it is hard to come to terms with the fact that these men who are generally jolly and pleased to be out on the golf course, will have been through experiences that the rest of us can scarcely imagine; have fought alongside and lost friends and colleagues in battle and, yes, been responsible, directly or indirectly, with death and destruction often on a large scale. To survive and emerge from all this in a balanced and level-headed frame of mind requires remarkable moral compass, courage and integrity. I always recall hearing the politician, Enoch Powell, on 'Desert Island Discs' being asked by programme's creator, Roy Plomley, whether there was anything he regretted looking back on his long and distinguished career. "Yes," said Powell (who, by the way, was a Brigadier before he was thirty), "I wish I'd been killed in the war." He went on to explain the sense of guilt he had felt for the rest of his life at having survived when all his friends and comrades had perished. It is not possible to elicit anything from these men when it comes to such experiences, although one knows they must have been through similar traumas.

One elderly general, a former honorary physician to the Queen and now well into his eighties (who I won't name but with whom I have been privileged to play on several occasions), still has a wonderful bearing, insists on walking the course and plays a mean round of golf. The last time we met he told me his wife had just been diagnosed with cancer and was fading fast. By then we had played eighteen holes, showered and changed and were sitting down for a drink before dinner. I had spent the best part of five hours with him and would never have known there was anything the matter. All he would add was that he had seen precious little of her during the first thirty years of their married life and felt blessed to have spent so much time with her since. It seemed obvious that he would cope with this setback and would get on with life on his own. I think the word for it is 'fortitude'.

It is too easy to be sceptical. I sometimes think that the Americans celebrate their heroes more readily and unquestioningly than we do. Which is a shame because when the opportunity presents itself, saying 'thank-you' is therapeutic for us all.

The Bevs

IT was inevitable that when our three daughters went to dancing school, they would find themselves learning the old Irving Berlin favourite 'Sisters'. I can't remember how many times they performed it at local shows and in front of friends and family, but I do recall they got pretty slick at it! Well, it led to us meeting three extra-ordinary women, undoubtedly amongst the biggest stars of their generation, and this is how it happened.

At the time, the late, subsequently disgraced, Jimmy Saville was at the height of his popularity hosting a show called 'Jim'll Fix It'. For those of you who never watched it, the format was based around viewers (especially children and young people) writing in describing something they had always wanted to do but never had the chance. It was the job of Jim and his backroom team to make these 'dreams' come true.

Well, I would like to say that our adventure began with a letter from our girls to Jim, but that wouldn't be quite true - although the letter did come later. The truth was that in 1988 we were on a family cruise and, through the children, met up with a lovely man called Roger Ordish with his wife and son. With our children safely playing together, we discovered over a glass or two that Roger was the producer of 'Jim'll Fix It'. That evening we hatched up a little ploy. Vicky, our eldest, who was eight at the time would mention to Roger that she and her sisters knew the song 'Sisters' very well and had heard that it was originally recorded by the Beverley Sisters - was that true? Would he take the hint? We'd have to wait and see.

The following morning over breakfast, Vicky raised the topic. Roger saw the possibility in the blink of an eye. If she would write in to Jim, not only would he arrange for the girls to meet the Bevs but it might even be possible for them to perform the number with them on the show. It was just the sort of the request he was looking for.

When we got back to the UK, Vicky composed the letter, which was duly dispatched. The answer was not long coming back and we were all invited up to the Television Centre in Shepherds Bush for a pre-production meeting. As we were sitting chatting with Roger and his PA, in swept three very glamorous ladies, all in identical outfits topped off with identical blonde hairstyles. Although a little older than I remembered them, there was no denying they looked great. Joy, Babs and Teddy were soon introduced to Vicky, Libby and Georgie, who the Bevs took great care to put at their ease. In fact, the two trios of sisters seemed to strike up quite a friendship.

I suppose at the time Joy, the older sister, would have been coming up to 60, with her younger twin sisters in their middle fifties. By now they would have thought they were nearing the end of a glorious career, during which they were reputed to have been the highest paid cabaret artists in the world - as one more recent commentator subsequently remarked, the 'Spice Girls' of their generation. But, although they didn't know it at the time, it transpired that there was much more to come.

Their rise to fame is fascinating. With a style similar to their American counterparts, the Andrews Sisters, the Bevs career eventually spanned nearly seventy years. They were born in Bethnal Green, East London and during World War II were evacuated to the

Midlands, where they answered an advertisement from the company behind 'The Ovalteenies,' a group of children who promoted the virtues of the malt drink Ovaltine, mainly through a catchy jingle on the radio. The agency was searching for "Bonnie Babies" to further the campaign, and when the auditions came up, the trio were asked what they could do. They replied that they could sing a little.

Their potential was spotted immediately, as the girls sang one of the hymns they had learned at school in perfect harmony, not unusual for such close siblings. They were offered a contract worth fifteen guineas, which was more money than they had ever seen in their short lives. Cecil Madden, who was second in command at the BBC in Alexandra Palace, saw the ads and asked them to audition at the BBC's wartime location in Bedford. It was during this audition that the girls unexpectedly met Glenn Miller who was recording in there. He was so enthralled with the young sisters that he offered them a choice of any of his musicians to make a recording with proper accompaniment. The BBC originally planned to feature the sisters on radio, and were amazed when the girls named several of Miller's band members who had agreed to perform with them. In 1944, those same musicians went to Paris to join their leader, but of course he never arrived, his plane crashing over the English Channel with all on board lost.

When the war was over, the BBC began broadcasting television from Alexandra Palace, and the Bevs were an early hit of the new medium, always singing live - although they retained their humble roots, with their mother making all their costumes due to the rationing of clothes that had continued long after the war. The Glen Miller band had not forgotten them, either, and they were invited to appear live on NBC with the boys backing them. The whole family, including their parents, moved to New York, but returned to London so that the sisters could star at the Bagatelle, where they were noticed by Vic Parnell, who wanted to book them to appear at the London Palladium with Gracie Fields, a huge star at the time. However, with contracts having been signed, she demanded that the sisters should not appear with her, and no further explanation was ever given. The following year presented a different situation, with Danny Kaye starring at the Palladium, and he had no such qualms about appearing with a group of gorgeous singing sisters. Following their success, the BBC gave the girls a TV show of their own, and so began the series 'Three Little Girls on View', featuring the girls singing top songs of the day. The show was so popular that the following year it was re-named 'Those Beverley Sisters', and ran for seven years.

While performing in Blackpool, the girls' talent was recognized by Irving Berlin, who wrote the song 'Sisters' especially for them. Although they liked the song, they were reluctant to record it at first, as they believed they would be thought arrogant singing a song about themselves. But they eventually relented and the song became their signature tune.

Although they had no ambition to be a recording act and preferring to sing live in theatres, they nevertheless made some records at Abbey Road Studios, their first hit being a harmony version of the Christmas song 'I Saw Mommy Kissing Santa Claus,' which reached number six on the charts. Most of their hits were released around Christmas, with further successes including the singles 'Little Drummer Boy' and 'Little Donkey' and an EP that hit the separate EP charts in 1960, 'The Bevs for Christmas'. They were in demand by advertisers and were featured singing the jingles for many products during the 1950s.

One fan of their music was English football captain Billy Wright who Joy fell in love with. After a short courtship they married in 1958 and their wedding was the media event of the year, in fact, probably the first truly international 'celebrity wed-ding'. Teddy also married a sportsman, Peter Felix, a British water skiing champion which, sadly, did not work out.

At the time Joy married Billy Wright in 1958, the Beverley Sisters were reportedly earning £1,000 a week. Billy, by contrast, was never paid more than £24 a week by Wolverhampton Wanderers , and in more than 100 matches for England he never walked away with more than £60. As Joy recalled, the life of a footballer's wife in the 1950s was very different from what it became in the high-rolling 1980s and 1990s: "We were boringly well behaved, and loyal. In marriage you have to keep telling yourself that your husband is very important. That is not fashionable now, is it? I am disappointed at the way some women behave." The disparity between their earning power seemed to have no effect on their relationship, however, and they remained happily married until Billy Wright's death in 1994.

During the 60s and 70s the sisters, who had five children between by now, only took local London bookings, preferring not to travel far from home. However, twenty years later, the children - who had inherited their mothers' talent for harmony - began singing under the stage name 'The Foxes' so as not to use the Beverley Sisters name. One night at the London Hippodrome nightclub where The Foxes were playing, Peter Stringfellow *(above)* requested that the mums, although by then in semi-retirement, appear on stage themselves, and although this was not their sort of venue (with loud amplified music and laser light shows), they finally agreed. The reception they received was beyond all expectations and led to an entirely new career.

It's amazing to think they remained active in the 21st century, performing for the Queen as part of her Golden Jubilee celebrations in 2002. They also signed up for a ten-date tour with Max Bygraves to re-create the 1952 Royal Variety Performance in which they appeared together for the first time. They took part in the D-Day 60th anniversary memorial in 2004, and in January 2006 all three sisters were awarded MBEs in the New Year's honours list. Joy died in September, 2015 at the age of 91.

At the time we met them, the three sisters were still the best part of fifteen years away from hanging up their heels and hairpieces. But they didn't know that then. In fact, if you Google the Bevs, you will find plenty of footage of their later work and you cannot help but marvel at the precision of their routines. These ladies were professionals through and through - as we were soon to discover.

But, back to my tale. Having met our girls, the Bevs were positively enthusiastic about performing with them and quickly worked out a routine. A rehearsal was arranged, the band parts commissioned and the date set for the show itself. 'Jim'll Fix It' was recorded in Studio Two at the Television Centre in front of a live audience and there would be one opportunity to rehearse with the band on set immediately prior to the audience arriving. Well, when the time came our three girls knew the routine backwards. The Bevs had arranged for them to wear identical dresses to theirs so they looked like miniature Bevs but without the blonde wigs! The afternoon rehearsal went well and soon it would be time for the actual recording, prior to which they would meet the great Jim himself.

He was charming with them and, again, he and the whole studio team worked hard to put them at their ease. This is very much part of the television process. Everyone on the studio floor knows that their job is to make sure they get the best out of their performers (whatever they might think of them) and the way to do this is to make sure that tension and nerves are kept to a minimum - whilst, at the same time, bolstering the performer's confidence. So, when it came to recording their routine with the Bevs, Vicky 10, Libby, 7 and Georgie (who was only six) were positively looking forward to it. And it showed.

The routine was straightforward enough. The set amounted to a large screen situated in the centre of the studio floor from behind which the three children would emerge singing the first chorus of 'Sisters' disappearing behind the screen at the end. The Bevs would then appear from behind the same screen to sing the second chorus and then, finally, all six would join together for a third chorus. This all went exceedingly well and was greeted with tumultuous applause by the studio audience. So far, so good. They then joined Jim on the sofa for a brief chat and the obligatory presentation of the 'Jim'll Fix It' medals - and the news that the Bevs were presenting our girls with the dresses to keep. As with all Mr Saville's work (and much of light entertainment for that matter), it was inconsequential in real terms but highly entertaining and a great thrill just the same.

Following the show the Bevs invited us back to their dressing rooms. After a good deal of mutual congratulation, Babs took me to one side and looked at me intensely. "Keep them together, Pip," she said. "Don't let them drift apart, family is the most important thing in the world." She said it with such passion that her words quite took me aback. Both her other sisters agreed strongly with her. Somewhere I had read that the three sisters, one widowed, one divorced and the other a spinster, lived with their children in three adjoining houses in Totteridge and had done for many years. I suspect that their mutual support had been very important during times of stress - Billy Wright's death, Teddy's divorce and who knows what else. They wanted us to know that.

Following the show they kept in touch, even inviting the girls to repeat their joint performance at a concert in Worthing. Again, they were delightfully welcoming, genuinely pleased to see us and generous with their praise. All very enjoyable.

After that we exchanged Christmas cards for many years before losing touch in the middle '90s.

In 2006 I was contacted by the BBC who were planning a tribute to the Bevs as part of their series 'Legends'. They asked me if I would like to take part and relate our experiences with them. I was pleased to accept the invitation and the BBC sent a recording team to our home to film my remarks. I was pleased to have had the opportunity and, watching the programme later, was delighted to see that everyone who appeared had nothing but praise for this remarkable trio. Joy Beverley died in September, 2015. She was 91.

* * *

I have thought long and hard about whether to include a piece about Jimmy Saville in this book. I accept that I am in no position to contradict what others, including the BBC and the police, subsequently alleged to be his crimes, but I have to say I never saw any sign of such predilections in my dealings with him. So, whether or not the vilification heaped upon him after his death was justified, and on the principle that we should judge people as we find them rather than on hearsay, I have decided to relate my own experience of this unusually complex character

I was first introduced to him by a man called Bob Brooksby who worked at an advertising agency called The London Press Exchange just off Trafalgar Square. Bob was what we called at the time a 'promotions man', meaning that if anything cropped up outside of the agency's normal business of placing and creating ads, it would most likely land on his desk. He was an unusual character to find in an agency: not only was he older than the majority of his colleagues, but he was distinctly not the 'type' - more of a second-hand car salesman than an account executive. Still, he was direct and to the point, which was a refreshing change in a business high on blarney.

Bob had heard of my company Design Counsellors and called me up with a very special job in mind. Jimmy Saville, with whom he appeared to have a close if somewhat undefined relationship, was about to appear in a new TV series called 'Clunk, Click'. Jim had been appearing in an advertising campaign for the government promoting seat belts in cars The catchphrase for the campaign was "Clunk, Click, Every Trip" and, unusually, if not uniquely, the BBC had agreed to produce a TV chat show whose title would reflect the campaign. The problem was how to feature car seatbelts in a light entertainment, chat show format.

The gimmick that Jim had come up with was a chair from which he would present the entire show. The chair, of course, would be fitted with a seatbelt - but that was not all: he wanted the chair to do other things too - like making tea, lighting his cigars, playing music and anything else we could dream up. Bob had no idea how to go about such a project and wondered if we could help. Frankly, I had no idea either. I knew we could design a superb looking chair but fitting it out with all the mechanics was another matter. I told Bob that I would be delighted to take on the challenge and would get back to him with a price within a few days.

Luckily I knew someone who might help, an ingenious friend called Tony Novissimo, who had set himself up as a kind of inventor in a workshop not far from the Television Centre at Shepherds Bush. I set our design team to work up a rough design for the chair and took the drawings round to see if he could make it work. Tony studied the brief and soon came up with a plan - the only thing he needed us to do was modify the design so that the armrests were big enough to house his mechanics. Once I was confident that we could successfully deliver what was wanted, we jointly worked out some costs and I went back to Bob. Needless to say a 'one-off' such as this was not cheap; not only did the chair have to be built and upholstered, it had to fitted with all the electrical gadgets, too. When

I gave Bob the estimate he gulped and swallowed hard. The day later he told us to go ahead.

It took several weeks to complete the assignment but we were still in good time for the show and that was the first time I met Mr Saville. He was greatly intrigued and quickly mastered how to operate his new toy. When the first of the series was recorded both Tony and I were in attendance to make sure nothing went wrong - but we needn't have worried, Tony's system of radio aerials acting as hydraulic rams, coupled with the car radio, a tea maker and the cigar lighter all worked perfectly and had the studio audience in fits of laughter. In fact, with its bulky 'cubist' look and bright orange upholstery - and appearing in almost every shot - it really caught the eye. Jim loved it and not only used it for several series of 'Clunk, Click' but also, by this time re-upholstered in a more sedate dark blue and without the gadgets, in 'Jim'll Fix It', too.

During these years I went to a number or recordings of Jim's shows and got to know him, although not well. That was simply not possible. On one occasion I was standing at the back of the studio and noticed an attractive young girl, sitting alone watching the show. As soon as it finished she left her seat and made a beeline backstage. A few minutes later she was back, clearly in distress and crying. I asked the producer who was standing next to me, what that was all about. "Happens quite often", he replied. "These girls somehow get tickets with the express intent of getting to see Jim afterwards. They are often under-age and Jim usually sends them away with a signed photograph. Hell hath no fury..." Whether that was the full story I will never know. If it wasn't, then there could have been a cover-up going on but it didn't occur to me at the time.

On another occasion we were running a promotion with The Health and Safety Executive which involved an exhibition of paintings from schoolchildren all over the country. There was a competition involved and our client had arranged for the Duke of Gloucester to chair the judging panel and present the prizes. Aware of the fact that the Duke's profile might not have been familiar to children, they asked us if we could arrange for a celebrity to be there as well. Jim was at the peak of his fame at the time and fitted the bill perfectly. Our contact at the H&SE didn't believe he would do it and, in any event, would expect an affordable fee. I 'phoned Bob and explained the situation. Within the hour he came back to me. Jim had agreed and would be pleased to do the job so long as we picked him up from his flat close to Broadcasting House and took him to the venue. "What about a fee?" I asked Bob. "He'd be pleased to do it for a box of cigars," came the reply.

I picked Jim up in my old Rover, which I'd had valeted especially for the event. He wasn't quite ready and asked me up to his first floor flat. Although in a perfect position in the centre of a glorious Nash terrace overlooking Regent's Park (and most likely worth a fortune) there wasn't a scrap of furniture that I could see. "It's just a pied-a-terre," Jim explained without a trace of embarrassment, "My home is in Leeds with my Mum," With that, he locked the front door behind us and we made our way over to the City.

According to protocol we arrived just before the Duke who immediately spotted Jim - as usual, unmissable in his trademark tracksuit and long white hair. The two of them shook hands like old friends and went on to judge the pictures and present the prizes together. Afterwards, when the Duke had departed, Jim was in no hurry to leave, mixing with the kids and signing autographs. He really gave value for money, even though the box of Havannah cigars (which Bob Brooksby mysteriously procured) were not the cheapest!

On the way back Jim told me that he was often asked to attend Royal events, largely because he was able to take the pressure off the Royals themselves. An interesting perspective from a strange but highly professional public servant.

Did he deserve the total dismantling of his reputation after he died? A lot of people would say 'yes' and if you believe everything you read in the media you can see why. However, it would be salutary to remind ourselves that, unlike the two or three celebrities who were subsequently arrested, charged with historic sex crimes and sent to prison, Jim was never arrested, charged, nor was he tried, let alone found guilty of anything.

So, for the time being at any rate, we still have three "Jim'll Fix It" medals on our mantleshelf, a black and white photograph and an old VHS recording of our girls and The Bevs appearing on his show nearly thirty years ago. And very entertaining it still is.

Barbara Windsor

THE first time I met Barbara Windsor was when I was Chief Barker of the Variety Club. She had been a great supporter of the charity for many years and I had proposed a tribute lunch in her honour at the Hilton in Park Lane. Needless to say this was a fundraising event with all the proceeds going to under privileged children so we were not surprised but nevertheless delighted when Babs agreed to take part.

I have been involved in a number of these events and the trick is to give the 'star' as little as possible to do so that she (or he) can relax and bask in the praise of the other celebrities present. So, with our main attraction lined up, it was a matter of recruiting the guest speakers.

Sometimes it is harder to fix up the speakers than the star in whose honour the event is being held - if only because they may not be available on the chosen date. There was no such problem with Barbara. At the time she was the longest running star of 'EastEnders' and the whole cast would have taken part if we had wanted them to.

As it was, we settled for Mike Reid, who was in his tenth year as Frank Butcher, Pam StClement and June Brown as our guests of honour. Still, many other cast members wanted to be there and happily bought tickets. We also contacted the BBC to offer them the opportunity to broadcast the lunch and I was surprised when the Controller of BBC1, Peter Salmon, asked if he could attend with his wife.

Babs Windsor has had an extraordinary career. Born in Shoreditch in 1937, the only child of a costermonger and a dressmaker, she passed her 11-plus and went to Our Lady's Convent in Stamford Hill. Her mother paid for her to have elocution lessons and she trained at the Aida Foster School in Golders Green, making her stage debut at thirteen and her West End debut in 1952 in the chorus of the musical 'Love From Judy'.

Her first film role was in 'The Belles of St Trinian's' in 1954. She went on to join Joan Littlewood's Theatre Workshop at Stratford East, coming to prominence in their stage production 'Fings Ain't Wot They Used to Be' and Littlewood's film 'Sparrers Can't Sing' in 1963, which earned her a BAFTA nomination for Best British Film Actress, and for which she recorded the theme song. In the sixties she appeared in the film comedy 'Crooks in Cloisters', the film 'Chitty Chitty Bang Bang' and in the TV sitcoms 'The Rag Trade' and 'Wild, Wild Women'. In 1980, Babs played Saucy Nancy in the second series of the ITV children's show 'Worzel Gummidge' with the late Jon Pertwee.

But she came to real prominence with her portrayals of a 'good time girl' in nine 'Carry On films'. One of her most iconic scenes was in 'Carry On Camping' when her bikini top flew off during outdoor aerobic exercises. In classic 'Carry On' style, bare breastedness was implied but very little actually seen! In the seventies she appeared with several of the 'Carry On' team in the West End revue 'Carry On London!' In fact, she became so strongly identified with her 'Carry On' characters that it restricted the variety of roles she was chosen to play later.

She also had an impressive and distinguished stage career, starring on Broadway in the Theatre Workshop's 'Oh, What a Lovely War!' for which she received a 1965 Tony Award nomination for Best Featured Actress in a Musical. She also appeared in Lionel Bart's musical flop 'Twang!' (directed by Joan Littlewood) and in the musical 'Come Spy with Me' with Danny La Rue.

In the seventies she starred as music hall legend Marie Lloyd in the musical-biopic 'Sing A Rude Song' and a year later appeared in the West End production of 'The Threepenny Opera' with Vanessa Redgrave. She also toured internationally in her own show, 'Carry On Barbara!' and followed this with the role of Maria in 'Twelfth Night' at the Chichester Festival Theatre. In 1981 she played sex-mad landlady Kath in Joe Orton's black comedy 'Entertaining Mr Sloane' directed by her friend Kenneth Williams.

When EastEnders began in 1985, the producers said they would only cast unknown actors. Shoreditch-born Babs said that she regretted this, as she would have liked to have taken part. Nine years later the BBC had a change of heart and Babs took over the role of Peggy Mitchell, landlady of the Queen Vic pub, for which she received the Best Actress award at the British Soap Awards. Illness forced a two-year absence from the role between 2003 to 2005 when she rejoined the cast full time initially on a one-year contract, although this was later extended. In 2009 she announced she was to quit her role as Peggy Mitchell, saying she wanted to spend more time with her husband.

Since then she provided the voice of the Dormouse in Walt Disney's live adaptation of Lewis Carroll's 'Alice in Wonderland', directed by Tim Burton with Johnny Depp, Helena Bonham Carter and Anne Hathaway and, for the last few years, has regularly stood in for Elaine Paige on her BBC Radio 2 show on Sunday afternoons and, in 2014, she was given her own series called 'Ladies Of Song'.

Alongside this busy professional career she has had an equally turbulent personal life. She had well-reported flings with Sid James,

footballer George Best and Reggie Kray and has been married three times. She has said that she never wanted children as a result of her father rejecting her. She was awarded an MBE in 2000 and, in 2010, was given the Freedom of the City of London. In 2014 she was awarded an honorary doctorate from the University of East London. Quite a CV for a Shoreditch girl.

When it came to the week of the lunch I sat down with the events team to arrange the seating plan. On the top table I sat myself and Christine in the centre with Babs to my right, then Pam and June and their partners. To Christine's left I seated Mike Reid who was unaccompanied, and then Peter Salmon, the Controller of BBC One and his wife. A pretty good arrangement, I thought. The office sent a copy to Babs to make sure she was happy.

Well, she wasn't - and a sharp note came back saying that she didn't want any other women at the top table! In hindsight I can see why - she probably had a picture in her mind of herself surrounded by adoring, middle-aged men. She would have been in her early sixties at the time and, although she still scrubbed up pretty well, I suppose she didn't welcome comparisons. She was also on her own (she didn't marry Scott Mitchell, 26 years her junior, until the following year). But then she was a star and, like all stars, believed that if she didn't look after her 'star status' no-one else would. The problem I had, however, was that if we excluded Pam, June, Christine and Peter Salmon's wife from the top table, it would only have left Mike, Peter and myself. And that assumed that Peter wouldn't mind his wife sitting somewhere else! Not to mention that we would have to draft in some other men to fill the gaps, which would have left their partners stranded in the body of the room! It was impossible and it fell to me to call Babs to explain.

I must say that I approached the task with some trepidation - if her tone on the 'phone was anything like her note, I was in for a real drubbing. However, when I carefully explained the position to her, she simply said it was fine, she quite understood. She also said that she was looking forward to the lunch and would like to sing for us as well. Did I mind picking up the cost of her pianist? Of course, this was a real bonus and I was delighted.

On the day of the lunch, everything seemed well set up. The room was packed, the TV cameras in place, the guests were all present and everyone was in a good mood, including Babs who looked positively radiant. The meal was delicious and the moment came to introduce the first speaker, June Brown. June is, of course, a fine actress but best known for Dot Cotton - and it always surprises people when she speaks in her cultured, beautifully enunciated natural voice. She kept her remarks brief and to the point and went down very well. I had deliberately asked Mike Reid to be the second speaker as I knew I could rely on him to gauge the audience and make a highly entertaining, professional job of it. This would then leave me as Chief Barker to briefly propose the toast to Babs, present her with her Variety Club Gold heart and draw the formalities to a close - although we still awaited the pleasure of hearing her sing.

Mistake number two - Mike was terrible. I have no idea why but he simply got it all wrong and instead of drawing on the dozens of amusing anecdotes he must have accumulated after years of acting alongside her, he attempted a 'stand-up' act which, partly because much of it was vulgar and totally inappropriate for the occasion, fell flat on its face. He sat down to a smattering of polite applause and a despairing comment from Babs of "Oh, Mike!" plainly audible, as she probably intended, over the sound system. And I was up next! There was clearly a rescue job to be done. It seemed best to change things around and I glanced over to the piano where Bab's pianist was already in position. I asked Babs if she was ready to sing right away. She nodded, obviously understanding why I was changing the running order. I turned to Brian Greenham, the toastmaster, and asked him to announce the next item. Babs made her way over to the piano to a round of renewed, enthusiastic applause. The recollection of Mike's ill-judged effort was already fading fast.

I recall that Babs sang more than one song that afternoon, but the one that stuck in my mind and everyone else's was "Sparrows Can't Sing" which she had first recorded in 1963 when she was twenty-six. She sung it beautifully, demonstrating that she still possessed a fine singing voice. It was a moving performance and she returned to the top table amidst a standing ovation from an adoring audience. All I had to do was to get up, thank her, and present her with her Gold Heart with the words: "Barbara, you are our original cockney sparrer." And that was it. Somehow we had managed to avoid Mr Reid spoiling the day and, needless to say, when extracts were broadcast later on, his contribution was not amongst them!

The next time I met Barbara was a year or two later at a Variety Club Annual Dinner and Ball at the Grosvenor House. I had been asked to conduct a money raising event called 'Heads and Tails'. You may well be familiar with this now popular fundraising game. The idea is for everyone participating to put a £20 note into the hat for the privilege of taking part. The Master of Ceremonies then tosses a coin and the audience has to put their hands on their heads or their bottoms depending which way they think the coin will land. Those who get it wrong sit down. It is surprising how quickly you can reduce six or seven hundred people down to a dozen or so. In the meantime you have raised £10 - £12,000 fairly effortlessly for the cost of one decent prize for the winner, the last person left standing. Usually, the whole game takes no more than fifteen minutes.

Well, I had thought of a variation to this. My idea was to compile a list of questions each with two possible answers - one representing 'heads' and the other 'tails'. The trick, of course, is to come up with the right questions. At worst (and I have seen it done since) the answers are a matter of public knowledge and the questions themselves boring. This is no time to adopt a general knowledge approach. If you do, more than half of your crowd will get the answers right, it becomes tedious and the game goes on for ever! You have to invent questions that are fun and to which the answers can only be guessed at. That evening we had a large number of celebrities in the audience and I had decided to prepare a list of questions centred around those individuals. So, for example, the question might be "Jeremy Beadle has presented more Saturday night shows on television than any other performer. Has he presented 2,038 shows (heads) or 3,012 (tails)?" Well, I got through about four questions like this and had those remaining on their feet down to about thirty, when I noticed Babs sitting in the audience. I didn't know she was going to be there and asked one of the girls assisting me to invite her onto the stage. While she was on the way, I asked another question reducing the numbers left to a dozen, who I then lined up on the stage. By this time Babs was beside me and, as always, was greeted warmly by the crowd. I whispered in her ear and she nodded enthusiastically. One more question and we would be down to four or five people. Here's how it went: "So, ladies and gentlemen, Barbara needs no introduction from me. And the next question is 'There were 31 'Carry On films. How many did Barbara appear in? Was it nine (heads) or twenty (tails)?'" Surprisingly, the answer was nine; generally people think it was more, but there was the lady herself to confirm the fact. The heads won and suddenly we were down to only two, a lady and a gentleman. You could sense the audience's interest in who might win. "Now", I said, "I'm not sure who will be the better judge of this. Barbara very nearly bared all in more than one of those films. Here's the question: 'what is her bra size? Is it 32B (heads) or 34D (Tails)?" Neither contestant rushed to commit and then the lady put her hands on her bottom and the man opted for heads. I asked Babs to announce the answer which was… 34D. The lady contestant had won!

My last encounter with this fun lady was on the telephone - although it wasn't me on the other end of it. Richard Desmond, owner of Northern and Shell, publishers of OK Magazine and, subsequent to my meeting, the Daily Express and Channel Five had asked me to go and see him to discuss the forthcoming Variety Showbiz Awards which he was supporting through OK magazine. Whilst there, I couldn't help noticing the latest copy of the magazine on a coffee table featuring a front cover picture of Babs on a holiday beach looking alluring in a bathing costume. I recalled that she was on honeymoon with her young new husband. For a sixty-five year-old, she looked extraordinary and I commented as much to Richard. Just then, the 'phone rang. It was the lady herself and, mischievously, Richard put in onto speaker so that I could hear both sides of the conversation. Not that there was much on his side - this was a virtuoso performance by a 'grande dame' of showbusiness who believed her privacy had been grossly invaded. "But, Babs," Richard protested, "you knew the pictures were being taken, it was arranged with you before you left the UK?" Not a bit of it, came the reply, and, anyway, it was a terrible picture. "You might have used a better shot," she went on, "or at least touched up the bags under my eyes. I haven't even got any make-up on!" I looked again at the front cover; I was certain she had. Anyway, it all came down to that. For once she hadn't seen the picture first, hadn't approved it and wasn't expecting to see it printed on the front cover of what at the time was fast becoming one of the UK's most popular weekly magazines. "You look great," smoothed Richard, "take another look in the morning, you'll see things differently." They said their good-byes amicably enough and I was reminded of my telephone conversation with her the previous year about the seating plan. "It wasn't what she was expecting, that's all," Richard said. "She'll calm down. What a smasher that woman is."

A real compliment from a Hampstead lad.

Bernard Coral

I was in my late forties when I first started to suffer from pain in my ankles and knees. I put it down to strain on the joints brought on by too much golf and tennis - coupled with a stressful lifestyle. Later, I discovered that my self-diagnosis was wide of the mark and, in more recent years, these problems have all but gone way. At the time, however, I thought what I needed was a good rest, some pampering - and, in particular, a self-imposed break from golf.

So, in order to address the matter and with Christine's encouragement, I booked myself into a health farm called Grayshott Manor near Hindhead for a week of dieting and gentle massage. As it transpired, this turned out to be seven days that would significantly change my life.

The first day was uneventful until, early in the evening, I was sitting in the bar drinking a fruit juice after dinner, when a tallish, dark haired, rather imposing man made a notable entrance flanked by two 'associates'. It felt a bit like something from 'The Godfather'. They took a look around and promptly sat next to me at the bar. Al Capone turned to me and proffered a hand. "Hello, I'm Bernard, pleased to meet you - I thought we were the only men here." He was right, I hadn't seen another male all day. We completed the introductions and Bernard ordered three drinks, offering to buy me another one, too. I noticed they were all drinking scotch, making my mixed fruit punch look a little tame. As if reading my mind he said: "We're not here for our health, we're here for some golf, but we've told the wives we've booked into a health farm." Which was true, or true enough.

We chatted on for a bit but, apart from discovering that the other two were either business colleagues or there at Bernard's expense, I found out little about them.

"Do you play?" Bernard asked. I explained that I did and was actually recuperating from a badly strained ankle. "Ever played Hindhead?" he asked, "it's a beautiful course, just down the road." I told him I hadn't, moreover, I was trying to avoid golf for a few days. "Nonsense," he said. "We're playing tomorrow, you can make up a four-ball." He got up - the other two quickly on their feet. "See you in reception at nine. I'll drive." With that they bid me goodnight and departed. Needles to say, my clubs were in the boot (as always) and I went to bed knowing that I was about to break my first resolve.

The next morning, following a sedate ride in Bernard's highly polished Bentley and sore ankle notwithstanding, I found myself on the first tee of Hindhead Golf Club, looking down the beautifully manicured fairway. I had not been asked for any money, so could only presume that this was on Bernard. Without more ado - let alone tossing for who should take the honour - Bernard executed a couple of powerful practice swings before hitting a fine, long drive down the centre of the fairway. He turned to me with a justified smirk and offered me the tee. I limped over and, somewhat impeded by my injury, followed with a decent if not spectacular drive of my own. As his two 'friends' drove off (which didn't seem to remotely interest him) he said: "How's the ankle?" I told him it was a bit bruised. "I thought about getting you a buggy," he said, "but they don't have any here. Too hilly. Still, I thought the walk would probably do you good." Thanks a bunch, I thought.

The round progressed very much in the same manner with Bernard playing excellent golf, cursing himself aloud for the smallest error, and the rest of us bumbling along providing an admiring audience.

In between shots he asked me what I did for a living. I explained that I was in the process of filming the second series of 'The Darling Buds of May'. "So, you're in show business?" he asked. "Well, I'm a producer, if that counts," I responded. He thought about this for a moment and then hit a perfect wedge to within a couple of feet of the flag. "You should join the Variety Club Golfing Society," he said, "they need a few more like you."

Now, I knew about the Society but never considered membership, which I had heard was strictly by invitation. "It does very good work," he went on, "raising money for Sunshine Coaches for disabled kids. I've raised a million myself over the years with the Bud Flanagan Classic." I was beginning to realise that I knew nothing about this man. "What do you do exactly," I enquired. "I run a chain of betting shops," he said, striding off towards his ball. One of his cronies nudged me. "I thought you'd recognised him, that's Bernard Coral, head of the Coral empire - oh, and by the way, its not just betting shops."

Of course, I'd heard the name, he was often in the papers, together with his father, the legendary Joe Coral. "He's a very generous and charitable man," the sidekick went on, "just like his old man. Ever been to the Wig and Pen Club?" I had, of course; the old lawyers' and journalists' haunt opposite the Law Courts was one of the few buildings in Fleet Street to have escaped the Great Fire of London. In my early publishing days I had met clients there more than once. "That belongs to the Corals. It was Joe's great passion and now Bernard's taken it over."

I caught up with Bernard who was still striding along the fairway. By now my ankle was really painful. "Bernard," I asked, "isn't the Golfing Society part of Variety Club? Shouldn't I join that first?"

This seemed to stop him in his tracks. "Yes, of course," he said eventually, "if you want to join Variety Club, I'm sure they'll be pleased to have you. I'll talk to Eric Morley."

We finished the round and Bernard drove us back to Grayshott. "You'd better get someone to look at that ankle," he said in parting, "it's interfering with your golf."

We didn't see much of each other for the rest of the week and I assumed he must have found a better/fitter golfing partner. However, we did meet up on our last evening for a game of snooker. I managed to beat him - which I was not too sure he appreciated. The following morning we bumped into each other in the car park. He was driving off in the Bentley when he spotted me and stopped, winding down the driver's window. "If you don't hear from Eric give me a call," he said and handed me his card. I waved him off not knowing whether we would meet again.

When I got home there was a note from Eric Morley enclosing an application form for membership. It appeared that Mr Morley was proposing me and someone else who I didn't know was seconding. There was no mention of Bernard. In his accompanying letter Eric suggested some dates when he could see me at his offices in Golden Square for an initial interview.

By now the remarkable Mr Morley had long since departed Mecca and was running his Miss World operation with the assistance of his wife Julia and his son Stephen. Now in his early seventies, he would still be at his desk, six days a week, at 7pm in the morning, often having cycled from his home in Dulwich. But more about him later. For the moment I had to get through his quizzing me about my circumstances and charitable intentions.

"Will you commit to taking a table at all our events?" he asked me.

"I'll take tables as often as I can, Mr Morley, but there will be times when I simply won't be around," I replied. "Understood," he nodded, "you're no use to the charity if your not earning a living."

I told him that Bernard had suggested I join the Golfing Society. "Good idea," Eric responded, "Bernard will propose you for that."

A couple of weeks later, I received my new members' pack from Variety Club. I was in. I telephoned Bernard's office and was referred by his secretary to Jerry Stevens who, at that time, was running the Variety Club Golf Society. Jerry already knew about me and confirmed that Bernard would act as my proposer. As I would discover over the next few years, I could not have been influenced or supported by two better men.

There was a lingering curiosity in my mind as to why the business of proposing me involved two people when I had thought Bernard might have stood as my proposer for the Variety Club and the Golf Society, but it was to be some years before that particular mystery unravelled. In the meantime I continued to enjoy my association with both men - which I like to think developed into friendships - Mr Coral on the golf course and Mr Morley at Variety Club meetings. However, never the twain met.

To digress for a moment, the story of how Corals came to be one of the country's largest betting, casino and hotel groups is fascinating and reads like a history of the betting industry during the latter part of the twentieth century.

Bernard's father, Joe Coral (real name Joseph Kagarlitsky) was born in into a Jewish family in Warsaw, Poland in 1904. His father, Abraham Kagarlitsky, died when he was at an early age and his mother, Jessica, joined a wave of migrants in 1912 from Eastern Europe who were seeking a better life in the United Kingdom.

The family took on the surname Coral and Joseph became 'Joe' to make it easier to get a job, of which he'd had many after leaving school at the age of fourteen. Having a flair for mathematics Joe took a clerk's position in a lamp-making firm, which gave him the connections to meet bookmakers and become a 'runner' (someone who takes bets on behalf of a bookmaker, which had been illegal since 1853).

Joe was sacked from the lamp-maker's workshop for, in Coral's words, 'concentrating on the wrong ledger'. From there he went to work at a small London advertising agency which gave him enough time off to begin taking bets in a billiards club in Stoke Newington during the General Strike of 1926. He left advertising to set up his own pitches at the Harringay and White City greyhound racing tracks. The introduction of the electric hare from the US in 1926 assisted his career as it created a legal context for trackside betting in London.

Joe Coral and his brother had failed to register as 'aliens' resident in the UK until 1924 and were fined £20 each at Thames Magistrates Court. It was the beginning of a long running feud that would see Joe on the wrong side of the law for the next thirty years.

Like many bookies of the time, Joe ran both a legal and an illegal business. The legitimate side was greyhound racing and credit betting with cheques, where no ready money changed hands, but the most lucrative wing of his business was street betting. He worked hard to develop a local network of agents to collect bets on his behalf in pubs, shops and back alleyways and by 1930 employed between seventy and eighty agents who collected ready-money bets for him. By then he had also taken over the pitches of Bill Chandler, a popular bookie, who was unable to compete with Coral.

Joe's success attracted the attention of Charles Sabini, commonly known as Darby Sabini, a gang leader of mixed Italian and English parentage. Darby was head of 'The Sabinis' and 'king of the racecourse gangs' that dominated the London underworld and racecourses throughout the south of England for much of the early twentieth century. Sabini had extensive police and political connections including judges, politicians and police officials. Sabini's power rested on an alliance of Italian and Jewish bookmakers, but Joe Coral somehow managed to fend off the protection rackets perpetrated against other bookmakers. It was a dangerous time but things improved when Sabini moved to Brighton. Sabini was later immortalized as the gangster Colleoni in Graham Greene's 'Brighton Rock'.

By now, Joe Coral was one of the largest regional bookmakers in England. War interrupted the betting business, owing to the huge reductions in the racing calendar, but Coral was still busy. He opened a credit betting office in Stoke Newington and moved to London's West End four years later. After the war he was one of a number of bookmakers who advertised betting by post in the major sporting newspapers such as the Sporting Life and the Sporting Chronicle. Postal betting was legal because no cash changed hands, only cheques or postal orders.

The illegal business continued to thrive, however, and in the 1950s the official attitudes to betting and gambling loosened. During an era of full employment and affluence the idea that the working classes would gamble themselves into poverty was misplaced. The police also took the opportunity to argue that the old law was unworkable, and that illegal betting was an open secret, which was impossible to stop. This change of mind led to the Betting and Gaming Act of 1960, which finally legalized off-course cash betting, and introduced the licensed betting office to the high streets and back streets of England and Wales.

Joe Coral, along with other bookmakers such as William Hill, were not keen about legalization. A requirement of the act was that any new betting office needed to show 'unstimulated demand' before being granted a lice nce. One way was to convert existing business premises to licensed betting offices. Coral paid to have the one of his agents sweetshcp turned into a betting shop. But the most efficient way to negotiate the new law was to buy up other offices and, by 1962, Coral had twenty-three shops. During the 1960s the corporate structure of bookmaking became more fully-fledged, and bookmaking firms became public companies, operating on a legal and commercial basis. Corals became a public company in 1963, and diversified into casinos, bingo halls, and hotels. The firm was eventually purchased by the brewing, hotels, and entertainments group Bass in 1970. Joe remained president of the bookmaking firm and a major shareholder.

By the mid-1970s expansion had led to 650 Corals betting

shops and by the end of the decade Corals was one of the 'big four' bookmaking firms - a status they retained well into the 1990s. In 1992 Corals entered into an arrangement with the Tote, the pool betting system based at the racecourses, whereby pool bets could be placed at Corals outlets.

Coral had married his wife, Dorothy Helen, in 1932. They brought up three sons, two of whom, Bernard and Nicholas, pursued careers in the family business from the early 1950s. Joe Coral died in 1996. An extraordinary story and an extraordinary man.

It was over a lunch with Eric Morley that the full facts of Bernard's history with Variety Club were finally revealed to me. Eric was clearly a great admirer of Bernard. "Best Chief Barker the Variety Club never had," he said. Now, perhaps I should explain again that the Chief Barker - a term derived from circus language like many others in this charity, which originated in the world of carnival and variety theatre - is elected by the Crew to effectively run the business for twelve months. So, I presumed from what Eric was saying that Bernard Coral had been elected Chief Barker but, for some reason, never served in office. "It was a mistake," Eric went on. "When he needed his friends to stand by him they turned against him." The story had begun to sound like a re-run of the Last Supper.

According to Eric, this is what happened. Bernard had been on the Crew for a number of years and done more than his fair share of raising funds for the children the Charity supports. Plus, he was a well-known and influential businessman and a leading light in the Golfing Society. It was inevitable that he would become Chief Barker at some point and he was duly and enthusiastically elected to serve in 1979.

Then, just before Christmas, Bernard was doing his customary round of the Coral casinos in the West End. One night in the early hours of the morning he had just arrived at The Curzon Club off Park Lane when it was raided by the police. All the patrons were asked to leave and, as the senior manager on the premises, Bernard, in full evening dress, was taken to Kensington police station for questioning. Suspecting a set-up, he refused to co-operate and demanded the presence of his lawyer. Since this was not possible until the next morning, Bernard found himself spending the night at Her Majesty's pleasure. By midday the following day he had been released pending further investigation. The Curzon Club was open again within 48 hours due to lack of evidence, but by then the story had been picked up by the media, complete with pictures of Bernard being led away in a police car, taken by a photographer who just 'happened' to be on the scene. No charges were ever brought against him or the company and Bernard always maintained that the 'tip-off' to which the police responded had come from Coral's arch competitor, Ladbrokes.

It was enough, however, for Variety Club to inform him that the nominating committee had re-convened and decided that following the widely publicised incident, and after 'due consideration', it was not possible for the charity to have a Chief Barker who had been in prison. His nomination had been withdrawn.

From subsequent conversations with Bernard, I discovered how hurt and betrayed he had felt by this turn of events. He'd felt the honour of being elected Chief Barker deeply and had been looking forward to putting his heart and soul into the role. He was both insulted and humiliated by his treatment at the hands of a group of people he had thought to be close friends and his reaction was to immediately resign from the charity. However, his belief and respect for the work of the charity raising funds for disadvantaged children remained undiminished and he resolved to continue to make his contribution via the Golfing Society only. This he did tirelessly for the rest of his life.

A decade later, when my year as Chief Barker was drawing to a close, I invited Bernard and his wife, Diane, to join me as my guests at the last function of the year, the charity's Christmas Lunch at the Hilton, Park Lane. I was delighted when they accepted, bearing in mind that Bernard had not attended a main Variety event for fifteen years. It was to be something of a special occasion, not least because I had arranged for two grand pianos to be set back to back onstage. My successor as Chief Barker was to be the great Tony Hatch and we had worked out a 'grand finale' involving the two pianos and a big entrance for Tony. But, before that was my farewell speech.

I started with a few formalities going on to briefly describe how I had been introduced to Variety Club all those years ago. "Without Bernard's encouragement," I said, "quite simply I would not be here. And I am delighted to say he is by my side today as my year as Chief Barker ends. Ladies and gentlemen, a man who has raised millions for our charity, Bernard Coral." I gestured to him to stand and acknowledge the great round of applause that greeted his presence. I think he must have known that amongst the 600 people present that day, there were a few guilty consciences.

The finale went well. As a clue to the identity of my successor, I played a chorus of Tony's famous hit 'Downtown', during which he made his way to the stage to more great applause. We then continued to play a medley of songs on the two pianos with other singers joining us at various points as we progressed to our last number 'White Christmas'. I had started the whole thing on an empty stage but, by the end, Tony and I were surrounded by fifty or sixty people including a children's choir! It was a good end to a good year, but my abiding memory of that lunch is the expression on Bernard's face when his beloved charity finally welcomed him back.

But that is not the end of the story. I mentioned that Bernard had taken over the running of the Wig & Pen Club in Fleet Street. One year he asked me if I would like to bring the family up to watch the Lord Mayor's Show as he was laying on a special day. We jumped at the opportunity, not least because the club had a unique view of the procession as it wound its way down Fleet Street. My three girls were in their teens by then and old enough to appreciate the history of their surroundings, including the remarkable collection of paintings, prints and artefacts that adorned the walls of the club itself. We had a great time and, despite the large number of regular clientele present, Bernard went to considerable trouble to look after us. It was to be the first of a number of visits to the Wig and Pen with the family.

By now Bernard had retired from the board of Corals, which had been taken over by Bass Charrington. However, the Wig & Pen was privately owned by the family and Bernard had made it his business to ensure that Joe's pride and joy continued as a going concern - not easy when all the major newspapers had deserted Fleet Street and headed to Docklands and the East End. He had also set up The Wig & Pen Golf Society, again with the intent of raising money for disadvantaged children. In short, Joe's passion had become Bernard's.

One day we decided we would like to go for dinner and I called the club to book in. Bernard wasn't there so I made the reservation with the manager. Within ten minutes my telephone rang. It was Bernard: "I gather you're coming up for dinner," he said, "I'm sorry I won't be around, but I'll make sure you get a good table and you're well looked after. Are you bringing the girls?" I told him we were. "I'll be sorry to miss you, then. Have a great evening."

Later on we drove up from Surrey, found a parking space in New Fetter Lane (those were the days) and made our way to the club. We were greeted and seated by the manager, ordered our drinks and were perusing the rather splendid all-English menu when who should appear but Bernard. There he was, making sure we were okay, happy with the table and the food choices on offer. "If it's not on the menu, just ask and we'll cook it for you," he said. We chatted for a few minutes more and then he left us to it. We didn't see him again that evening.

When we'd finished, there was no sign of him and I asked the manager when he had left. "Oh, soon after you arrived," came the reply. "That's odd," I said, "he told me he wouldn't be in tonight. Was he here earlier?" The waiter looked surprised. "No, he arrived ten minutes before you did. We weren't expecting him."

Bernard lived in St Albans. I could be wrong, but I believe he came down to the Wig & Pen that night especially to see us and make sure we were properly looked after. Which we were.

Not many months afterwards I heard that he was in St Thomas' Hospital, just across the road from our apartment at County Hall. I dropped everything and went round to see him immediately. Just as I was entering the ward, I met two familiar figures coming out, Bruce Forsyth and Henry Cooper. I asked them how he was. "Not good," said Henry. "He's got cancer of the spine. They've operated but the wound won't heal. They're treating it with leeches". This sounded strange and I wondered if Henry had got it right. I looked at Bruce. "That's right," he confirmed, "leeches - another great advance in medical research!" We said our goodbyes and they went on their way.

Bernard was in a private room with a view of the river, looking rather uncomfortable propped up against a pile of pillows. I was struck by how much smaller he looked. But he seemed in good spirits, anxious to know what was going on, keen to get back on the golf course and to work. We chatted for nearly an hour by which time he was getting tired. "I can't believe Henry and Bruce came to see me," he said, "why would they do that? Jerry came in yesterday, Jimmy the day before. Extraordinary, I didn't expect that in a million years." This was said with such sincerity that I have no doubt he was genuinely surprised; he clearly had no idea of the esteem in which he was held.

When I got back to the flat I sat down and wrote a letter to him attempting to explain why he was held in such high regard. Unlike his father, he had been born into a life of wealth and luxury. It would have been so easy to take it all for granted, to sit back and do little for others. Instead, he had chosen to return his good fortune in spades, aware of the sacrifices his parents had made, compelled to do as much as he could to repay his debt to them and society. His many kindnesses, not just to me - others told of similar experiences - his directness, his charm; these and more were the reasons why people loved and respected him and why they were visiting him in his hour of need. All this I put in the letter and posted it to him at St Thomas'.

Sadly, the operation to remove the tumour was not a success. He was discharged from St Thomas' to recuperate at home. I only saw him twice after that. Once at his golf club, Dyrham Park, when Variety held a golf day there. To him it would have been unthinkable not to be in attendance, although, needless to say, his playing days were over. By now he had shrunk to little more than five foot, presumably as his spine continued to collapse. But, as always, he appeared in good spirits, chatting away to all concerned. He didn't mention my letter and I was beginning to think he hadn't received it.

The last time I saw him was at the renowned Variety Club Stag Do, held every year at the Royal Lancaster Hotel on the first Sunday of December. It is always a top event with six or seven hundred men, not just golfers, togged up in evening dress, eating steak and kidney pie and splitting their sides as the country's top comedians regale them with one-liners, jokes and speeches with the media barred from entry.

Bernard was there at the top table, which must have been an enormous effort for him. He died the following month.

I wrote a letter of sympathy to his wife, Diane. The reply was not long coming. In it, she referred to my letter. She said he had been very moved and read it several times - although didn't know how to respond. His only comment had been: "I had no idea."

L. Ron Hubbard

ONE of the most extraordinary men I have encountered, I never met. Probably because he was already dead - although no-one was sure about that. This would have been around 1986-7. The man in question was L Ron Hubbard.

By this time my magazine business was doing well, really well, in fact, and we were looking to expand. Book publishing was an obvious extension to our existing operation, although I personally knew very little about it. As it happened, my old friend and fellow director, Tony Tanner, mentioned that a relative of his had just left New English Library where he had been MD and might be interested in starting up a new book publishing business with us. We arranged to meet him - his name was Trevor de Cruz - got on famously and it didn't take long to set up and launch Quadrant Books.

Of course, we were totally dependent on Trevor's existing contacts to get us started, including a couple of projects which either his previous employers didn't know about or weren't interested in. One of these was a book called "Battlefield Earth" by, you've guessed it, L. Ron Hubbard. Naturally, I had heard of him - the man who had 'invented' Scientology. But, I didn't know that before all that, he had been a science fiction writer. "Battlefield Earth", Trevor had been told, was his greatest work. The story of the book goes something like this:

In the year AD 3000, Earth has been ruled by an alien race, the Psychlos, for a millennium. After a thousand years, humanity has been reduced to a few tribes in isolated parts of the world while the Psychlos strip the planet of its mineral wealth. Our hero, Jonnie Goodboy Tyler, a young warrior of one such tribe, lives in the shadow of the Rocky Mountains. Depressed by the death and disease affecting his tribe due to irradiation from decaying unused nuclear land mines, he leaves his village to explore the lowlands and to disprove the superstitions long held by his people. He is captured in the ruins of Denver by Terl, the Psychlo chief of security - a hairy nine-foot tall, 1,000-pound sociopath.

Terl has been assigned to Earth, and eventually learns that his term has been extended, with no word of relief. Fearful at the thought of spending several more years on Earth, he decides to make himself a millionaire to escape, by secretly mining gold in the Rocky Mountains. However, the gold is surrounded by uranium deposits that make Psychlo mining impossible, so Terl captures Jonnie to mine the gold. After the last teleportation of gold to Psychlo, led by Jonnie, the humans use the Psychlos' own weapons against them and regain control of Earth. Like all good heroes, Johnnie has saved the Earth. There's a bit more to it than that. It's a very long book - more than 1,000 pages in paperback!

In December 1980, two months after he completed "Battlefield Earth", Hubbard told fellow Scientologists that "I was a bit disgusted with the way the psychologists and brain surgeons mess people up so I wrote a fiction story based in part on the consequences that could occur if the shrinks continued to do it."

Written in the style of the pulp fiction era the novel was Hubbard's first openly science fiction novel since his pulp magazine days of the 1940s, and was being promoted by Hubbard's agents as his "return" to science fiction after a long hiatus.

So, this was the opportunity Trevor brought to us - whether his previous employers knew nothing about it or simply didn't want to know, I never found out.

The 'agents' were called Author Services, based in LA, and the head honcho turned out to be one Norman Starkey who we met together with a couple of British 'assistants' who were based at the Scientologists' headquarters near East Grinstead. All went well at this initial meeting; Norman, a large, bluff man in his forties, seemed to accept our brand new company status and may have even considered it an advantage. Contracts were exchanged and the heavy manuscript delivered. Norman left to take his flight back to LA leaving us with the two lads from East Grinstead to oversee the day-to-day business.

Our first task was to set a publishing date for the hardback; the paperback version would come later. Whilst there was no budget for a heavyweight publicity campaign, nevertheless, to achieve the sort of sales that Norman wanted, it was important to make a serious impression on the book trade. We told the lads at East Grinstead what we wanted to do by way of promotion and they agreed to share the additional costs with us.

At this stage everything seemed to be in order. I was quite prepared to give the Scientologists the benefit of the doubt, regardless of what I had heard and read. They seemed pleasant enough, although it was a little unnerving to be working with people who appeared to be slavishly towing some transatlantic party line, which we mere mortals found difficult to comprehend. Probably more out of curiosity than necessity, I found myself wanting to know more about this so-called religion and, before long, was invited down to East Grinstead to find out.

I had passed their UK headquarters many times. It was situated south of the town; an impressive Georgian mansion called Saint Hill Manor, formerly owned by the Maharajah of Jaipur and situated in lovely parkland grounds. Hubbard had purchased Saint Hill in

1959, and made it his worldwide headquarters declaring it to be the 'organization' by which all other organizations would be measured.

Without going into any great detail about Scientology (if you are interested you can find more than you would ever want to know on the internet), suffice to say that he described the religious aims of Scientology thus: "A civilization without insanity, without criminals and without war, where the able can prosper and honest beings can have rights, and where man is free to rise to greater heights." Lofty and worthwhile, indeed.

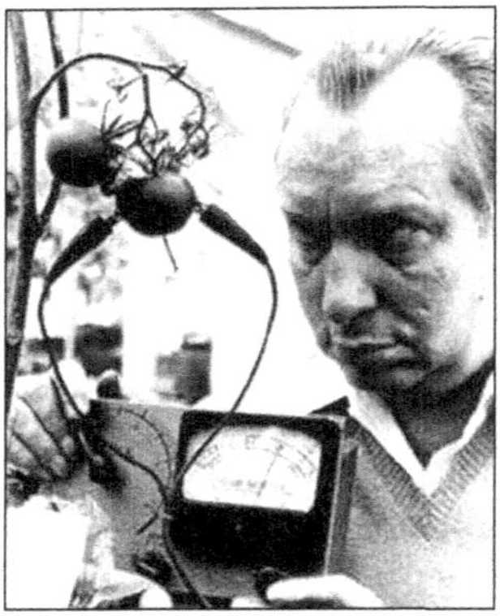

On my arrival at Saint Hill, I was met by a couple of young men in sailor suits - the 'uniform' for scientologists on duty as I later found out, apparently explained by the fact that RH had founded his 'religion' on a ship. All Scientology churches built after Hubbard's death include a corporate-style office set aside for Hubbard's reincarnation. It was to this room that I was taken by my new 'friends'. The room was a good size but sparsely furnished, containing a large mahogany desk and a captain's chair, with a plaque on the desk bearing LRH's name, and a pad of paper with a pen for him to continue writing novels when he returned. There was also a strange looking contraption that looked like an old voltmeter. They explained that this was an E-meter, one of LRH's greatest inventions and a fundamental tool of the trade - in particular for 'auditing' new members.

I later found out that the E-Meter was similar in mechanism to the commonly used polygraph or lie detector used by police forces all over the world, which measures variations in skin response that can be highly sensitive to emotions. Fear, anger, being startled or disoriented and sexual feelings are among the responses that account for the changes picked up by the E-Meter. One account tells about Hubbard using the E-meter to determine whether or not fruits can experience pain, as in his 1968 assertion that tomatoes "scream when sliced." I also discovered that Hubbard had not invented it - although he probably did devise his rather specialized use for it!

I was given the 'tourist' version that day which, I have to say, was not an uninteresting experience. I came away better informed but with absolutely no intention of getting more deeply involved with these people than was absolutely necessary to succeed at the job in hand - namely, to make a success of "Battlefield Earth". Fortunately, Trevor knew his job and before long the hardback was out and in the shops.

Sales took off pretty well. Reviews were mixed but, unusually, it didn't seem to make any difference. In fact, to sell nearly 10,000 copies of a hardback in the UK at launch is considered very good indeed. This we managed with comparative ease. However, far from being pleased as we had expected, our friends at Saint Hill suddenly became very engaged in the project. The first sign of this was when they told us they had imported a couple of eight-foot tall 'Terls' from LA and wanted us to organize 'personal' appearances for them at major towns and cities all over the country. Quite apart from the scale and cost of setting up such an operation, we advised them that such activity would be far more appropriate to support the forthcoming launch of the paperback which would, of course, have much greater appeal to the mass market and at a correspondingly lower price. To be honest, we had been surprised at the rapid sales for the hardback. Science fiction was not hugely popular at the time and to get a sci-fi book into the hardback best-seller list was pretty unusual in itself, let alone so rapidly. Still a success is a success and we weren't too concerned about the whys and wherefores.

That was when we got our next surprise. Apparently (our friends from Saint Hall told us smugly), a directive had gone out from LA Org telling all scientologists based in the UK to go out and buy ten copies each. This is why the book had sold so well - it had nothing to do with us or our marketing efforts! Now, they wanted us to do our bit and promote the book city by city - in other words, start to make "Battlefield Earth" the best-selling hardback of all time! Frankly, we were not too impressed either with the content or tone of their demands. It all smacked of eccentricity bordering on fanaticism. Still, it was early days, and we continued to give them the benefit of the doubt. So, without any great conviction, we approached some friends who ran an established and successful PR and events business and rowed them in to handle Terl's nationwide promotional tour.

Then we received another invitation. "Battlefield Earth" was going to become a major Hollywood film starring John Travolta, himself a committed Scientologist and we were invited to LA to meet the producers and sketch out a joint marketing approach. This sounded like fun and Trevor and I decided to go. When it came to it, however, it emerged that we were expected to pick up our own travel and accommodation costs - so the 'invitation' was not quite as generous as we had at first assumed! Nevertheless, we decided to put four days aside (including a weekend) and make the trip - if only to meet Mr Travolta!

When we had checked in to the rather modest hotel they had booked for us in LA - apparently not far from the 'Org' - there was a message from Norman Starkey telling us we would be collected for dinner at 7pm - which gave us an hour for a quick shower and change of clothes. Soon after that we were sitting in the back of a large black limo with tinted windows heading for - well, frankly we didn't know.

It turned out to be in a smallish dining room at the Scientologists' headquarters. The dinner was so bizarre that I can only recall it sketchily. Present were Trevor and I, Norman Starkey, a middle-aged couple (who were introduced as the producer of the film and his wife) and a young lady who was simply addressed by her Christian name. That made six of us. The large round table was set for eight. Just then a waitress arrived with two sashes, which she draped ceremoniously on the two empty chairs - one carrying the name of L.Ron Hubbard, the other, his wife, Mary Sue. Of Mr Travolta there was no sign.

Little of substance was discussed over dinner, other than Norman again relating that "Battlefield Earth" was undoubtedly one of the greatest-ever works of science fiction and how, together, we were all going to make the book and the film a huge worldwide success, amassing our own fortunes in the process. No-one else said very much at all and it seemed to me that it had been simply another opportunity to regurgitate the 'positive-thinking' propaganda to which we had been subjected already - although I got the impression that the film producer might have been hearing much of this for the first time. An uneventful evening that concluded with the film producer inviting us all round to his house for lunch the following day.

Credit where credit's due, he laid on a good Sunday lunch. We arrived at his house around noon - a pleasant enough residence situated in a Hollywood suburb, but by no means the sort of mansion you might associate with a top film producer. The food and drink was arranged as a help-yourself buffet and, again, it was the same six people with a couple of newcomers who were introduced by the producer as his development executives assigned to the project. In fact, he made a beeline for me, keen to discover how our relationship with Norman and the Scientologists was going. I told him it was early days but, as far as I could tell, things were going okay. He enquired what I thought of the book and I replied honestly that although it was not my personal cup of tea, as science fiction went, it was a good enough read and excellent value at over 1,000 pages. In turn, he explained that he was primarily in the business of developing projects to the point where he would hope to sell them on to a major studio. Apparently there was a good living to be made out of developing movies in Hollywood without ever making one! I asked him if he was a Scientologist himself. He said he wasn't and had concluded that Norman and his colleagues believed they would have more success in the wider commercial market by contracting people from outside of their 'church' - the exception in this case being John Travolta, who was a big star in his own right and, despite being a Scientologist, a huge asset to have attached to the project. I asked him whether he had a script yet and he explained that his team was working on the adaptation as we spoke. We exchanged a few other pleasantries and then were interrupted by yet another of Norman Starkey's motivational addresses.

The afternoon meandered on until it was time for us to leave and return to our hotel. There had been no discussion whatsoever about a joint marketing plan or anything else and, despite Norman's enthusiasm, I knew enough about the film business to guess that the film of "Battlefield Earth" was many years away. We caught the plane home the following day.

Back in London, sales of the hardback continued to go well with the provincial Terl promotions picking up a lot of coverage in local press. It was time to start planning the publication of the paperback which we were confident would sell well on the back of the hardback launch. This is when things started to go awry. Our two young contacts from East Grinstead had been told by LA that we were not to proceed with the paperback until sales of the hardback reached 25,000 copies. Trevor explained that this was as good as impossible in the UK; anything over 10,000 copies was a huge success - it was the paperback which would generate the much larger numbers, quite possibly 50,000 to 100,000 copies, depending upon, amongst other things, the marketing spend. Well, they wouldn't accept his advice and we reached a stalemate. As a last resort we reminded them that we had a contract with Author Services, which included the publication of the paperback version as well as the hardback. There were no conditions attached, no references to the paperback launch being dependent on the sales of the hardback, and we were keen to get the paperback out in time for the holiday market. Of course, if they were unhappy with the situation they had the option to buy us out of our contract - an option we were quite happy to discuss as we really did not want to continue without goodwill on both sides.

A few days went past and then an extraordinary thing happened. We were working happily away in our offices one afternoon when, without any warning, there was a commotion at reception. The next thing I saw was a group of people making their way towards Trevor's office, which was next to mine. The little procession was headed up by Mr Starkey and included his two sidekicks from Saint Hill and a tallish man I had never seen before. This was all unannounced and totally unexpected. Clearly, our receptionist had managed to alert Trevor to the fact that these people had barged in because, as I emerged from my office, Trevor was coming out of his, all smiles, to greet them. There were no smiles from the other side, however, and we repaired to the boardroom for what was clearly going to be a confrontation.

Norman's attitude was bullying and aggressive. The tallish man was introduced as the lawyer acting on behalf of Author Services and his presence was explained by the fact that they wanted the paperback rights back without paying us a penny. Their case was that Quadrant Books were incompetent, had no clout in the marketplace and the success of the hardback was entirely due to their efforts and not ours. In fact, if we didn't agree to give them back the paperback rights they would counter sue us for negligence, lack of best endeavors, misrepresentation, you name it, etc, etc.

After suffering two or three tirades of abuse, I looked at my colleagues seeing that nothing good was going to come out of this - not to mention that we really didn't want to persevere with any kind of future relationship with these people. We signed the papers they wanted, except for one - a further agreement which bound us to never say anything nasty or detrimental about Scientology, Scientologists, their founder L Ron Hubbard or our experiences in dealing with them. It was a 'gagging' order. Again they were insistent, saying that this was a routine part of their way of handling disputes of this nature. On the presumption that their experience of handling such disputes was extensive, I could see why. Anyway, we signed that, too, under some duress and, until now, I have abided by it. I leave it to you to decide whether what I have written is detrimental or not.

We never heard from them again - although curiosity led me to pick up some of what subsequently transpired. "Battlefield Earth" went on to be published by the Church of Scientology's own publishing companies, Bridge Publications and Galaxy Press. The film finally got made (needless to say with the original producer kicked into touch in the same way that we were) but not for a further twenty years. It was released in 2000 with John Travolta playing Terl, as he was by then far too old to play the young hero. It was met with appallingly bad reviews and rapidly faded into obscurity. The book was re-released at the same time to capitalize on the publicity the film received.

It had mixed reviews again, although much better than the film! *The Economist*, for instance, called it "an unsubtle saga, atrociously written, windy and out of control" while the science fiction magazine *Analog* criticized it as "a wish-fulfillment fantasy wholly populated by the most one-dimensional of cardboard characters." Other critics pointed to the book's slipshod writing, such as "the ineffably klutzy destruction of the planet of the evil Psychlos by atomic bombs, which turns it into a 'radioactive sun'. *Punch* sarcastically commended Hubbard's "excellent understanding of evil impulses, particularly deviousness, which helps with the plot, and he is well-enough aware of his weaknesses not to dwell upon frailties like love, generosity and compassion." British sci-fi critic David Langford, after criticizing the plot, style and scientific implausibility, concluded: "From this, 'Battlefield Earth' may sound almost worth looking at for its sheer laughable badness. No. It's dreadful and tedious beyond endurance".

Despite this, "Battlefield Earth" went to the top of the New

York Times Bestseller List. It came as no surprise to us, of course, when not long afterwards, stories emerged of a reported Church of Scientology book-buying campaign mounted to ensure that the book would appear on the bestseller lists. The *New York Times* reported: "two Scientology organizations bought a total of 30,000 copies of the book at discount directly from the publisher, apparently to sell or to give to current or prospective Scientology members." Booksellers told the newspaper that they had seen unusual purchasing patterns, including individuals buying as many as 800 copies of the book at a time. It was suggested that "church members could be trying to buy themselves a bestseller in order to obtain a large paperback or movie sale, both of which are often contingent on a book's first becoming a bestseller in hard cover.'

So, what would founder Mr Hubbard thought about all this? He had achieved success beyond his wildest dreams - wealth, fame and the adulation of thousands of devoted adherents. Yet for the last five years of his life, Hubbard, a virtual prisoner of his own paranoia, lived as a recluse in self-imposed exile, on a ranch in the desert of Creston, California. Surrounded by a handful of trusted aides, he handed over the running of his multi-million dollar empire to a chosen few. Even his wife was cut off and never saw him again.

In fact, few did. Fearing indictment in the Snow White case (an attempt by the Church of Scientology to eradicate anti-Scientology material from public files by covert and illegal means), Hubbard fled to the desert in the early 80s, leaving behind his role as de facto controller of the Scientology empire and taking with him only a handful of close aides, mostly those now-grown messengers from the Commodore's Messenger Org, who had, in some cases literally, grown up under Hubbard's Machiavellian tutelage, and became his emissaries to the empire he oversaw.

Of these former messengers turned executives, the future head of Scientology, David Miscavige (originally LRH's personal photographer) was amongst those angling to take control of the church upon its founder's death. But despite chronic ill health, the founder lived on, leaving Miscavige - and others, including Norman Starkey - in a state of flux. They controlled the church but their authority came only through their appointed - some say self-appointed - role as the controllers of LRH's communication with the world. As LRH himself may have written, he who controls communications controls the game. But events were spinning out of control for these so-called young rulers of Scientology.

It was only later that the details of Hubbard's death unfurled. On January 24th 1986, under circumstances that can at best be perceived as 'suspicious', he died. Although his condition had been steadily deteriorating for years, the coroner noted that there were irregularities surrounding his death, including the presence in his body of vast quantities of Vistaril, a powerful anti-psychotic drug. Just days before Hubbard's death, his personal physician, a Scientologist called Gene Denk, left for a gambling vacation in Las Vegas with some of Hubbard's top aides. By the time they returned, there was nothing to be done. Hubbard had died, and the battle for control of his legacy, which had been simmering for years, took centre stage.

He left behind a vast corporate empire, including millions of dollars' worth of copyrights and trademarks, as well as a personal fortune rumoured to be in the hundreds of millions. Rumour, though, is all we have - the vast portion of Hubbard's riches were buried far inside the CoS ledgers, safe from the prying eyes of the IRS, which had been threatening an audit of Hubbard for years, right up until his death. But even leaving aside his personal fortune, Hubbard's legacy was rich - and there was no shortage of people eager to take a cut.

The day before Hubbard died, his will was redrafted. The new executor, who would oversee the transfer of all Hubbard's intellectual property to a trust known as Author's Family Trust-B, and from there, into a newly created vessel, the Church of Spiritual Technology, was our friend Norman Starkey.

Starkey became Hubbard's executor, and David Miscavige took the reins of power as effortlessly as he had disposed of his rivals to the throne in previous internal skirmishes. There was no explanation for this last minute changing of the guard and it was not long before those most likely to raise questions about the new regime - Hubbard's old retainers, including Pat Broeker - had disappeared from the eye of the storm as though they had never existed. With them out of the picture, there was no one to pose a significant threat to Miscavige, and, like one born with the divine right of kings, he took his place as titular head of the church, highest ranking officer in the 'Sea Org' and ruler of the Scientology empire without firing a single shot.

He remains there to this day. Oh, and another thing - in all the material I have researched about the Scientologists and "Battlefield Earth" (book and film), there isn't a single mention of Quadrant Books Ltd. It is as if we were erased from history. Which I don't mind one little bit.

Eric Morley

I was a great admirer of Eric Morley whose deeds transcended his reputation. Like many people who find themselves in the public eye, Eric is remembered mainly for creating Miss World - the televised beauty pageant that held us glued to our seats during the seventies and eighties. In fact, there was much more to him, as I discovered during the ten or so years I worked alongside him in our charitable endeavours.

Eric was an impresario and highly successful businessman and his life was a prime example of someone from a disadvantaged background making it to the very top of the tree - something he never allowed himself to forget. Orphaned at the age of 11, Eric attended Whitstable Grammar School in Kent followed by the Royal Naval Training Ship 'Exmouth; and an Army school, where he played the French horn in the band. Later, in the Royal Fusiliers, he reached the rank of captain. He was one of the last out of Dunkirk.

After demob in 1946, he got a job as head of publicity in a small company called Mecca. Six years later he was general manager of Mecca Dancing and soon after was made a director. Finally, as CEO, he built up the Mecca empire into an entertainment giant and became a household name all over the world when he appeared on stage at the climax of a Miss World contest announcing the winners "in reverse order".

The Miss World competition had its roots in the fashion shows organized by Mecca, culminating in a bathing beauty contest devised by Eric in 1951 to tie in with the Festival of Britain. After that it became an annual event. Eric was revered by Mecca's 15,000 employees for whom he had set up a generous bonus scheme; but others found him difficult to take. Rumbustious, hard-working and abrasive, not even his admirers considered him modest. "I can frankly say I'm gifted with a bit of brain," he said once, "and I'm the sort of man who'll walk in where angels fear to tread."

In 1978 he was effectively forced to leave Mecca, of which he was then chairman, after falling out with the parent company, Grand Metropolitan. He left with an agreement that he could continue as "Mr World". Rights to the show were later sold to Belhaven Brewery, where Morley was joint chairman from 1979 to 1984 and later in 1983 to a company owned by the Morleys.

Together with his wife Julia, herself an ex-Miss World, he presided over a competition that was watched by more than 20 million viewers in Britain at its peak in the seventies and eighties. But, even back then, it was dogged by protestors angry at what they regarded as the exploitative nature of the competition. In fact, in one memorable incident at The Royal Albert Hall, compère, Bob Hope, was hit by flour bombs thrown by protesters as he introduced the contestants. Eric's reply to his critics was: "If it is shameful to women, then the best thing they can do is turn it off".

But despite these troubles, the competition survived raising millions for charity in the process. In the end, however, the protesters prevailed and 'Miss World' disappeared from terrestrial TV screens and from the UK, heading instead to a string of exotic overseas locations. Later, for a brief period, Channel 5 brought the competition back, pushing the pageant temporarily into the spotlight again.

Eric also created the equally successful TV phenomenon 'Come Dancing', the ballroom dancing competition show that ran on and off on the BBC from 1949 to 1998, becoming one of television's longest-running shows. Early episodes were broadcast from regional ballroom studios with professional dancers on hand to offer teaching. Later the format changed to become a competition, with regional teams going head to head for the coveted trophy. The many presenters over the years included Peter West, McDonald Hobley, Charles Nove, Terry Wogan, Brian Johnston, Angela Rippon, Michael Aspel, Noel Edmonds, David Jacobs, Judith Chalmers and Pete Murray. The Morleys insisted on strict family values being preserved by the contestants and the light banter between the presenters made the show strangely irresistible viewing.

In 2004 (four years after Eric had died), a re-launched celebrity version entitled 'Strictly Come Dancing', hosted by Bruce Forsyth and Tess Daly and broadcast at Saturday peaktime on BBC One, became hugely popular. The title is a pastiche of the titles of both the 1992 Australian film 'Strictly Ballroom' and 'Come Dancing'. The format of the newer show has been successfully exported to other countries under the name 'Dancing with the Stars'.

Eric was a loyal supporter of the Variety Club for forty years, and was a past international president. In fact, as I remember him saying one evening when being introduced to a new group of members: "I'm past Chief Barker, past International President, past Chair of Fundraising, past Chair of Appeals - in fact, past everything."

By the time I knew him he was well into his seventies, but as spry and energetic as a forty year old. He was still running Miss World from his offices in Golden Square; cycling there every morning, including Saturdays, from his rather grand home in Dulwich. By then much of his time was spent on his charity work; not only Variety Club, where he was heavily involved in raising funds for the Variety Club Children's Hospital at Kings' at Denmark Hill not far from where he lived, but also the Duke of Edinburgh's Outward Bound Trust which he had been instrumental in setting up in and subsequently becoming Chairman. Both thrive to this day. The Variety Club Children's Hospital, which I have visited many times, remains one of the UK's leading children's units, treating and caring for more than 40,000 sick children every year from all over the UK who come to receive the highest quality medical care at the hospital. The unit also provides a general pediatric and pediatric surgical service to the local community, as well as neonatal intensive care for very sick and preterm babies. The Outward Bound Trust, now with the Duke as its Patron, continues to flourish using demanding outdoor activities to help develop young people from all walks of life.

I worked alongside Eric on a number of his projects and was always impressed by his ability to get the best out of people, as well as his powers of delegation and attention to detail. It is hard to imagine anyone who grasped the opportunities provided by e-mail more keenly than Eric. In fact, if you were amongst his circle, it was not unusual to receive half a dozen e-mails a day from him as he argued some point or other, usually managing to win everyone round to his point-of-view - and this was long before the rest of us had got used to the potential of this fantastic invention. He was a man who led naturally and others were content to follow.

I remember once taking him out to lunch, just around the corner from his office. By now he was over eighty and it was beginning to show. As always, we had an engaging and entertaining lunch. Over the coffee I asked him why he drove himself at such a relentless pace when he had a young wife and family and a beautiful home he could be enjoying. He hesitated for a moment before saying: "You're quite right, of course. I should have stopped years ago. Now, it's too late. I'll just have to go on like this until I drop." I am not sure but there may just have been a hint of remorse in that remark.

Not long afterwards his health started to deteriorate and he admitted himself to the London Clinic in Devonshire Place. I went to see him and announced myself at reception. "Oh, yes, Mr Burley, we are expecting you - you've come to see Sir Eric Morley, haven't you?" I assented and was given directions to his room. When I arrived, I noticed that on the door was a nameplate again saying 'Sir Eric Morley'. It seemed entirely appropriate and why he was never awarded a knighthood in real life we shall never know. No-one could have deserved one more, nor done more, both to keep the nation entertained and to raise huge sums to good causes. Despite his Royal connections, perhaps he was simply in the wrong trade.

Having partially recovered from illness, he went home, only to collapse again a few weeks later. On his own at the time, he must have somehow managed to raise the alarm and was rushed by paramedics to his beloved Kings College Hospital for whom he had worked tirelessly for more than thirty years. Ironically, unrecognized, he lay in a corridor for several hours awaiting a bed, which is where his wife, Julia, found him having returned from a prior engagement. He died some hours later. *The Telegraph* described him as "one of the most successful entertainment entrepreneurs in the world."

Eric Morley was an unashamed Thatcherite. He once said: "I would do anything for that woman." He also had political ambitions of his own and came within a whisker of entering parliament himself. In the 1979 General Election he slashed the Labour 7,500 majority of then-Attorney General Sam Silkin to a mere 122 in his seat in Dulwich, south London. Days later he remarked: "Unlike Sam Silkin, I didn't go to Dulwich College and to Cambridge. I went to the college of hard knocks and last week I received my doctorate."

Even Briefer Encounters

You will have gathered by now that most of those I have written about in this book I have come to know through spending time with them, usually through business or, in the case of some, through repeated social contact. There are a few, however, who have made a lasting impression on me (good or bad) as a result of a single meeting or even a chance encounter.

A good example is **Sarah Ferguson**, Duchess of York, who I sat next at a businessmen's dinner in Leeds when she was presenting the awards. It was not long after she had separated from Prince Andrew and she was working hard to earn a living to pay back a sizeable mountain of debt that she had run up when the Queen had unceremoniously removed her from the Civil List. No doubt she was receiving a fee for her services to the Leeds business community that day. Why not?

Again, contrary to the image of her that the media were portraying at the time, I found her to be excellent company; chatty, vivacious, open, frank and entirely without affectation of any kind. She had not had an easy time of it - either with the Royal Family or the press - but by the time I met her she was making a pretty good fist of getting on with her life. In fact, she described herself as a writer, charity patron, public speaker, film producer and television personality. Plenty of options to choose from you might think and I have no doubt she was having a go at all of them. It was in the latter category that she was keen to seek my advice since she had obviously done her research and already knew of my involvement in that industry.

She told me that she had just returned from the States where she had landed a deal with one of the US broadcasters to host a TV interview series. She was unhappy with the format that the producers had come up with. Apparently they wanted her to conduct interviews with a number of people she didn't feel comfortable with - including the former first lady of the Philippines, Imelda Marcos, better known for her vast collection of shoes than her contribution to the betterment of her fellow countrymen. Should she do as they asked, she wanted to know, or stand up to them and risk losing the series altogether? I asked how many times in the past had she gone along with what other people wanted her to do, perhaps against her better judgement. "Too often", she answered, "I never really had the self-confidence to say 'no'". I said that maybe this would be a good time to start. If she felt uneasy in the studio talking to someone she didn't like, the chances are it would show onscreen, the interview would be unsuccessful and the show would fail. After all, she was not a professional journalist; her attraction to the broadcaster was her fame as a member of the British aristocracy, and the fact that on the other side of the Atlantic they love a princess. She thought about this for a few seconds. "So, I should tell them that I want approval of the people I get to interview, then?" she asked. "Absolutely", I replied. "Don't fall into the trap of thinking they know better than you do. They don't. It will be perceived as your show, not theirs. Put your foot down, they won't take the show away from you."

After the dinner she was being photographed, no doubt for the next morning's tabloids, and I didn't get the chance to say goodbye. I returned home and didn't think any more about it. Three or four weeks later I received a letter from her thanking me for the advice. She had followed it and, as I predicted, the producers hadn't cancelled the show. The series was going ahead but with a list of interviewees which she had approved. It was a nice letter, signed 'Fergie'.

Since then she has been getting on with things, working hard, raising her daughters and gradually recovering from the public ridicule heaped upon her as a result of her escapades in the nineties.

Sometimes we need to give people time to grow up.

* * *

WE purchased an Andy Warhol once - or at least we thought we had.

I'd bumped into **Jeffrey Archer** a few times at various events and had the odd chat with him. He always seemed very focused and a bit detached, but, other than that, a perfectly pleasant, well-mannered man. In fact, despite what happened subsequently, leading to a spell at Her Majesty's pleasure in HMP Belmarsh, I don't think anyone ever accused him of being rude or discourteous. Certainly, the fragrant Mary stood by him during that most difficult period, and she seems far too intelligent and lovely to have shared her entire married life with an out-and-out rogue.

One also has to bear in mind his extraordinarily successful literary output, although I know there are those who would question the word 'literary' in this context. Nonetheless, his twenty books and novels have sold at least 250 million copies worldwide so far and he shows no sign of stopping! Furthermore, it is hard not to have a grudging admiration for people who, in the words of the song, 'pick themselves up, brush themselves down, and start all over again'. Archer was bankrupt when he took up writing.

He was well known for owning an extensive collection of modern art, including a number of Warhols, which he eventually decided to sell off. We had received an invitation to attend the sale, which was to be conducted at a Mayfair gallery. On our arrival, we were greeted by Jeffrey, champagne in hand, who encouraged us to take a leisurely look around. It was a smallish gallery and rather hot and overcrowded, which made viewing awkward, nevertheless, we soon alighted on a prominently displayed limited edition Warhol print, one of that familiar series of multi-coloured silk-screen pictures of Marilyn Monroe. Although expensive, we were furnishing our London apartment at the time, so we decided to make an offer. We tracked Jeffrey down and he accepted without hesitation saying that we getting a 'real bargain' but, then again, why shouldn't we? He was happy if we were. He pointed us in the direction of the gallery manager who, he said, would take our details and mark the picture as sold. All very nice.

The manager immediately went to put a little red sticker on the picture, which, he said, would remain on exhibition until the end of the week. We explained that we were about to go abroad for a week, so would it be okay if we collected it on our return? "Of course," he replied, "you can pay for it on collection. See you when you get back." Excellent.

As soon as were back, I telephoned the gallery only to be told that they had sold the picture to someone else. No amount of argument got me anywhere, so, in the end, we decided to leave it at that, consoling ourselves in the knowledge we had saved a few thousand pounds. But I would still rather have had the picture.

The other time we met him was at a small birthday party held at a hotel just off Marble Arch in honour of our great friend, Robin Moffat. Robin had been my family doctor as a child, had looked after me all my life, and presided over the delivery of all three of our daughters at home. A truly great guy. There were only about twenty people present, including, to our surprise, Lord Archer. Apparently,

Robin had met him briefly at an event a day or so earlier, got chatting and ended up inviting him to his birthday party - never expecting him to turn up. Well, he did, complete with a box full of copies of his new book! It was also at the time he was campaigning to be Mayor of London, so I presumed he must have been putting in appearances at as many gatherings, large and small, as he could.

Consequently, when Robin formally introduced his Lordship over coffee, we all expected a semi-political address coupled with some hefty promotion for the book. Again, the enigmatic Jeffrey had other ideas. His speech, delivered with great modesty and eloquence, was a birthday tribute to Robin, a man who he had never met until a few days earlier, painstakingly researched to make sure there was nothing that the rest of us who had known Robin all our lives could take exception to. It was a masterful performance with only a very few brief references to himself. Why did he go to all that trouble? I have no idea. But I don't suppose I am the only one to have been mystified by this contradictory and unpredictable character.

* * *

THE restaurateur, **Peter Langan**, was another enigma. A self-confessed alcoholic, he prided himself on being living proof that an alcoholic could function successfully enough to run a well-ordered and profitable business. He had a point. Despite him spending many a night at the local police station rather than going home drunk and disorderly, no-one could deny the success of Langans Brasserie, the Parisian-style café/restaurant opposite the Ritz which, by the mid-eighties, had become London's most fashionable haunt for stars like Elizabeth Taylor, Cassius Clay, Mick Jagger, Jack Nicholson - to name but a few.

Apart from the abundance of artwork, the carefully mis-matched lamps and furniture and the lack of a dress code, one of the attractions to its regular customers was the proprietor's rudeness and effrontery. There was no-one he wouldn't cut down to size, no-one with whom he wouldn't trade impolite remarks. When the actor Mel Smith died, Sir Michael Caine, Langan's longstanding investor and partner, said: "Mel died with a dream unfulfilled - to portray Peter Langan whose signature dish was insults."

Although many would disagree, personally, I always thought Langans was overrated with its oversimplified menu and exorbitant pricing, but you couldn't be in the advertising industry in the eighties without sometimes finding yourself there, for better or for worse - and not always through your own choice.

One day I was reading a copy of 'Campaign' and came across a story about an advertising agency called C. P. Vernon, a well-known and old-established business which in its heyday had held down some very big clients indeed. Apparently, they were in financial difficulties and I wondered whether there was any possibility that what was left of the business might come up for sale. Although my company specialised mainly in promotional and below-the-line work and was smaller than theirs, nevertheless we were highly profitable and the acquisition of an above-the-line business would be a good fit and a quick way to expand. I didn't know the people at Vernons at all, but that didn't stop me picking up the 'phone and asking to speak to their managing director. I was put through to a secretary who explained that Miss J (I won't use her full name) was not in the office but if I would kindly explain the nature of my call she would arrange for her to return it later. With nothing to lose, I said I was interested in buying their company and would be pleased to talk further about it.

As soon as Miss J's' name was mentioned, I knew who she was. She was known as 'Mo' and was one of those strident females, typical of the mid-eighties media world, who had clawed her way up the ladder through a mixture of good, old-fashioned chutzpah and an appetite for self-promotion. She was well-known for her frequent appearances in the trade media wearing outlandish outfits accompanied by equally controversial quotes and comments. She was a journalist's dream and equal to any male counterpart who might take her on. A tough cookie, you might think. The only question was why was the agency she headed up going into liquidation? Still, I had nothing against the young lady personally, so awaited her call with interest.

When it came it was everything you might expect - effusive, flattering, even flirty. We were to meet at Langan's where she and the owner, the marvellous Peter, were on close terms and where she assured me he would make certain we enjoyed the comfort of her 'usual' table. What's more, lunch was on her. I was beginning to look forward to it.

The day came and I dutifully arrived at the Brasserie dead on 12.30 and, having announced that I was a guest of Miss J, was shown to a pleasant table by the window. She was, of course, ten minutes late and made a grand (if somewhat wasted) entrance as the restaurant that day was actually not very full. As I recall she was dressed all in black, with a short skirt and glossy high heels, which matched her jet black Sassoon-coiffed hair. Her sole accessory was a transparent Perspex briefcase, containing her designer Filo-Fax (de rigeuer at the time), a small purse-like make-up bag and, as far as I could see, nothing else. I stood as she approached and was greeted like a long-lost friend with kisses on both cheeks.

Conversation was loud, relentless and one-sided - did I know so-and-so (mostly, no), was I at such-and-such (definitely no) and was I a member of some fashionable club (wouldn't be seen dead there, but that's not what I said). I was beginning to think I might be a disappointment to her. In fact, I wasn't sure whether to feel sorry for her or for myself, anticipating the likelihood of another hour of this nonsense. During all of this she was constantly looking over my shoulders to see who else might arriving, avoiding any reference to the purpose of our meeting. Then suddenly, she became very excited indeed. "Its Peter!" she gasped, waving frantically to someone in a far corner, "I'll get him over so that you can meet him, we're such good friends, Peter and I".

And there he was, shambling over towards us in an open-necked checked shirt, a rather soiled brown jacket and a pair of grey flannels. It wasn't yet 1pm but he looked as though he was already two sheets to the wind.

"Ah, the lovely Mo!" he drawled solicitously in his Irish dialect as she bathed in the compliment.

"Hello, darling," she responded, her voice having alarmingly dropped half an octave, "this is Pip, he's been dying to meet you, haven't you, my love?" I nodded co-operatively.

Now, of course, Mr Langan had no way of telling who I was or what my relationship might be with this decorous creature. I could have been her current boyfriend for all he knew. He turned to me: "Isn't she gorgeous, Pip, a lovely woman, indeed, you're so lucky. And do you know she's got the largest c--------s I've ever seen". With which he shambled off, mumbling: "Enjoy your lunch" as he went.

Well, the effect on Mo was catatonic. She turned bright scarlet, started to tremble, tears appeared in her eyes and she buried her face in her hands. Collapse of stout party. I didn't know what to say or do. What Peter had said was, of course, unforgivable, but, he was a drunk and she must have known that - as Michael Caine had said, insults were his stock-in-trade. But, much as other clients might have been game for his jibes, this one, clearly, was beyond the pale for Mo. For all I know, despite her bravado, she might have had a strict Jewish upbringing and never heard language like that before. I thought the best thing I could do was excuse myself from the table on the pretext of a visit to the gents, thus giving her the chance to collect herself. When I returned there was no sign of her. By now Mr Langan was back at his table near to the kitchen, demolishing a bottle of red wine.

"She appears to have left," he shouted across the restaurant, "it must have been something I said."

A couple of years later in 1998 he died in a raging fire that demolished his house in Essex. He was forty-seven. There was much speculation that he had started it himself. "Must have gone up a treat", was the rather unsympathetic comment from one of his most famous clients.

* * *

MANY would agree that the greatest Hollywood leading man of them all was **Cary Grant.** Apart from his looks (how do you think George Clooney compares?), he possessed great charm and, without attempting to be an 'action' hero in the same vein as his contemporaries such as Kirk Douglas or John Wayne, nevertheless, he had great physical presence onscreen, an ease of movement, flawless timing and a natural sophistication which was uniquely his own. And he was English!

However, as if often the case, the character he portrayed bore little resemblance to reality. After an unhappy childhood, the handsome young 16-year old Bristolian made his way to the States and performed as a stilt walker and acrobat under his real name, Archie Leach. Soon, he was appearing onstage in New York and it wasn t long before he travelled to Hollywood to seek stardom in the movies. His film debut was in 1925, which is when the studio encouraged him to change his name to Cary Grant, the name he kept for the rest of his life. His career in films lasted until 1966, by which time he had made 72 films, after which he retired from movies at the relatively young age of 62.

He first foray into the world of business was when he joined the board of Faberge, the American fragrance company famous for it's Brut aftershave. By all accounts this position was not honorary as some had assumed; Grant regularly attended meetings and his mere appearance at a product launch would almost certainly guarantee its success. The position also permitted use of a private plane, which he could use to fly to see his daughter wherever her mother, Dyan Cannon, was working.

It was at a Faberge launch event in the West End that I met him. He looked incredibly fit, tanned and in excellent shape. I was one of the few males present in my capacity as publisher of the trade magazine 'Beauty Counter' - this was one job I wasn't going to delegate to a member of my editorial staff! There was a bunch of consumer journalists present, mostly female, and, once he had done his duty presenting the new Faberge product, it was announced that Mr Grant would take questions from the floor. Needless to say, there was little interest in the Faberge side of things and an awful lot of questions about him, his career and colourful domestic life. At the time he was on his fourth marriage, although, in fairness, he seemed more or less settled with Ms Cannon with whom he had recently fathered a little girl. The lady journalists were anxious to find out every current detail about his marriage and his first child, no doubt seeking tomorrow's 'sensational' headline to run with the inevitable photo.

That was when I made an error. I thought he looked a little peeved and, although expertly fielding all this intrusive questioning like the past master he was, he was becoming impatient. So, I asked my question: "Mr Grant, as possibly one of the world's greatest experts on the opposite sex, how do you think women have changed during your lifetime?" Now, I should say in defense of what even now appears to be a juvenile and naïve question, that this was the seventies and there was, indeed, much going on in the world of women's rights. Whether I intended the question to elicit a response such as "I preferred women the way they were," or "I like women to be feminine and compliant," I can't honestly recall. I hadn't really thought it through. Well, for a moment you couldn't hear a pin drop, then, starting from the back of the room, came an outraged response from the ladies. I was jeered, insulted and booed, before Mr Grant came to my rescue. This is what he said: "Ladies, the young man is asking a question that is puzzling a lot of us men at the present time. My answer? Women will always be women and men will always be men whether they like it or not." And with that he left the podium.

Some years later in 1986 he was at a hotel in Iowa preparing for a public appearance, when he collapsed with a cerebral hemorrhage. His then fifth wife, Barbara Harris, unaware of what was ailing him, went to a local pharmacy to get some aspirin. That was not what he needed and he died later the same day. He was 82. The bulk of his huge estate went to Barbara and his daughter Jennifer Grant.

Like all great leading actors Cary Grant mastered the art of acting a part whilst remaining himself - a difficult trick to pull. Great leading men? - you can count them on the fingers of one hand.

* * *

FOR some years after I had sold the magazine publishing business, Tony and I carried on publishing a magazine down in Marbella. To start with we called it 'The Marbella Times' but, eventually, it metamorphosed into 'Marbella Life'. If you go to Marbella today (as we frequently do) you'll find umpteen high-gloss magazines lying around in hotel lobbies, estate agents and so on, but then, thirty years ago, we had the market to ourselves. After a brief spell when it was edited by a lady called Elisabeth Coty, a member of the famous French fragrance dynasty, we settled on a local writer - well-known for his social and business connections on the coast, called **Peter Bond.**

In fact, Peter had lived in Marbella for many years and become quite a local 'character', having mastered the art of rubbing shoulders with the multifarious types who inhabited the town in those days, stretching from exiled and dispossessed European royals and aristocrats on the one hand, to stars of stage and screen on the other and everything you can possibly imagine in between. Whether kings, commoners or crooks, everyone wanted to be a celebrity in Marbella in those days and Peter was part of their rites of passage.

He was an interesting chap, well-educated, short and dapper, with bright blue eyes and a shock of blonde hair. He had his own style, too, and was a familiar sight walking around the town with his big straw hat and raffia bag containing his papers. I never saw him carrying a briefcase and seldom behind the wheel of a car.

I once asked him what had drawn him to the Golden Mile originally. He told me it was the climate mainly, but also the opportunity to try and earn a living as a writer, which, he thought would be easier in Marbella than in the UK. Well, he seemed to have got that one right. I rather liked this 'jack-of-all-trades' approach to life, possibly because it rang true with me, too.

During the course of one of these conversations he told me that for some years he had worked as a valet for the abdicated King, Edward VIII, after he and Wallis Simpson had come to live in Marbella in the fifties. Peter explained that despite their immediate history and recent exile from the UK, the couple conducted themselves in an inordinately 'royal' manner and had quickly gathered around them a 'court' of fawning, aspiring locals. Concentrating their social activities around the newly-opened Marbella Club, they seemed to have found a Mediterranean 'haven' where past sins were quickly forgiven.

Things were much the same at home in their villa, apparently, and it intrigued me that Peter had seen all of this very much at first hand. However, he drew the line at divulging any specific recollections of them personally and refused to be drawn into criticising or condemning them. What a gentleman!

I did ask him on one occasion whether, with the benefit of hindsight, and his close acquaintanceship with them, he thought the abdication had been a good or bad thing. He thought about this for a moment and then answered: "A disastrous thing for him, but very good for the country."

He continued to edit 'Marbella Life' for the best part of the next fifteen years and that was the closest we ever got…

* * *

Richard Price is one of those 'old-fashioned' producers who recognises no boundaries between film, television and theatre, all you have to do is make sure that whatever you do is worthwhile, entertaining and produced to the highest possible standards. This he has done with great success for a very long time. And, actually, I don't think that's old fashioned at all. For twenty tears he handled all LWTs programme sales, including 'Upstairs Downstairs'; after that he went on to produce his own television shows, as well as making feature films, TV series, and producing West End musicals and plays for the National Theatre.

In the early days of Excelsior, I made it my business to get to know as many people in the business as possible. Televison and film are collaborative industries and you never know where the next co-production or development deal might come from - and, after the success of "The Darling Buds of May", there was some curiosity around as to what we might come up with next. So, one of the names on my list was Mr Price.

I met him for the first time at his offices near Oxford Street. He was welcoming and friendly and genuinely interested in what we were doing. In fact, we enjoyed a lengthy discussion about how to structure a long-form television drama series, mixing series and serial elements, which we later pioneered successfully when scripting

'A Touch of Frost'. I liked him immediately and, although very much more established than most, he was quite open about his own frustrations with broadcasters (especially the BBC) as well as the difficulty of funding the development of new projects. He pointed across the open plan office to a young woman sitting at a desk in a corner. "There's a bright girl" he said, "no experience in the business, only interested in horses, but she's got an idea for a musical that she's passionate about. So, I've given her a desk and a bit of financial support; we'll just have to wait and see whether she gets anywhere with it. If she does, then, hopefully, she'll return the compliment."

I could see that there might have been some commercial benefit to Richard in the future, but it seemed a terribly long shot and I still believe to this day that it was more important to him to encourage her youthful enthusiasm and passion than to make money out of her. I asked him what her idea for a musical was. "Something to do with Abba," he replied. "She wants to make a musical based around their songs." I looked again at the young woman talking animatedly on the 'phone. "Good luck to her," I said.

Well, the 'girl' turned out to be Judy Craymer and the musical was 'Mama Mia!', one of the highest grossing stage musicals of all time. It transpired that Richard had put up half of the development money for Catherine Johnson's script. The stage musical was then adapted to become the blockbuster film starring Meryl Streep, Colin Firth and Pierce Brosnan. A truly sensational success and one of the best examples you'll ever see of an old hand helping a younger colleague up the ladder of success. Nowadays, as with everything else, we have a name for it. Mentoring.

If that doesn't encourage young people to have a go in showbusiness, nothing will. Talk about dreaming the dream...

Acknowledgements

IN writing this book I have almost certainly omitted to give sufficient credit to my wife and family. They have been with me every step of the way and without their faith and support I would never have been able to live the life I have. From the day we married more than forty years ago, Christine gave me freedom to go off and do what I wanted, when I wanted, whilst she took care of the really important things such as bringing up the family – often with little help from me. She has also been a wise counsel, editor, proof-reader and occasional manager. I never embarked upon a new idea or project without checking it out with her first. Neither of us has enjoyed a monopoly of what's right, nor always agreed, but overall we have moved forward together and things have worked out. She has also been wonderfully enthusiastic - and looked after my health.

During the course of my jack-of-all-trades existence, we somehow managed to bring into the world three glorious, level-headed, independently minded daughters. I am tremendously proud of them and what they have achieved - even though they terrify me on occasions. I know that when they were younger they sometimes found it difficult to comprehend some of the twists and turns that happened along the way. When I sold the publishing company my middle daughter, who would have been about seven at the time, said: "But Daddy, does that mean the magazines (and she named them) have all gone?" When I told her they had, she replied: "You're mad." Perhaps she was right, but then I started up again in a different business and, as luck would have it, that worked out okay, too.

I have always believed that if you get it right seven or eight times out of ten you'll be ahead of the field. The important thing is to have the confidence to take a calculated risk in the first place. And every time you succeed, that confidence grows. You never know what you are capable of unless you try. If I have had any underlying philosophy underpinning an irregular career, that has been it.

I have never done anything I haven't enjoyed, but I am aware that for many, if not most people, this is not an option. During those years when I was commuting on the train to and from Brighton, it was hard not to observe people just ticking off the days til their retirement. As I got to know some of my fellow passengers better, many were only too happy to admit it; it was their favourite topic of conversation! Men in their fifties with another ten years to go, already planning the end of their working life, browsing the property pages for their dream retirement cottage by the sea. In a better world no-one should have to think like that. But then we don't bring up our children to follow their noses or their instincts - or, to put it more romantically, to 'dream the dream'. In fact, quite the reverse, we seem pretty keen to knock all that nonsense out of them by the time they emerge into the world - mostly, I suspect, in an illusory quest for security. What security? Surely the one lesson we should have learnt in the turbulent years around the turn of the century is that there is no such thing. Nobody has a job for life for the simple reason there aren't any. Nothing is guaranteed, no matter how much we would wish it to be. I doubt whether any of the people I have written about have spent too much time worrying about such things and, with only a very few casualties, that hasn't mattered in the end.

For me (so far) it has all stayed together; the careers, the marriage and the family, with comparatively few ups and downs. We have been lucky, worked as a team – and it isn't over yet.

Thank you for reading this book.

About the Author

Pip Burley was born and educated in Croydon and left Whitgift School in 1962. He subsequently went on to study graphic design at the London College of Printing, now the University of the Arts, at the Elephant and Castle. He was a self-taught pianist from the age of four and, although destined to be an engineer, a late change of heart led him to a career spanning music, marketing, advertising, publishing and broadcasting. He has founded three companies including most recently Excelsior, best known for its television dramas *The Darling Buds Of May* and *A Touch Of Frost* starring David Jason and *My Uncle Silas* with Albert Finney.

As a writer, director and producer he has been active in the theatre, particularly as Festival Director for the National Trust at Polesden Lacey, and has produced at the Edinburgh Festival. He has written and directed four plays as well as the stage adaptation of *The Slipper and the Rose* which has been performed all over the world. In 1992 he composed the theme music for *The Darling Buds Of May* for which he received an Ivor Novello Award. His first book, written under the name of Philip Walsh, *Views from the Back of a Taxi*, was published in 2007.

Pip has been involved with Variety the Children's Charity, formerly the Variety Club of Great Britain, since 1995 and was Chief Barker in 1999, the charity's 50th Anniversary year. He lives in Surrey and has been married for more than forty years. He has three daughters and five grandchildren.

Index